16 HINDU SAMSKĀRS

From before
the birth till Death
and even after Death
— with RITUALS
and PUJAN VIDHI

16 HINDU SAMSKĀRS

From before
the birth till Death
and even after Death
— with RITUALS
and PUJAN VIDHI

PROF. SHRIKANT PRASOON

Published by

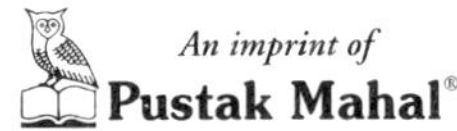

Administrative office and sale centre
J-3/16 , Daryaganj, New Delhi-110002
☎ 23276539, 23272783, 23272784 • *Fax:* 011-23260518
E-mail: info@pustakmahal.com • *Website:* www.pustakmahal.com

Branches
Bengaluru: ☎ 080-22234025 • *Telefax:* 080-22240209
E-mail: pustakmahalblr@gmail.com
Mumbai: ☎ 022-22010941, 022-22053387
E-mail: unicornbooksmumbai@gmail.com
Patna: ☎ 0612-3294193 • *Telefax:* 0612-2302719
E-mail: rapidexptn@gmail.com

ISBN 978-81-223-1053-5

Edition 2017

Printed at : Radha Offset, Delhi

DEDICATION

These sixteen steps to
spiritual progress,
culture, refinement
and salvation
are dedicated to
those who possess and spread
Happiness, Sweetness,
Light** and **Fragrance
And
To my father
Late Pt. Rambhawan Pandey
who gave Samskārs to
numerous people,
including me.

Late Pt. Rambhawan Pandey &
Prof. Shrikant Prasoon (1968)

Prof. Shrikant Prasoon

Contents

Preface

This book on Samskārs, particularly Sixteen Samskārs, was planned originally by Shri Ram Avtār Gupta, Chairman of Pustak Mahal.

It is a great service to human beings, specially the modern Indians, and a laudable effort to bring forth the most essential things in life in order to create a cultured and refined society that he is doing with his Hindoology Books.

If man becomes sensitive enough to realise the value of being cultured as human being by not simply changing dress, language, formal behaviour and amenities but by becoming religious, spiritual and diligent and by leading a life free from fears and inhibitions then all the honest and sincere efforts of the Chairman and the author will be amply rewarded.

In this book, you will find all the Samskārs as I have left nothing out. In other words, I have incorporated everything related to Samskārs that I have ever heard of or read about. I have incorporated the ways and means of performing all such Samskārs and of worshipping various gods and goddesses in a separate section. It is the most essential part of the Samskārs. Without the *Poojan Vidhi* the book would have been incomplete.

Nowadays, people are not aware of the Samskārs. They are only living for *Artha* (wealth) and *Kāma* (desire). So, they are unhappy, depressed and live under fear. Only the Samskārs will make them live a complete and blissful life by including *Dharma* (righteousness) and *Moksha* (liberation) in their life. The Samskārs can chart the path and give them inner strength to follow the path of righteousness that will eventually lead a man to bliss and beatitude.

Only **ā** has been taken from scriptural transliteration for long 'a' sound which is otherwise impossible to write in the Roman script. Everything else is written in the same way as given in government papers, magazines, newspapers and general books. Most of the longer compound words have been separated in shorter simple words. It will help the readers to read the *Mantras* and *Shlokas* quoted in the book.

Prof. Shrikant Prasoon

Mobile: 09868082133
E-mail: shrikantprasoon@yahoo.co.in

❋❋❋

Prayers

At the beginning and end of every day, and the start and finish of every work we must pray to the *Param Brahma* (Almighty God) who is *Sattva* (truth), *Chitta* (consciousness) and *Ānand* (happiness).

Say *AUM* every time you go out and on returning home. Keep your heart pure and free from lust. You are bound to get both success and happiness.

Gāyatri Mantra

ॐ भूर्भुवः स्वः।
तत्सवितुर्वरेण्यं भर्गो देवस्य धीमहि।
धियो यो नः प्रचोदयात्।

Aum bhoorbhuvah swah
Tatsaviturvarenyam bhargo devasya dheemahi
Dhiyo yo nah prachodayāt.

Rig Veda (10:3)

(Aum is the name of *Param Brahma,* the Almighty God. That is the life of all lives; He is the Protector of all; He is the dispeller of pain and misery; He bestows pleasure and prosperity on devotees. We must embody and possess the Almighty who created and creates all. He is the light of all lighted celestial bodies and qualities. He is the illuminator of the souls of all and the imparter of bliss. May He always protect our intellectual faculties from evil. May He inspire us to do only good.)

Namaskāram (Obeisance)

ॐ नमः शम्भवाय च मयोभवाय च नमः शंकराय च मयस्कराय च नमः शिवाय च शिवतराय च ।

Aum namah shambhawāya cha mayobhawāya cha namah shankarāya cha mayaskarāya cha namah shivāya cha shivatarāya cha.

Yajur Veda (16:41)

(We pay our adoration and salutation to God, the blissful; and the One that bestows all bliss; Benefactor of the devotees; the tranquil and the giver of tranquility. We offer obeisance to the Holy One who showers blessings and emancipates.)

Wish for Sweetness

जिह्वाया अग्रे मधुमे जिह्वामूले मधुलकम् ।
ममेदह क्रतावासो मम चित्तमुपायसि ।

Jihwāyā agre madhumey jihwāmule madhulakam;
Mamedah kratāwāso mama chittamupāyasi.

- Atharva Veda

(May there be sweetness on the tip of my tongue! May there be sweetness at the beginning of my tongue! May sweetness be in all my actions and deeds! And, O Sweetness! Reach up to my heart.)

Wish for Purity

ओ३म् भूः पुनातु शिरसि । ओ३म् भुवः पुनातु नेत्र्योः । ओ३म् स्वः पुनातु कण्ठे । ओ३म् महः पुनातु हृदये । ओ३म् जनः पुनातु नाभ्याम् । ओ३म् तपः पुनातु पादयोः । ओ३म् सत्यं पुनातु पुनषिशरसि । ओ३म् खं ब्रह्म पुनातु सर्वत्र ।

Aum bhuh punātu shirasi.
Aum bhuwah punātu netrayoh.
Aum swah punātu kanthe.
Aum mahah punātu hridaye.
Aum janah punātu nābhyām.
Aum tapah punātu pādayoh.
Aum satyam punātu punashisharasi.
Aum khang Brahma punātu sarvartra.

(May the self-subsistent God purify my head! May the all-seeing God purify my eyes! May the sublime God purify my heart! May the blissful God purify my throat! May the Creator of all purify my navel! May the righteous God purify my feet! Once again I pray to God, the Truth, to purify my head! May the all-pervading God purify everything.)

Refinement and Qualities

Kāma krodh vihinashcha pākhand sparsh varjitah;
Jitendriyah satyavādi cha sarva karma prashasyate.

काम क्रोध विहीनश्च पाखण्ड स्पर्श वर्जितः।
जितेन्द्रीयः सत्यवादी च सर्व कर्म प्रशस्यते॥

(The man who has no lust for physical passion, no anger and no pretensions; who has control over his senses and is truthful, can accomplish any work. The Brāhmin who has no lust for physical passion, no anger and no pretensions;

who has control over his senses and is truthful, is fit for performing all rituals.)

Eight Best Qualities in the Self

According to Maharishi Gautama the following eight are the best qualities that make a person pure and refined, and endow him with peace and prosperity; health and happiness, riches and bliss; fulfilment in the world and salvation after it.

Dayā sarvabhuteshukshāntiransuyā shauchamanāyāso mangalam kārpanyam aspriheti.

Only these eight qualities can make a person cultured and refined, humane and sublime. It is easier to fall down from a height but it is difficult to achieve a height. Human beings are the best creation only because they always strive hard to be better. The men who fail to grow better, remain animals and demons:

1. *Dayā sarvabhuteshu* - Kindness, compassion, pity and sympathy towards every living being.
2. *Kshamā* - Forgiveness.
3. *Anusuyā, anirmatsaratā* - No jealousy.
4. *Shauch, antar-bāhya-shuchirbhutatā* - The state of being pure from outside and inside.
5. *Anāyāsa* - Not to indulge in the petty and meaningless.
6. *Mangala* - To think, wish and work for bliss, well-being and prosperity of all.
7. *Akārpanya* - Neither to be nor to show weakness and miserliness.
8. *Asprihā* - Neither lust nor wish to possess whatever belonged to others.)

The Pilgrimages

Satyam teertham kshamā teertham teertham indriyanigrahah;

Sarvabhutadayā teertham teerthamārjavamewa cha.

Dānam teertham damasteertham santoshah teertham uchyate;

Brahmacharyam param teertham teertham cha priyavāditā.

Gyānam teertham dhritih teertham tapasteertham udāhritam;

Teerthānamapi tatteertham vishuddhih manasah parā.

Skand Purāna (6:30-33)

सत्यं तीर्थं क्षमा तीर्थं तीर्थं इन्द्रियनिग्रहः।
सर्वभूतदया तीर्थं तीर्थमार्जवमेव च॥
दानं तीर्थं दमस्तीर्थं संतोषः तीर्थं उच्यते।
ब्रह्मचर्यं परं तीर्थं तीर्थं च प्रियवादिता॥
ज्ञानं तीर्थं धृतिः तीर्थं तपस्तीर्थं उदाहृतम्।
तीर्थानामपि तत्तीर्थं विशुद्धिः मनसः परा।

(Truth is like a pilgrimage in the same way as forgiveness is called a pilgrimage. The control over senses, pity and sympathy towards all living beings and simplicity are also treated as pilgrimage. Charity, self-restraint, control over mind and contentment are also called pilgrimages. Celibacy is greater pilgrimage. Speaking sweetly is also pilgrimage. Knowledge, patience, and penance have also been accepted as such pious places and the greatest pilgrimage is the immediate purification of the inner self.)

❁❁❁

Samskārs in Spiritual Quadruplets

1. ॐ

Samskārs are performed to add confidence to faith,
To purge the body and mind and to gain health.
To refine the sensibility and to define culture,
And to free one from complexes and the fear of death.

2. ॐ

Samskārs are ways of natural and happy living,
Collective effort to strengthen an individual being.
Assistance and gradual teaching at the time ripe,
To be able to store energy, wisdom for doing, keeping.

3. ॐ

Samskārs are scientifically checking and testing an individual,
They are psychologically learning traits: both visual and spiritual.
They are looking into fitness, social set-up, and economic status,
And preparing to face the difficult days: imaginary and actual.

4. ॐ

Samskārs are ultimate outcome of centuries of medical research,
Study of natural phenomenon and man's regular celestial search.
Of behavioural science and the need of inner growth, strength,
It is performed to give stability, control, know-how and clutch.

5. ॐ

Early Samskārs pave way to give pleasure, power, and vision,
Others show grand success because of balanced living, decision.
They empower one with dedication, devotion and discipline,
The last has deep psychological advantage and definite reason.

6. ॐ

Samskārs are foolishly looked down upon by people sloth,
Neither performed at ripe time nor in ecstasy, joy and mirth,
They are hurriedly finished setting aside rites, on pretext of time,
By those who waste hours on checking and testing fitness of cloth.

7. ॐ

It is better to know and understand apparent and hidden meaning,
Numerous benefits that make, maintain healthy moral, social setting.

The growing anxieties, tensions, depressions, suicides and murders,
Can be done away if we follow traditional rites, rituals and teachings.

8. ॐ

Samskār is a process of increasing potential, acquiring qualities,
Knowing, behaving well in broader sense and following technicalities.
It is improving, purifying the existing, and removing shortcomings,
In short, it adds and develops positive values and capabilities.

9. ॐ

With garbhādhāna the rituals of Samskārs begin from before birth,
One by one it takes the complete cycle of life in its wider girth.
Through punswan, seemāntonnayan, jātakarma and nishkraman etc,
With the son performing the pitri-tarpan it continues well after death.

From Spiritual Quadruptets

SECTION 1

The Samskãrs

Samskārs : Meaning and Philosophy

Samskārs can be defined as the process of increasing the potential and the refining steps towards inner and outer progress. Each Samskār leads one to a better, healthier and *Sāttvika* (righteous) way of life.

Pāṇini defines it as: *Samparyupebhyah karotau bhushane:* that which decorates the personality.

Another definition of Samskār says: *Samdkaranam gunāntarādhānam samskārah*: Samskār is absorbing other qualities or characteristics.

Samskārs are for the all-round development of a person. They give the ability to face life well, endow it with dexterity for better performance and enable us to lead a complete and contented life.

Samskārs for Progress

Samskārs are gradual steps for definite progress, development and prosperity. There is no setback for the person who performs all the Samskārs. On the one hand Samskārs make us pure and on the other hand they bring us the grace and blessings of the Lord.

Samskārs are as much physical as psychological and spiritual. Some lay greater stress on spiritual progress and minimise its physical aspect. As the law of Nature is to achieve balance, so physical pleasure and spiritual progress should also be equal in proportion. Hence, it is achieving perfection in purifying ideas and actions, thinking and deeds.

Samskārs should be such an integrated part of our being that one can easily say: *Swabhāvasunderam vastuna samskāramapekshate*: that which is beautiful by nature expects no further refinement.

It is integral because it is inner purification, the cultivation of higher thoughts and doing greater deeds for the betterment of all. It is the force of pure emotions and pious growth: *Samskārārtham sharirasya*: the body is for the purification of the soul.

Samskāro hi gunāntarādhānam uchyate: only Samskārs plant better qualities, replacing the rotten ones.

Virtues of Samskārs

Physical faults and deformities, dirt and sins, impious attitude and vices are washed out by the Samskārs and the person is able to achieve spirituality. Samskārs are the elements of obedience to Scriptures and classical behaviour. Better and higher aims are achieved easily when a person's life is enriched with philanthropic ideas and deeds. Only such men fulfil their duties and responsibilities. Purity, piety, compassion and other virtues are found in abundance in the *Samskāri Purush*. He leads a disciplined, balanced and rich life according to the moral rules and ethical codes. Indian cultural heritage has always given priority to Samskārs, the cultivation of greater qualities. That way man, who takes birth as Shudra becomes a *Dwija*, gets another life; grows from inside, absorbs and incorporates sublime and divine qualities; then becomes a Brahmin and then a Rishi.

Hence, Samskārs are essential and must be performed to be alert and remain pious throughout life.

The Gods of Different Samskārs

S.N.	Samskārs	Gods
1.	Garbhādhāna	Brahmā/ Prajāpati
2.	Punsawan	Prajāpati
3.	Seemantonnayan	Dhātā
4.	Jāta Karma	Savitā
5.	Chudākarma, Keshānta Karma	Prajāpati
6.	Upanayan	Indra
7.	Vedārambha	Apāwaka
8.	Pious Rites	Shraddhā
9.	Utsarga	Sushravā
10.	Upākarma	Savitā
11.	Vivāh	Prajāpati
12.	Nāndi Shrāddha (as part of Garbhādhāna)	Kutudaksha
13.	In other Rites	Satyabasu
14.	Upāsana Hoama	Agni; Sun and Prajāpati
15.	Sthālipāka Karma Devatā	Agnigarbha

❁❁❁

Rishis on Samskārs

Rishis have always declared higher goals for life and shown different ways and means to achieve that goal. Samskār, the act of refining body and mind for greater health, purity, work and accomplishment, is one of them.

Rishis divided our possessions in two definite categories: one that we are born with and the other that we acquire in this life. They proved that a child is never born with a blank mind. There is always something in the child's not-so-conscious consciousness. Not everything is written afresh on it. Some new things are added to the already existing writing which may be unknown but not mysterious. This writing is known only to the inner self.

However, the new writing which may be natural and spontaneous added by the environment, situations, thinking and deeds; or deliberately created, refined, improved, changed and cultivated, can change the existing writing.

So, the *Rishis* devised many Samskārs that created a lasting impression, changed the thought and deeds of a person and in this way improved his life-style and made him cultured, refined, more human, sublime and divine.

Samskārs changed the negative thoughts, destructive tendencies and demonic philosophies.

Religious Rites and Rituals

In other words, Samskārs are scientific and psychological, and deliberate means to purify and refine the life and mind of a person.

These are not mere religious rites and rituals. To make the ignorant people follow good values, the Samskārs have been made a part of religious rituals. Since they were thought to be essential, *Rishis* made them part and parcel of our life.

Hence, it will be a great mistake to take them to be only religious activities. They are essential for life; they are very scientific, they have deeper psychological advantages and are deeply related to our inner unknown self. A body and mind devoid of the Samskārs is like a dead skeleton with skin, flesh and organs. It lacks the flow of life that makes a man human and different from animals and beasts.

Meaning of Samskar

The word Samskār has been used in many ways.

Kaushitaki, *Chhāndogya* and *Brihadakāranya Upanishads* have used it in the sense of *Samskaroti* (to grow and prosper).

Maharishi Pānini has used it in three different ways:

i. *Utakarshasādhanam Samskāram*: Samskār gives prosperity.

ii. *Samawāya* or *Sanghāta:* A thing that happens at the same time as something else.

iii. *Ābhushana*: Ornaments.

Brahmin Granthas and *Sutras* have used Samskārs as *Shuddhikāraka*, purifier.

In *Boddha Tripitaka*, it is many things besides being the one among the twelve wheels of the worldly cycle:

- *Nirmāna* (creation)
- *Ābhushana* (ornament)
- *Samawāya* (multitude)
- *Prakriti* (Nature)
- *Satkarma* (wholesome deeds)
- *Skandha* (canto), *Shabda, Sparsh, rupa, rasa, gandha*

Maharishi Kanāda in his *Vaisheshika Sutras* has accepted Samskārs as one of the 24 qualities of human beings.

Samskār has a very wide range of meanings. By adding prefix *sam* (balance) to the verb *kri* and adding the suffix *ghyanz* the word *Samskār* is formed.

Samskār is rubbing off the dust, dirt and impurities from the self and soul. Such a soul could be purified by wholesome ideas and deeds. Only they can be called *Samskrit* or *Susamskrit*. **All the lasting impressions on our mind are due to our Samskārs.** They change with the changing time, feelings, emotions, knowledge and experience.

Samskār may mean any one or all of the following:

i. *Shikshā* (education)
ii. *Chamaka* (brightness)
iii. *Sajāwata* (decoration)
iv. *Ābhushana* (ornament)
v. *Chhāpa*(impression)

vi. *Ākāra* (shape)
vii. *Sānchā* (mould)
viii. *Kriyā* (action)
ix. *Prabhāvasmriti* (the lasting impression in the memory)
x. *Pāwaka Karma* (the nature and quality of fire)
xi. *Vichāra* (thought)
xii. *Dhāranā* (firmness)
xiii. *Punya* (virtues)

Thus, Samskār means to be good and to make others good; to get purified and to purify others; to be healthy and aesthetically satisfying and to provide health and beauty to others; to purge the inner and outer self and to purge others for greater attraction and better use.

The actions that add human and sublime qualities and provide nourishment and protection are called Samskārs. **Samskārs are processes that add value to life.**

A Samskār has such depth, height and width that it can not be summarised in any one definition. Samskār embodies and symbolises many things.

Veermitrodaya in his *Samskār Prakāsh* has claimed that Samskār is an indescribable strange religious act that gives rise to virtues:

Atmasharirānyatarnishtho vihitkriyājanyo atishayavisheshah samskārah.

❁❁❁

Samskārs as Culture

Usually, Samskār as culture stands for the way of living, art, customs, beliefs and social organisation. But in India it is far more significant than one can attach to the word. It is a deliberate and conscious act of making one cultured after forcing one to learn by observing certain rules to maintain a standard of thinking. It is followed by the rigorous tests to establish that one has absorbed them and has successfully made them a part of his life.

It is the quality of being polite and the ability to judge others. It is also the state of having the kind of character that is considered typical of a higher personal, social and spiritual order. The process of baptism and refinement begins even before the conception and continues even after the death.

That is one great reason which Dayanand Saraswati has suggested:

"Before conception, during pregnancy and after delivery, the mother and the father should abstain from intoxicant drugs, wine, decomposed or sour substances injurious to the brain; and use such nutritious foodstuffs as clarified butter, milk, sugar, grain, water and the like, pure food and drink; which conduce to health, strength, sedateness, the clear brain, courage, moral conduct, and decent habits. Such a pure diet will purge the ova and sperms of all defects and endue them with germs of excellent constitution of the embryo."

(Light of Truth – 29)

Physical and Spiritual Growth

Samskār can be good or bad. But only the good ones are taken as Samskārs and the rest are rejected as Kusamskārs. Indians have, since time immemorial, been trying consistently to improve the existing refinements by performing different acts, teachings, rites and rituals called Samskārs.

They have divided the body into two: physical and spiritual. With the help of Samskārs they have tried to achieve a balance between the two. They work towards the healthy growth of both the physical body and the spiritual body. Since, only by performing good deeds with the physical body the spiritual body can grow, so, the *Rishis* never ignored the physical body; rather they laid stress on keeping it healthier and stronger. They had their scientific reasons that by eating less, by forcing the body to tolerate, endure and sustain difficult and hostile climate, the body could be made stronger. So, when there was rain or cold wind or scorching hot sun, they would sit in the open.

In *Chandrāyan Vrat*, a fast that starts from a full moon night and ends with another full moon night, the food-intake is reduced in equal proportion to the phases of the moon, and is increased with the increasing shape of the moon to equalise the intake on another full moon night with that of the first full moon night. On the moonless night no food would be taken. It has been proved time and again that the health of the body depends upon the digestive system. The food is a complete waste if it is not digested well and if the blood does not absorb its essence.

The physical body and the spiritual body played a vital role in the concept and origin of the Samskārs. They were actually so effective that performing the Samskārs was made essential for all those who wanted a better, healthier, happier and blissful life. The body was prepared for the immense, tremendous, marvellous and divine experience of *Param Brahma* through *Swādhyāya* (self-study), *Vrat* (fasting), *Homa* (offerings), *Vedābhyasa* (study of Scriptures), *Yagyas* (rituals) and, of course, with different Samskārs. Through womb-purifying sacraments the impurities related to seed and womb are removed.

Kāryah sharira samskārah pāwanah pretya cheha cha.

Manusmriti (2:26)

कार्यः शरीर संस्कारः पावनः प्रेत्य चेह च॥

Mahāyagyascha yagyascha brāhmiyam kriyate tanuh.

Ibid (2:28)

महायज्ञैश्च यज्ञैश्च ब्राह्मीयं क्रियते तनुः॥

(This body is made fit for attaining Brahmahood through scriptural studies.)

It is claimed by the sages that by performing the Samskārs and by following those pious ways Brahmninhood and union with Brahma is easily achieved: *Brāhmanyapi tadwatasyāt samskārai vidhipu vakam.*

The sages were neither the materialists who consider the physical pleasure to be all nor were they eccentrics who did not attach value to body. They kept both the things in mind. The physical health was as important to them as the spiritual health. They lived a controlled life based on natural products, herbal medicines and enjoyed good health and long life.

Brahmcharya (no or less sex) was considered the best way to be healthy. So, the *Rishis* admonished sex to the *Vānaprasthis* who left their homes even with their wife. They preferred regulated sex during *Grihasthāshram* mostly for giving birth to children. This is one of the basics of Samskārs.

❋❋❋

Importance of Samskārs

Samskārs play a vital role in making a better society. They have made the development and progress possible. If our ancestors had not strived hard for the betterment and achieved near perfection in almost every field; and protected that knowledge for the generations then man would never have become civilised.

Lack of Samskars

The Samskārs have made man great and sublime but the lack of Samskārs resulted in the growth of animal instincts. Among such people, criminal and demonic feelings grew stronger and resulted into degeneration. All the loss of natural wealth and ecological balance is due to the lack of Samskārs. The men with no humanity and sublimity turn into materialists and remain thoroughly absorbed in physical pleasure, luxury, money and crime. They try to prove themselves right in every possible way and with their foolish deeds they bring destruction and ruin. Security withers out, and life comes to the brink of total annihilation.

Samskārs give the ability and acumen to make steady and balanced progress in all the four 'great eternal human pursuits' known as *Dharma* (religiosity), *Artha* (finance), *Kāma* (physical work and pleasure) and *Moksha* (the final accomplishment in the form of peace, blessing and salvation). They make a better man out of us and give healthier and better children that ensure both the continuation of life and definite progress towards perfection.

Samskārs for Growth

The Samskārs are really important as they ensure progress, prosperity, knowledge, wisdom, moral character and ethical deeds; and **thus guarantee a better and prosperous social set-up and continuity of life.** The good, moral deeds make the world a better and peaceful place to live in harmony with others and make collective progress.

The men with Samskārs get respect. They do not indulge in too much physical pleasure and remain absorbed in religious, moral and spiritual deeds. They follow the rules formulated by the wise forefathers and followed by others through the ages. In place of only personal growth they think of all, work for all and ensure overall growth and prosperity.

So, Samskārs in India stand for the ways, extent and quality of formation, growth and effect. The formation and growth may be in phases but Samskārs refer to the totality. Hence, the disbursement of Samskārs is as important as their possession. One must show in daily life that he/she is cultured, refined, aesthetically and spiritually cultivated and graceful. It can be compared only to the process the bees use to make honey. In a nutshell, the final product i.e. honey is the Samskār.

Dwija – *Born Again*

Samskārs are like second birth. They make one *Dwija*, born again. This second birth is not physical, it is the inner change. Those that are unable to take Samskārs remain Shudra. It is misquoted and wrongly explained that Shudras have no right to take Samskārs. In fact all are born as Shudra. They became *Dwija* that took Samskārs and refined themselves and the rest remained Shudra. They also can try for refinement, first without Mantras, and after attaining some purity with Mantras. It applies to women also because they too get physically impure and are hardly able to free themselves from physical pleasure, lust and jealousy. But women in India have risen to great heights to become deities and *Rishikās*. They are the embodiment and incarnation of power. They have greatly influenced Indian life, art, music, culture and civilisation. Similar is the case with Shudras. They too attained great heights but after making themselves pious, cultured and refined; they no longer remained Shudra, they got rebirth, and were treated as *Dwija*, Brahmin and even *Rishis*. There are many saints that were born in Shudra family but it is a social, moral and spiritual crime to call them Shudra. Once the saints became *Dwija* and got the Brahminhood they can't be called Shudras. This is the greatness of Samskār and Indian life, philosophy, culture and civilisation.

Persons born in Shudras family that got higher education, higher post and possess mental, economic and political power should ask a question and answer to themselves: are they still Shudra? Then there will be no fight on caste-basis.

There are many good and bad influences which we carry from one birth to another and experience almost everyday from the moment we gain subtle and unknown consciousness in the mother's lap. *Samskārs give us power to distinguish between good and bad influences; and help in opting for good influences and rejecting the bad ones.* If we study well, take on the required articles and medicines and perform the Samskārs with pure soul, then we are able to absorb a lot of power, grow better and achieve significant success.

❁❁❁

List of Samskārs

Everything and anything written about Samskārs in the *Veda Samhitās* has been explained in the *Smritis* and *Grihyasutras*.

Samskārs are the main subject matter of the *Grihyasutras*. However, they do not deal with all the Samskārs. Most of them deal with only the physical and social Samskārs beginning with '*Vivah*' up to '*Samāvartan*'. Some others like *Pāraskar Grihyasutra, Āswalāyana Grihyasutra* and *Bauddhāyana Grihyasutras* also discuss the '*Antyeshti*', which is performed as last rites after death.

Most of the *Granthas* differ on both the numbers and names of Samskārs. *Āswalāyana Grihyasutra* mentions only 11 Samskārs while *Pāraskar, Bauddhāyana* and *Vārāha Grihyasutra* claim 13 Samskārs but *Vaikhānas* deals with 18 Samskārs. The maximum number of Samskārs have been inculcated and explained to be sixty-four. But Maharishi Gautam, in his *Gautam Grihyasutra* reduced them to 48 that included 40 Samskārs and 8 qualities of the self.

They are the following:

List of Samskārs by Maharishi Gautam

1. Garbhādhān	2. Punswan	3. Seemantonnayana	4. Jātakarma
5. Nāmakaran	6. Annaprāshana	7. Chaulakarma	8. Upanayana
9. Rigvedavrat	10. Sāmavedavrat	11. Ajurvedavrat	12. Atharvedavrat
13. Samāvartan Snāna	14. Vivāh	15. Devayagya	16. Pitriyagya
17. Manusya Yagya	18. Bhutayagya	19. Brahmayagya	20. Ashtaka Shrāddha
21. Pārvana	22.Masika Shrāddha	23. Shrāvani	24. Āgrahāyani
25. Chaitrakarma	26. Āswayuji	27. Agnyādhān	28. Agnihotra
29. Darshapurna māsa	30. Āgrayan	31. Chāturmasya	32. Nirudha pashubandha
33. Sautrāmani	34. Somayāga	35. Atyagnishtoma	36. Ukathya
37. Shodashi	38. Vājapeya	39. Atirātra	40. Āptoryāma

Qualities for the Self

41. Dayā	42. Kshamā	43. Anusuyā	54. Shauch
45. Anāyāsa	46. Mangala	47. Akārpanya	48. Asprihā

Maharishi Angirā further reduced these 40 Samskars to twenty-five. Later Veda Vyāsa gave the list of 16 Samskārs.

These sixteen Samskars have been accepted and followed throughout India.

They are:

Garbhādhānam punswanam seemanto jātkarma cha Nāmkriyāniskramane annāhsanam vapankriyā. Karnvedho vratādesho vedārambhakriyāvidhih Keshānto snānmudwānho vivāhāgniparigrahah. Tretāgnisangrahashcheti samskārāh shodas smritāh

Vyās Smriti (1/13-15)

गर्भाधानं पुंसवनं सीमान्तो जातकर्म च।
नामक्रियानिष्क्रमणेऽन्नाशनं वपनक्रिया।।
कर्णवेधो व्रतोदेशो वेदारम्भक्रियाविधिः।
केशान्तो स्नानमुद्वान्हो विवाहाग्नि परिग्रहः।।
त्रेताग्नि संग्रहश्चेति संस्काराः षोडस स्मृताः।

1. Conception (*Garbhādhān*) - For better children.
2. Fertilisation (*Punswan*) - Three months after conception for life-being and safety.
3. Upgradation of limitations (*Seemantonnayan*) - A month before delivery for safe and secure birth.
4. The ceremony performed at the birth of a child (*Jātkarma*) - Performed just after the birth to be sure that all necessary precautions have been taken.
5. Naming (*Nāmkaran*) - Eleven days after the birth to give him/her an individual identity.

6. Ceremoniously going out (*Niskraman*) - After four months the child is taken out into the open to face the wind and sunshine.
7. Ceremoniously giving a child its first cereal food (*Annaprāshana*) - After six months.
8. Cutting off hair (*Chudākarma*) - Cutting all the hair.
9. Piercing of ears (*Karnavedha*) - For therapeutic effect.
10. Investiture ceremony (*Upanayan*) - With the sacred thread.
11. Initiation into study (*Vedārambh*) - To start study.
12. Convocation (*Samāvartan*) - Baptism into the *Vedas*.
13. Marriage (*Vivāh*) - Entering *grihasthashram*.
14. Marriage-fire (*Āwasthyādhāna/Vivāhagni parigrah*) - Encircling the sacred fire.
15. Baptism into the conservation of fire (*Tretāgnisangrah*) - To start a domestic life.
16. The last rite (*Antyeshti*) – After the death.

The changes in the names, numbers and preferences of Samskārs clearly indicate that there were acceptable variations in Samskārs from time to time. It seems that the need of a particular period prompted the wise men to bring about changes.

Thus, it gives a clear message that Samskārs can be altered according to the need of time, society and person. It also shows that the followers of the Eternal Religion, which is now known as Hindu Religion, were quite flexible and never against incorporating new and better ideas.

❁❁❁

Governing Factors in Samskārs

Our forefathers did their best to save everything essential during slavery period. But in the process they missed the fine details and the real scientific and psychological reasons behind those saved rites and rituals; spiritual and celestial deeds and religious and social functions. Naturally, we have greater responsibilities on our shoulders **to save and keep intact what they had saved and to search out the missing links as well as the meanings and details.** In place of fighting among ourselves over petty political and economic gains we must try hard to regain those healthier activities for greater peace, satisfaction, health, happiness and bliss.

Restoring the Old Order

Of course, it is not easy to know everything behind each ritual and Samskār as there have been numerous changes over the years; when we were fighting hard for our survival and failed to add new and valuable things to our rich heritage.

The trouble with today's generation is that they know a part and derive all their conclusions based on it. We are still not able to see the entire thing as a whole and many essential parts are still missing. Happily enough, some people are working in the right direction and trying their level best to restore the old order and incorporate meaningful and healthy changes.

It is due to their effort that we know some of the essential factors that were behind the Samskārs.

The most essential thing in Indian life was **faith, devotion** and **surrender** that brought us to **meditation** and s**pirituality** and gave us capacity to connect and fuse to **natural** and **celestial energy.** This gave us **control, hope, contentment, solace** and **satisfaction.**

These unseen abstract things are our real assets. In place of losing them, we have to accumulate them for richer and fuller life. With it we can be human and divine, without it we will turn into beasts. Indians have always fought against the demonic and barbarous acts and **only Indians have the power, ability and aspiration to fight against them.**

We don't pray with true devotion for sublime and divine spirit and character; we only pray for wealth and luxurious living.

Living without Life

Of course, we are getting it but at the cost of severe bloodshed. We are killing and we get killed; we are deceiving and we are deceived; we steal property and our property is stolen; we capture the love of others and our love is taken away; we are throwing bombs in others' courtyard and bombs fall in ours; we fire bullets on others and we are fired at by others; we snatch others' happiness and our happiness is gone.

Even in winning, we are the losers. We are killing animals and getting killed like animals: from road, rail, sea and air accidents; from serial killing to serial blasts; and from human bombs to the weapons used for mass destruction.

We can't shed blood and claim to be refined and cultured. We can't create fatal weapons and claim to be wise scientists. We fail to protect life and yet claim to be the rulers. We have to accept the fact that we have surrendered to Satan. We have lost the blissful, heavenly natural paradise; and stake big claims in drunken state to be living in paradise. In this way our control over senses is gone.

There is no place safe and none without fear. We are living without life; working without ideal. We are dying without fulfilling our responsibilities and without paying our debts.

What a life! We are born in debt, live in debt, and die in debt! What a great irony!

It is all because we have lost the Samskārs. We are not trying our level best to incorporate good Samskārs. We are not giving Samskārs to our children because we don't have them in the first place. It is imperative to get Samskārs for better, healthier, happier and prosperous life. There may not be money or luxury but there must be refinement, culture, sublimity and divinity in life.

This may be a dream. All this may not come true. But even if some people opt for Samskārs and get purged then this world will become a better place to live.

Fire

Since our thinking has become negative so has our life, hence we always talk of the destructive powers of fire. We have forgotten that fire is one of the five fundamental gross elements; that it gives life; that there won't be life without fire, heat and light; that fire has a great healing capacity; that fire is energy and preserves life; that fire does not destroy on its own. We are the ones who create the cause of destruction. It is our fault and not the fault of fire that cylinders burst, airplanes catch fire, multi-storey buildings are gutted and factories are burnt. We are behind all the loss of life and property and very conveniently we blame fire.

Our forefathers remained cautious and prayed to fire for giving energy and power, and for not engulfing life and property. The prayers gave them time and kept them cautious. Now we don't pray, hence we find it easy to blame fire for the numerous accidents that occur everyday all around the world.

Earlier, no single Indian lady would start a fire in the kitchen without bowing and praying to fire; today not a single Indian woman follows that tradition. As a result hundred of women die in mishaps with kitchen fire. When we pray we take conscious steps to go through the rituals of precautions. At present they light gas in a sleepy state or just after coming out of deep slumber. Sometimes they forget closing the knob of the cylinder or sometimes they fail to feel the smell of the gas that had filled up the kitchen. A prayer could easily stop them from doing anything in a hurry and avert any mishap.

We talk only of the loss of life and property by fire and unfortunately we have forgotten that fire purifies and heals pain.

Agnibadhu Swāhā engulfs all the impurities if the impurities are offered to her with the pronouncement of '*Swāhāh*'.

The fragrant smell that rises with the smoke of the sacred fire fills the nostrils, enters the lungs and blood along with the oxygen and instantly purifies the blood. It energises and the extent of energy depends on the capacity to absorb heat.

The *Rishis* preferred to sit under the open bright sky during the noon hours of the hot summer for absorbing heat. So, they were able to sit outside during icy cold winter nights. They had conditioned their body and adapted the organs to sustain during extreme weather conditions. The farmers and the labourers still have that kind of conditioning in their body but the city dwellers are unable to bear general heat, cold, rain or wind.

We need to pass through highly inflamed fire to burn all the numerous impurities that we have accumulated and absorb enough heat to sustain during bad climatic conditions.

We must know fire. There are different types of fire:

- *Gārhapatya* - the fire that we use at homes.
- *Āwāhaniya* - the fire started for poojā and *Yagyas*.
- *Dakshinagni* - Southern, the natural Fire.
- *Jatharāgni* - the inner heat of the body essential for digestion.

Fire has seven tongues:

Karāli dhumini shwetā lohitā neelalohitā,
Suvarnāpadmarāgachajihwāh saptavibhawaso.

कराली धुमिनि श्वेता लोहिता नीललोहिता।
सुवर्णा पद्मराग च जिह्वा सप्त विभावसो॥

(*Karāli, Dhumini, Shwetā, Lohitā, Neelalohitā; Suvarnā* and *Padmarāga* are the seven tongues of fire.)

Thus fire is capable of doing a lot. It is needless to state that the fire of the loin is the passion and is responsible for the conception of life.

Till not so long ago, fire was tended with care and caution. Those were treated as honourable who kept fire alive. Now, we have forgotten the Agnihotra, the offering to fire; and substituted fire with electric bulbs.

Fire rejuvenates. We are alive till our body is hot. A cold body is a dead body. Fire is the liveliest part of all the Samskārs. We must get it and keep it as part of our Samskār. Incidentally, the name of Agni is different in each Samskār.

In every Samskār, at the initial stage, the first ritual always belongs to Agni then to the main Deity and after that other rituals are performed. At the time of *Upanayan Samskār* (sacred thread ceremony), the *Batuka* or the *Brahmachāri* prays to fire while offering *āhuti:*

O Fire! Give me talent and intelligence; wisdom and brightness and make me glow with your brightness.

Prayer

Prārthanā siddhi shansinah

(Prayers give fulfilment.)

It is intriguing that we pray to many gods in Yagya but our main prayer is to the God we are mainly worshipping and for whom the Yagya has been arranged.

We must pray from the inner core of our being to become human after getting rid of all inhuman and satanic emotions and instincts, wishes and deeds.

As Shankārāchārya prays:

Kukarmi kusangi kubuddhi kudāsah,
Kulāchārheenah kadāchārleenah.
Kudrishti kuvākyaprabanddhah sadāham,
Gatistwam, gatistwam twamekā Bhawāni.

कुकर्मी कुसंगी कुबुद्धिः कुदासः।
कुलाचारहीनः कदाचारलीनः॥
कुदृष्टि कुवाक्य प्रबंन्धः सदाहं।
गतिस्त्वं गतिस्त्वं त्वमेका भवानि॥

(O Goddess Bhawāni your are the only saviour to men who indulge in misdeeds, live in bad company, have ghastly ideas and are slaves to vile emotions; who lack culture and refinement and are deeply indulged in immoral acts; who have lustful eyes; and who utter abusive language.)

Goddess Bhawāni, the incarnation of power and energy is the only saviour. Only she can keep happy and give bliss provided that we act and take Saṃskārs for refinement. All the prayers, from *Tamaso ma jyotirgamaya*: to *Yad bhadram tanna yā suwa* are aimed at that, including the prayers offered at the time of each Samskār.

During *Upanayan Samskār* (sacred thread ceremony), the *Brahmachāri* prays for incorporation of sublime qualities and for the removal of everything vile. The famous *Gāyatri Mantra* that is given to the *Brahmchāri* at this time is also a prayer to *Savitā*.

At the time of marriage ceremony the newly wed couple, while performing *Saptapadi*, pray to Lord Vishnu at every step they take forward together. The first for the growth of crop, the second for energy, the third for wealth, the fourth for happiness, the fifth for animal wealth, the sixth for growth of seasonal produce and the seventh for love and affection. All these prayers, which the couple takes as oath, are enough for a pleasant, healthy, happy and prosperous life provided they remain united and move forward together with complete faith and utmost sincerity.

Prayers go with duties. If one is not doing justice to his power, ability, skill, duty and responsibility then his prayers will not be accepted and fulfilled. This is the crux of the situation one must keep in mind, and before talking of the rights one must fulfil his duties.

Blessings

Blessings are assurance and guarantee of assistance and help whenever needed. They are the recognition of the ability of the person and the chances of success.

Blessings are the sanctions to the expenses, mode and place; and above all, blessings are the no objection certificates. These are the virtues of blessings that people know in different forms but hardly realise.

Blessings are tradition. At each important occasion, ceremony and Samskār, and at the completion of each function we salute the gods, deities, saints, *Brahmins* and elders to get their blessings.

We must get the blessings of the angels, saints, seers, relatives, elders, demigods and gods to be able to do justice to our birth as a human being. God must have created us with many general and higher purposes. We need the blessings of all to fulfil these expectations.

Coronation

Coronation is sacred and the symbol of piety and clear thinking. Though it is done in many ways but two ways are very popular:

1. By placing the mark on the forehead with sandal paste or sacred ash or something similar
2. By sprinkling clean and *Abhimantrita Jal* (sanctified and medicated water).

As a part of coronation, we throw rice mixed with water and turmeric. It is also done as a part of blessing that marks the end of the major function. Local and family rituals are performed after that.

We must coronate our forehead with *Vijay Tilak* (the mark of victory) to move ahead on the wholesome path and do away with anything vile and filthy.

Directives

We have been given wisdom. We have to consciously use this wisdom under the guidance of awakened conscience and consciousness. We have the directives that we need to follow.

We may not know the meaning of these directives but their effect is known and established. The words of the scriptures and the preceptors must be followed honestly and without questioning their validity.

Symbols

These symbols stand for something vital and sublime. We have to use them for our inner strength and growth.

1. **Mangal Kalash** (Decorated pitcher with water and mango leaves)
   It is the symbol of a complete life, prosperity, good omen, happiness and fulfilment.
2. **Gobar** (Cow dung)
   Cow dung is a good conductor of electricity and symbolises both energy and power.
3. **Gangā Jala** (Pure water)
   It represents fluidity and flow of life; coolness and peace.
4. **Shilā** (Stone)
   It is a symbol of stability, hardness, durability and absolute freedom from suspicion, worries and anxieties; and readiness to face the realities and difficulties of life. That is the reason that the bride is asked to stand on a stone slab while these *Mantras* are chanted:
   Emamashmānamārohashwamewa twam sthirā bhawa.
   (O bride! Step on to this stone and be stone-like strong and stable in life.)
5. **Prasāda** (Offering)
   It represents the sweet fruit of good deeds, sweetness, completeness and fulfilment.
6. **Rakshā Sutra** (A thread)
   It brings a sense of security and good omen.
7. **Tilak** (Holy dot adorning the forehead)
   It is a sign of religiosity, piety and wholesome deeds; readiness to work.

8. **Pallava** (Surrounding the *Yagya sthal*)
It symbolises prohibiting the bad elements and vile creatures from entering the *Yagya* place; freedom from harm, trouble and danger.
9. **Patram, Pushapam and Phalam** (Leaves, flowers and fruits)
It symbolises being close to Nature. Purifying the air with fragrance.
10. **Madhu *and* Mishri** (Honey and sugar)
It symbolises sweetness in tongue and attitude.
11. **Open Yagya Sthal** (Performing *Yagya* in open ground)
It is a declaration that the *Yagya* is for all; open heartedness; honesty, sincerity, candidness, guilelessness; straight and square dealing.
12. **Kusha** (A grass mat)
It indicates simplicity, ready to face tough situation, without wiles, ensuring the uninterrupted flow of energy.
13. **Dhruvatāra Darshan (**Looking at the Pole Star)
It presents the stability in life and relation; strength to bear the heavy burden of the life of a householder.
14. **Lawā and Chāwala** (Rice and baked rice)
It is the symbol of good omen and great start of prosperity, richness, enormous wealth and many children.
15. **Samanjan** (Taking refined butter on the tip of the middle finger and touching own heart)
It symbolises health, compassion and love.
In the same way often the palm is placed on the chest of the other person performing *Yagya* by the *Brāhmin* while chanting this Mantra:
Mama vrate te hridayam dadhāmi mama chittamanuchittam te astu

(I am placing my penance at your heart. Your heart must follow my wishes.)

16. **Ārati** (Showing light in a dish to the deities and gods) It symbolises good omen, prosperity, long life, light and blessings.

❁❁❁

Need of Samskārs

The need of Samskārs can be easily understood. We eat all natural products like cereals, vegetables, fruits, herbs, minerals etc. after refining them in some way - either after washing them or after taking their skin off either cutting them or cooking them. Even gold is refined before it is used and diamond is cut and polished before it can be made into a ring. In other words, we can say that a raw thing turns into finished product after going through its Samskār.

It is a simple logical thinking then that if everything needs a Samskār for its refining then why not refine the man too with Samskār?

If turmeric, oil, spices and salt can enrich our food and make it healthier and tastier then why will Samskārs not make us better, healthier and happier?

In this way, Samskārs are as natural as other things.

Cultivating Samskārs

Samskārāh ati durlabhah (Samskārs are rare).

In the same way *Samskāri* persons are rare because refinement does not come easily, Samskārs are cultivated with conscious effort during a long period. So far as perfection is concerned, one keeps on cultivating Samskārs throughout his life.

Life is a span, not a moment. It is a period of time not a point of time. Moments make the span. So, moments must be won over to give life its span. Naturally, life and living moments are both important. Samskārs, culture and refinements make life and its moments lively, meaningful and worth living. Hence, Samskārs are important and needed.

Conception is a moment, birth is another moment, death is also a moment but life is a complete cycle. We are born, we grow, weather out and die. For proper and healthy birth, for right growth and full living we need Samskārs. For better utilisation of the living time; for greater gains during weathering out, we need Samskārs.

The span of living is important. So, one must be ready and be well equipped to face the moments. It is important to sustain during the whole span of one's existence. When there is readiness and better equipments there are higher chances of survival and sustenance. That is why Samskārs are important and most needed.

Samskārs are there to keep us well equipped. These Samskārs have many parts and are given in many phases. Proper education is one such part. The modern men lay total stress on only bookish knowledge and forget all other phases of education. What they are doing is only collecting information and foolishly claiming it to be education.

We are learning one, two or may be three languages and claiming to have accumulated knowledge. We know only a part and think that we know everything.

Unfortunately, we don't know the Earth, Nature, life, society, even the self. Hence, we fail to live happily and with ease. Life, the greatest celestial gift, has become a burden today. Many persons are taking their own life and many other are taking the life of others. They are not thinking of adding life to their own life and make the life of others better.

In this way, we are all spending a fruitless life. We must get the Samskārs, refine ourselves and our children from the very beginning for better living so that life becomes fruitful and it is not wasted. In this way, we can avoid running after luxury, money and physical pleasure which are momentary. We must try to get maximum satisfaction from our life in the total span we spend on this planet earth.

Time of Samskār

The Samskārs are the need of the time as the *Grabhādhān* and *Punswan Samskārs* are performed on eligible women at the time of their first conception for better, healthier, refined and sublime embryo. These two Samskārs are performed to avoid the birth of a physically deformed or mentally crippled child.

This is not all. It is claimed that *Punswan Samskār* was powerful enough to ensure the birth of a male child. What a wonder! Modern science is still not as advanced as our ancient Indian science.

Seemantonnayan Samskār was capable of freeing the child from any contagious disease and from other misdeeds and sins of the parents. The newly born child was purged from blood impurities and the side effects of womb with the help of *Jātakarma*, *Nāmakaran* and *Annaprāshana Samskārs.*

Social Consciousness

Social sense in Samskārs can be understood easily if we can distinguish between nature, degradation and Samskārs.

- We feel hungry or thirsty and we take food or water, it is nature.
- We snatch food or other articles from others. It is degradation.
- We find a hungry man who needs food. We give him food and then we eat. It is Samskār.

A Samskār has a sense of sacrifice, tolerance, endurance, kindness, compassion, humility and benevolence. Possession of all these qualities which are a part of Samskār and their wise, intelligent, timely, conscious and confident use is what makes a man *Samskāri*. It is for all, hence, it has a social sense and social consciousness. Conscience plays a vital rôle as our conscience develops in many decades and many lives. A demon cannot change into a sublime figure overnight.

The collected and developed Samskārs from previous lives help us. The Samskārs taken from family, society and environment shape us in this life. This combined effort guides our life and controls our actions throughout the life. Slowly the Samskārs become a part and parcel of our being.

Care and Protection

We are human beings – weak and feeble. We need care and protection for survival. Most of the animals start to stand on their own feet within days. A human child takes years to stand on his own – on legs in more than one year and on self in no less than twenty-five years.

We are dependent on others for food, clothes and shelter for a good part of our life. We can never grow ourselves even one per cent of the things that are essential for our existence. Hence, we need a family and society. This is a debt we will have to pay towards them.

We should not take anything from the society without paying for it. We are nowadays earning and paying in cash. It will not free us from the debt.

- The crops, trees and other eatables are produced with labour and not out of money, so the environmental debt is to be paid back in the form of physical labour.
- The debt of the parents is repaid by becoming parents ourselves and taking all the troubles to raise children.
- The social debt is paid back by producing things essential for the society.
- Similarly love must be reciprocated with love; it can not be paid in currency.

❁❁❁

Lack of Samskārs

Those who fail to get Samskārs remain like animals, beasts and demons throughout their lives. They indulge in all sorts of corrupt practices for simple livelihood and yet fail to get a single square and balanced diet.

As a result they keep on complaining. They have complaints to each person living in and around their vicinity. As a result they never feel satisfied.

They fail to learn how to live, how to make use of the things available to them and how to spend time in useful deeds.

They are unable to incorporate changes and other good qualities and spend their lives like an animal without tail: *Sākshāt pashu puchhbihinah.*

Naturally, they fail to utilise their precious moments and fail to give meaning to this rare gift of life.

Lack of Samskārs turns a person into a thief, a criminal, a murderer, a terrorist – in a nutshell – a vile creature. Such a person has no control over his exuberant emotions and activities.

Indulging in Vices

Lack of Samskārs forces people to indulge in immoral, unethical, arbitrary works. It creates pessimists, sadists, hedonists, atheists and anti social persons who give no value to anything. Such men feel pride in doing something against the social norms, legal dictates and claim their misdeeds to be valiant heroic deeds. This gives rise to the concept of anti-heroes. The thieves and criminals are presented as heroes and all good men are sidelined. They keep on exploiting the natural resources and create natural and ecological imbalance.

Our world, today, is unfortunately passing through that phase. We can not break down the hills and mountains; we can not allow the miles deep ice of Antarctica to melt; we can not do away with the trees, water reservoirs, birds and animals; we dare not pollute the air and allow the heat to go beyond the affable 22 degrees. Unfortunately the pollution is growing fast and heat level has touched around 45 degrees. Neither man nor animals; neither crops nor plants can survive in such extreme hot conditions.

We are not living in coordination with Nature. We have forgotton the Samskars and become laws in ourselves. The words of the wise men hold no value to us. Material gain and luxurious living is all that we want. We are falsely claiming to control Nature. But we can not; instead we have created disparity and imbalance. We are losing everything because we have lost our Samskārs.

❋❋❋

The Scriptures on Samskārs

Most of the scriptures and the sages have something to say about the Samskārs. All can't be collected and quoted here. Yet, it will illuminate the mind to see, read and understand some of them.

Maharishi Hārit says,

"The person cultured and refined with conception and other outer Samskārs becomes comparable to Rishis and gets respect like them."

The quality that pervades both the general qualities and the special quality of the soul is called Samskār:

Sāmānya guna ātmavisheshaguno bhayavritigunatwa vyāpta jatim twam samskāratwam.

Both the *Nyāya Shāstra* and *Vaisheshika Darshan* have accepted three kinds of Samskārs:

Samskārbhedo vegoatha sthitisthāpakabhāwane: vega (force); *bhāwanā* (feeling) and *sthitisthāpaka* (that which maintains the status quo or returns back to the original state). This can be understood by the samskār of the heart that forces the blood out by contraction and regains its original shape.

In the *Mahābhārata* (Shāntiparva 235:24) Veda Vyāsa says,

"It is easy for that wise man to achieve *siddhi* (rare success) in this life and the life after it whose Samskārs have been duly and rightly performed, and who follows the rules and has control over the sense organs."

Samskritasya hi dāntasya niyatasya yatātmanah;
Prāgyasyānantarā siddhirihloke paratra cha.

संस्कृतस्य हि दानतस्य नीयतस्य यतात्मनः।
प्रज्ञास्यानन्तरा सिद्धिरिहलोके परन्न च॥

The scriptures lay stress that a person is not good or bad by birth. One takes on better or worse qualities after birth. Only in that sense we are our master if we control ourselves and become cultured and sublime. It depends upon our learning and absorbing better qualities and then following them. Learning is of no use if it is not followed. To be respectable or not depends entirely on us and on our Samskārs:

Āchārah paramo dharmah sarveshāmiti nishchayah;
Hināchāra paritātmā pretya āheha vinashyati.

आचारः परमो धर्मः सर्वेसामिति निश्चयः।
हीनाचारः परितात्मा प्रेत्याहेः विनश्यति॥

(It is certain that cultured behaviour is the essence of religion. Persons with unwholesome nature are destroyed soon, and suffer even after death.)

The same thing has been reiterated in *Vashishtha Smriti's* next *Shloka*:

Nainam tapānsi na brahma nāgnihotram na dakshināh; Hināchāramito bhrashtam tāryanti kadachana.

नैनं तपांसि न ब्रह्म नाग्निहोत्रं न दक्षिणाः।
हीनाचारमितो भ्रष्टं तारयन्ति कदाचन॥

(Persons with ill-cultured behaviour can't be emancipated; neither by penance nor by obeisance to fire and charity.)

sarvalakshanahinoapi yah sadāchārwānnarah; shraddhādāno anusuyashcha shatam varshāni jeevati.

Manusmriti (4:158)

सर्वलक्षणहीनोऽपि यः सदाचारवान्नरः।
श्रद्धादानोऽनसूयश्च शतं वर्षाणि जीवति॥

(The persons who have respect for all and are free from misdeeds live well for hundred years and accomplish all that they wish for.)

All the scriptures have laid stress on cleanliness and purging the inner self. Everything depends on mental and spiritual piety. Samskārs make good and lasting effect on the mind of the person whose Samskārs are performed, and also on his family members as well as on others who attend it. Our sublimity is the creation of our goodness and good moral and ethical values. It is the collection of virtuous inner qualities. It is up to us how far high we can raise our nature and refine our behaviour.

❁❁❁

Samskārs and the Problems of the World

Since long, the invaders, the Muslim rulers and the British rulers tried to wipe out the culture and history of our country. They did it vehemently and in many apparent and secret ways. It is due to the power of the ancient system of education; the character, devotion and dedication of Indians that they were able to save something out of everything.

It is unfortunate that the Indians of free India are destroying all our ancient knowledge with their ignorance, negligence and their foolish love for money. In the year 2005, 1,500 manuscripts from a temple of South were sent to USA, without keeping a zerox copy. They were lost. It's a dubious question why are we not able to save our wealth. India was *Vishwaguru* and ruled over the world not with arms but with love, knowledge, spirituality, and character. Why are we not able to attain that height again? We are not trying to regain our lost glory. Rupee, Dollar or Pound is temporary wealth, the real knowledge and power lies in the inner growth. We get things in lieu there of but we can't get everything with the currency notes, promissory notes or ATM cards.

Eternal Human Religion

There has been a deliberate attempt for a long time, to keep the Indians away from their powerful Samskārs; to make them forget the Samskārs; to force them to be aloof from their culture and to make them *Samskārheena* (uncultured) so that they may not become sublime and divine again. In this way, the demonic forces may rule easily all over the world.

The life of Indian gods, sages, seers, wise men and common people is full of the stories and incidents that describe and glorify their numerous, incessant and unfinished battle against sins, sinners, *Rākshasas* and other beasts of vile nature. It happens because they follow the Eternal Human Religion; because their cultural life, religious rites and social custom keep them united; because they achieve and enjoy a rare personal, family, social, religious and cultural relation and unity; because only they make honest efforts to grow from inside and because they possess the pure, spiritual and celestial power.

The country that fought the greatest battle in human history, the *Mahābhārata*, for complete disarmament and followed the peaceful ways of non-violence, benevolence and compassion; the country whose most valiant kings abandoned war; whose gods, saints and *Mahātmās* taught purity of character and deeds and detachment from everything worldly have something of illumined energy and power that saves them from breaking into pieces and getting scattered. Despite the incessant attempts for centuries and despite many weaknesses infesting Indian life and culture, it has something of a mixed unknown, undefined but deeply felt force that has saved them during the threats of total annihilation. They have taken that hidden but divine from their great and spiritual forefathers and carried them in every subsequent birth down the ages.

Cycle of Birth and Rebirth

The country that laid all the emphasis on rebirth and on making conscious, painstaking and deliberate attempt to grow from inside and to improve the inner self, take another life after birth, by taking rebirth (*Dwija*) by cultivating, harvesting and possessing culture and refinement, and thus by imbibing humanity, sublimity and divinity, has now virtually no knowledge of those Samskārs. They do not know how they are performed and why they are important; why they should be performed and what are the ultimate gains and immediate benefits, and why did the forefathers lay so much of emphasis on them that changed most of the *Shudras* (It is believed that all are born as *Shudras*) into *Dwija* (The *Vaishyas* and *Kshatriyas* are *Dwija* too for they get rebirth); and most of the *Dwijas* into *Brāhmins* (The *Brāhmins* are only those who possess all the great qualities of a cultured and refined human being); and most of the *Brāhmins* into *Rishis* and some of the *Rishis* into *Maharishis* and *Brahmarishis*. No one can be a *Rishi* without being a *Brāhmin*. So, the *Rishis*, who are being foolishly claimed to be *Shudras* (born out of a *Shudra* parent) are *Brāhmins* because they took rebirth and they kept on growing, gaining knowledge, accumulating spiritual power, storing up celestial energy and finally getting divinity.

They are divine, and the modern man, indulged in physical pleasure and luxury, has no social, political, moral, and religious or human rights to pass comments on them or to criticise them. Modern men and women will have to accept that they don't know all about them and they can't describe them fully. Since their inner wisdom and power is not known hence, the modern generation can't pass comments or judgments over them. It is beyond their conception and right.

Knowledge and Information

The modern sons and daughters of those sublime *Gotras*, of the *Rishis* that created the concept of Samskārs have, deliberately but foolishly, taken away all the reading materials related to the Samskārs from the syllabi to keep the new generation from knowing them and growing strong by following the time tested ways and methods of pure, peaceful, happy, healthy and prosperous life.

Subhāsits (great teachings of *Rishis* in the form of couplets) and other quotable and didactic *Shlokas* have been replaced by ordinary physical, material and shallow quotations of the foreign writers who have not read these scriptures or gone deep inside them. Even in the Samskrit texts, the numbers have been reduced and only a few are repeated in every class, in such a way and to such an extent that they make a lasting imprint on the minds of growing children that there are only a fistful of such *Shlokas*. The fact is that Germans have been trying for more than a hundred and fifty years to prepare a list of all the books in Samskrit. The list is still growing and the end is not in sight yet; then how can one count the number of *Shlokas*. Thousands of Encyclopedias will lack space to print them. The fact is that the European books give only **information** while the Indian books give **knowledge.** There is a very broad and fine line of demarcation between information and knowledge. In the educational institutions today only information is given. Students are collecting only information. They are not getting knowledge. Ironically enough, they boast that it is the age of Information Technology. Knowledge about the Earth, Nature, natural elements and wealth, living beings and that of the needs of real, healthier and happier life is no longer there. The roads are full of advertisements. Printed ads and ways of advertisement have been introduced and inducted into syllabus; and everything worth knowing and keeping and capable of making great and sublime persons out of the materialists has been mercilessly thrown out of educational curricula.

Health Hazards

Due to deep and centuries-old conspiracy by the invaders, the Indians are not being allowed that great knowledge which is the life of humanity and capable of saving the Earth and life on it. Life devoid of peace, pleasure, health, happiness and prosperity is no life at all.

As a result almost all the human beings of the world are suffering from some physical or mental disease. They are surviving not on healthy food, atmosphere, ideas and physical labour but on junk food, unhealthy habits, artificial equipments and numerous medicines. They know they are suffering, yet they opt for periodical tests. They know there are natural ways to get rid of the diseases but they prefer medicines. There are uncountable touts to lull you into their webs; ironically enough, they are also known as websites. Once, you connect your computer to Internet and enter any of numerous such attractive website, the virus is bound to enter your computer It is like the snake that paralyses its victim by injecting poison into its blood, before swallowing it bit by bit. Better check your body, check your mind and take an inventory of your physical possessions in the form of household articles of everyday use from utensils to bed and clothes, habits of eating, sleeping, sitting and working and spiritual possessions in the form of purity, sociability, morality and religiosity. You will easily know what are you doing that should not be done and what you are not doing that must be done. If human beings claim to be the master of their life and fate, then prove it; don't be a slave to the market, market products, attractive ads, physical pleasure and immoral acts.

Wealth of Knowledge

The modern Indians are not being allowed to get at the much needed knowledge imparted by their forefathers but that knowledge made the remaining world modern as the Europeans learnt this great and wide knowledge that brought about the Golden Age in England, Renaissance and Industrial Revolution in Europe when this knowledge reached there through Persian translations and mostly through Vasco da Gama who followed the Indian merchants and anchored his ship at Calicut in India in 1488 AD. For your own satisfaction as a proof, you can see the list of inventions and inventors. You won't find a single name from Europe before that period, barring the ancient Greeks who were in constant touch with India.

Incidentally, Vasco de Gama did not discover India, as was taught by the British and retained by modern Indians; he discovered only a sea-route for the Europeans and paved the route for their insurgence. It is no wonder that Europe became wise after that, and because of the 1000 years long slavery we are accepting them, reading and learning and following them blindfolded. They are still swimming on the surface, unable to dive deep into the secret truths of life or to make inward journey into space to connect the celestial electromagnetic energy with the physical energy; that yoga (union, better: fusion) is not as yet possible with them. The modern Indians should not be deprived of that great classical and Vedic wisdom or the culture and refinement. They have every right to grow healthy: physically and spiritually.

A few people who come into contact with our wealth of knowledge are so overwhelmed by its enormity that they forget everything else. They fail to take what comes first and what next. In this way, they neither get the systematic view nor confidently prescribe a system to follow in knowing and understanding the indomitable knowledge of the ancient Indian *Rishis*. They busy themselves in knowing more and more during the remaining days of their life. In that hurry they fail to co-relate the discordant and missing links. The fact is that there is wealth everywhere in it. One can't get or know everything in one single and short life, for generally, the life of the learned begins after forty and is finished before seventy.

Law of Cosmos

Don't search for the essential, take and use what you get. The most essential thing is that which you possess.

Possession and utilisation is all that is needed. This is the way to grow. And, believe it, all growth comes from within; growth is always inner, it can't come from outside, though the outside world, element and phenomenon influence the inner growth. The five senses are inner growth. They appear from inside. They get the feed-back, needed energy and support from inside and in return they are responsible to the inner self. They are fed and they feed back to that self. This is the law of cosmos.

Living in dens has caused the maximum damage. On different pretext we prefer to remain inside: closed and aloof; at home in locked gates and call it big house or spacious room and in office we call it cabins. They deny openness and help in avoiding others. Free mixing and normal communication is a dream. You take prior permission and fix a time to meet your relatives. We claim that we don't have time while the fact is that we waste a lot of our precious time in clubs (for fake freshness), in unnecessary transport (as we prefer to live far away from our workplace); in watching virtually nonsense on TV or talking to fixed persons about fixed topics on phone. We never calculate the loss: damages done to body, mind, relations; becoming non-existent in social set-up; doing nothing for preserving life and ensure peace, security, health and prosperity to our grandchildren. We falsely feel that by depositing a lot of money we can ensure the birth and happiness of the great-grand children of our great-grand children; and ignore the statements that we usually see in the newspapers about the growing dangers on the Earth and atmosphere. When there will be no Earth and no atmosphere, how and where will the 'den', or 'cabin' be?

Race for Modernisation

There are certain organisations, spiritual, religious, political and non-political, that have been trying to bring these facts, the foul play, into the fore but they are not getting adequate support and not making satisfactory progress. No one is taking heed to it. The race of modernisation, which is following European ways and adopting European means, is on and most of the people are participants, and each one of them wishes to be declared modern or ultra modern.

In spite of that race they have not completely abolished the Samskārs. Some of the Samskārs are performed. It is more correct to say that some of the Samskārs are hurriedly performed, that misses the essence, appears like a caricature and results in mediocrity. It is degeneration.

Places of Worship

In recent times, incidents of attacks on temples and Hindus' abodes and places of worship have started and the frequency has increased. Famous temples have security arrangements and checking at different places. It is neither safe nor easy to visit temples and worship the deity in peace and at ease. Some temples are so crowded that they provide smooth access to the sanctum only at a payment of very high premium as if it's a trade. So the number of personal temples and corners for worship in the residence are growing fast. In the same way, the number of general and local visitors to general and famous temples is naturally and substantially coming down. Pseudo-*Brāhmins*, illiterate *Brāhmins* (by birth), non-*Brāhmins* with least knowledge and profane people have started helping the devotees and the householders in performing

Poojā and *Samskārs*. The situation is alarming. The quality and sanctity has deteriorated and faith has been shattered. The things must change, and can change only with the will power and strong moral character. In this light the Samskārs become more significant than ever before.

The tendency in the modern man to prove that the ancient scriptural and classical Samskārs are uncivilised and uncultured is the greatest cause of concern. We are very far away from reality; and scientifically junk and rotten ideas, food, life, songs, dances and festivals are being integrated in our life. These have already created havoc in the western life. The people in other countries and in the metro cities of India are only living; they have no life, no laughter and no smile, nothing natural: neither love nor hatred.

Sticking to Tradition

There are certain heartening and encouraging features also. Only Indians perform *Poojā* and only Indians make conscious efforts and try many ways to become cultured and refined. There are many adamant and determined persons who are not ready to wipe out the tradition, and try their level best to perform and make others perform the rites, rituals and Samskārs in the best possible manner under the prevalent socio-economic and religious milieu.

In spite of all these facts, there is a very happy and encouraging trend that even in this age of excessive materialism all feel exhilarated whose Samskārs are to be ceremoniously arranged. It is Indian-ness and the inner and latent power of India.

❋❋❋

Samskārs and Supernatural Power

Samskārs can develop inner power to an extent to give superhuman and supernatural power. It develops inner mental working, ability and prowess. The western psychologists and philosophers discuss only three states of the development of mind. Indians see many layers of mental development. Sri Aurobindo claims nine layers including over mind and illumined mind. These rare layers of super consciousness can be developed with only Samskārs and Yoga, concentration and meditation, and purification and refinement.

Eternal Triangle

What we find in the imagined sketches of *Rishis* performing *Yagyas* sitting around fire and praying with folded hands drawn by artists during the ages are created by imagination on the basis of the information collected or popular anecdotes. They show outer and physical aspects of *Yagyas*. They are unable to depict the inner power and working which is still a mystery.

It is still not clear what sort of superhuman and supernatural powers are acquired. Through the analysis of the scriptures we can conclude that they got both positive and negative powers, but there must be some neutral force otherwise the eternal triangle won't be complete.

Indian eternal triangle is quite different to the western eternal triangle, which is limited to lover, beloved and villain; or husband, wife and lover. It is totally worldly and physical. While Indian philosophers, scientists and spiritual thinkers have drawn umpteen tri and triangles, they declare that balance in the universe as well as in life or Nature can't be achieved without the eternal triangle. So, beginning with the three-lettered word and sound *Aum* followed by *Trideva* and *Trimurti,* they went on to claim *Trikāl, Triguna, Trikuta, Tridhula, Trikatuka, Trayambaka, Tridarshi, Triphala, Trikshār, Trijagat, Tritāpa, Tridosha, Tridhātu, Trinetra, Tripadi, Triveda, Tripinda, Triputi* to *Trilawan, Triloka* and *Trishakti.* The list is unbelievably long. A part of it is given here only to suggest that just by the presence of three things the power was increased many hundredfolds because it completes the eternal triangle.

Samskārs for Indians

Samskārs are different for the Indians. By physically mixing different sets of three things and by making others eat, drink or smell they achieved wonders psychologically and spiritually. The outer activities helped the inner self to glow and endowed them with different supernatural powers. With only *Vashikār Siddhi* they were able to travel inwardly into time and space; witnessed the happenings at distant places in the present, past or future and even able to read the books at remote places. This inward journey was their speciality. It is a wonder that human consciousness can grow to such heights with only purity, humanity, concentration, devotion and fusion with the cosmic energy. But none of these are easy to achieve, and in the modern material world, each one is impossible to accomplish. All sorts of dirty ideas have been stuffed in our mind. We are unable to think clearly and act humanely. Only Samskārs can get the dirty stuff out because there are some factors related to the Samskārs that work as 'mind-wash'.

Attention must be drawn towards the fact that Samskārs take their own time to settle in mind and character as a part of being. Only then they show the maximum advantage while they start showing some outward effect from the time the preparations start for holding a particular Samskār ceremony. These two are very obvious in the attitude of the boy at the time of *Upanayan* and that of the girl when marriage is being settled before actual *Vaivāhika Samskār*. In girls there is a complete metamorphosis within twenty-four hours of marriage.

❋❋❋

Benefits from Samskārs

There are numerous benefits from Samskārs. Mental and physical health is the best gift of and greatest benefit from Samskārs. Blood is purified. It gives needed energy and adequate oxygen to each organ and every part of the body. It is rejuvenation and revitalisation. That way our physical stamina and mental strength are increased manifold, and we are able to work hard with freshness for longer duration, with concentration and consciousness to achieve greater success everywhere and in everything.

Better and Refined Life

Samskārs make the whole life better and refined. They give culture and refined sensibility for better control over intellect and its higher and deeper use. The intellect works in a fine manner. All the great intellectuals (not the pseudo-intellectuals) were and are men with Samskār.

Samskārs distil the character; direct the energy positively for benevolent causes. Selfishness, lust, anger and other vile traits of personality die. They never regain power to destroy the character. Once the balance is achieved, the equilibrium is maintained throughout the life.

Samskārs make us lead a complete and most satisfying life. A man with Samskārs is able to confidently and successfully face the problems of life. He is not afraid of anything or anyone. He knows that he has done the best and will get the best. This is the poetic justice. If one has not sown the seeds of thorns and poisons then thorns won't prick him and his life will not be poisonous. He won't suffer from the poisons of life.

Faith and Confidence

Samskārs give enough faith and confidence that a dying person is not afraid of the unknown life after death because he/she has done nothing wrong in life. It is wrong that incites wrong and it is right that offers and makes everything right. The hurricanes may rise, problems may come but they will pass over without doing serious damage. The faith and confidence is the reward for the troubles taken for acquiring Samskārs. The labour and tension, the penance and pains are amply rewarded.

❁❁❁

Essentials and Forbidden in Samskārs

Performing the rituals and rites are not as easy as we think them to be, and they are never superfluous. And, practicing them is all the more difficult. We may not know them that is one thing, we may not be following them, that is another thing, but each instruction is meaningful and essential to follow for the near perfect effect.

While performing a *Poojā* or a Samskār, it is essential to follow some formalities, rules and acts; in the same way there are many forbidden acts that should never be followed.

Pious Bath

Pavitra Snāna or pious bath or bath for piety is actually a medicated bath. The things that are known to rejuvenate the organs are used in such baths. Many minerals, metals, medicines, fruit-skins are mixed, liquidated and smeared over the body. In earlier days people used to take bath in ponds or rivers and the smeared paste got time to enter through the skin. Such things were mixed in water when the bath was taken inside a bathing pool.

The most popular things, *Sarva-ausadhi, Sarva-gandha, Til* (sesamum seeds) pestled *Āmlā* (myrobalan) are pestled together and smeared all over the body. At many places *Haldi* (turmeric) powder, and mustard seeds or orange peels are also used. Usually *Haldi* is mixed with curd. Then, *Chameli* (jasmine) oil is smeared.

All the family members and all the priests performing the *Poojā* or *Yagya* or Samskār should take such a bath. Nowadays, the priests claim that they have already taken the bath and only one selected or designated member or the person involved in the Samskār performs a similar bath. Sesamum seeds are put in the bucket of water. The water fails to suck in its essence during that short period.

Cloth

If you are wearing a *Dhoti*, wear it in such a way that it surrounds the navel, and the left side of navel and the back is covered. With three folds a person or a *Brāhmin* is ready for *Poojā*. These days the rituals are being performed in western and other dresses that give least movement and virtually no latitude; no freedom for moving hands, or to legs for bending or standing.

At the time of *Smārta* or *Shrout Karma*, one should wear two sacred threads and a scarf-like cloth. If such a cloth is not available then take a third sacred thread.

Wear two pieces of clothes in *Poojā* and rituals. Never perform *Sandhyā, Japa, Deva-Poojan* and *Homa* in one cloth.

One can not come to the place of *Poojā* or perform rites in wet clothes. In the same way, one can not change clothes after taking bath and can not perform '*Sāndhya Japa'* in a pond, in dry clothes. The clothes worn at the time of visiting toilet or copulation are strictly prohibited in all sorts of rituals and rites, *Poojan* and *Japa*.

❁❁❁

The Samskārs of the Previous Life

Prashnopanishad claims that when *Udān Vāyu* goes out of the body, the body becomes cold. The moment the heat of the body goes out and enters another body, the living element goes out along with the senses amalgamated with the mind. It is known as rebirth:

Tejo ha wā udānasta asmād upashāntatejāh
punarbhavam indriyairmanasi sampadyamānaih

Prashnopanishad (3:9)

Two things are very important in rebirth:

- The life element that takes rebirth
- The senses amalgamated into mind

It means that in some unknown form, the knowledge, deeds and misdeeds and inner achievements remain alive in the 'self' that takes rebirth.

Good and Bad Deeds

The *Garuda Purāna* takes recourse and claims that the good and bad deeds of the previous life show up as prosperity or disease in this life:

सुकृतं दुश्कृतं वा अपि भुक्त्वा पूर्वं यथा अर्जितम् ।
कर्मयोगात्तदा तस्य कश्चिद् व्याधिः प्रजायते ।

Sukritam dushkritam wā api bhuktwā purvam yathā arjitam;
Karmayogāttadā tasya kashchid vyādhih prajāyate.

Garuda Purāna (1:19)

शरीरं यदवाप्नोति यच्चाप्युत्क्रामतीश्वरः ।
गृहीत्वैतानि संयाति वार्युगन्धानिवाश्यात् ॥

Shariram yadwāpnoti achchāpyutakrāmatishwarh;
Grihitwaitāni samyāti vāyurgandhā aniwāshyāt.

Gitā (15:8)

(Lord Krishna has said that as the air carries away fragrance from one to another place, in the same manner, the living element takes away mind and soul from one body to another.)

In the *Gitā,* Sri Krishna clarifies that there are two types of Samskārs:

- Permanent - Its effect is to be faced by hook or crook
- Temporary - That keeps on changing with bigger changes in life; purged or improved through the recitation of name, spirituality, yoga, yagya, penance and oblation etc at different times and in different forms.

It is clear then that we carry our qualities, virtues or vices, Samskārs, deeds and misdeeds to the next life.

❋❋❋

The Samskārs of Grihastha Dharma

The wishes, feelings and emotions of a person and the deeds accordingly are called Samskārs. If a person has pure, correct and wholesome feelings and he works for the good of all, then he has good and refined Samskārs; if otherwise, then he has *Kusamskārs*.

Aim of Samskārs

All the Samskārs are aimed at happy, healthy, pleasant and full living; for keeping better relations with others, for making the world a better place to live and finally to get bliss and salvation.

The *Rishis* in the scriptures have dictated details of the Samskārs for all; for each division in society and for each age group. They have specially mentioned Samskārs for the *Grihasthas*. If one follows them then life will be pleasant; if not then despite all the material wealth and luxury, life will be hell.

Types of Samskārs

The Samskārs for the *Grihasthas* can be divided in two types:

- Fundamental Samskārs
- Outer Samskārs

Fundamental Samskārs include faith in God, oneness with other living beings, decent behaviour, helping attitude, forgiveness, not to torture others, not to be angry, moral acts, discipline and obedience, detachment, not to wish anything from anyone, not to be sad at loss etc.

The outer Samskārs include rising early, drinking water in the morning and before eating anything, wishes and salutation to every member of the family and society whenever they appear (*Abhivādan* and *Pranām*), worshipping, visits to temple and other sacred places, working hard, looking after own body and that of others, remaining physically fit, giving security and guarding the people and wealth, best utilisation of body, mind and of resources etc.

❁❁❁

The Samskārs Given during Childhood

Childhood is a tender age. It takes the impressions easily and whatever is imprinted in the mind remains there forever. So, all the good Samskārs should be given during childhood like the power to distinguish between good and bad and other qualities that can help a child grow into a better human being. In fact, childhood is not the age to make a child learned, wise and strong but all the seeds are sown and all the saplings are planted in a child during this age so that the child can become learned, wise and strong; so that the child can win over the overwhelming restlessness, sadness and depression that has gripped the whole world.

Mother, the Best Teacher

What a mother gives to her child is the real Samskār that never fades away. The importance of mother and mother's teaching can be understood from the fact that *Manusmriti* claims:

Upādhyāyāndashāchārya āchāryānām shatam pitā;
Sahastram tu pitrin mātā gauravenātirichyate
Manusmriti (2:145)

उपाध्यायान्दशाचार्य आचार्याणां शतं पिता।
सहस्तं तु पितृन्माता गौरवेणातिरिच्यते।।

(One *Āchārya* is better than ten *Upādhyāyas*; a father is greater than hundred *Āchāryas* but a mother is greater than one thousand fathers)

A mother is said to be the best teacher but she is far greater than any university, and the Saṁskārs given by her during the childhood are permanent Samskārs that mould a child and shape his whole life.

Modern Parents

Here it seems to be very pertinent to mention that the modern parents have become so much money-minded that they are unable to give what their children deserve from them. They don't have and so they do not give good Samskārs to their children. Modern mothers are foolish enough to send their children to schools, particularly preparatory schools, at the age of two and a half or three. Some of the conscious guardians are very alert about the education of their children up to the age of eight after that they lose interest or get otherwise busy. They forget one very important fact that in the life of a boy or a girl the age from 8 to 16 is very important, very critical and very dangerous because the secretion of male and female hormones starts and there is obvious growth in male and female organs. Their voice changes and their mind starts getting mature. If utmost care is not taken then they can go astray, perceive all the wrong notions and fall in all sorts of bad habits. They may get addicted to drugs, smoking, perverted sex, bad company etc.

They are the best guardians who keep their children under constant watch during the age of 8 to 16 and save them from going astray. If a boy or girl is given good Samskārs during this period, then there is perhaps no chance of them ever falling to bad company or forming bad habits. Then life can be better.

The Samskārs for the Children

Here is a list of the Samskārs which should be instilled in the children:

Rise before the sunrise.	Serve others.	Don't be angry.
Remember God.	Help others.	Never fight.
Salute the elders.	Be virtuous.	Never use abusive words.
Get fresh.	Learn and observe manners.	Don't shake the body.
Take exercises.	Share your things.	Avoid luxury.
Pray to God.	Be courteous.	Behave well.
Study the *Gita*.	Be disciplined.	Eat only fresh food.
Study the syllabus.	Be polite and humble.	Eat less than needed.
Study at school.	Be obedient.	Don't eat junk food.
Think to be the best.	Take bath.	Don't eat stale food.
Concentrate.	Remain clean and tidy.	Don't deceive.
Grow confident.	Study with pleasure.	Avoid expensive articles.
Encourage others.	Play for pleasure.	Avoid reflection, radiation and vibration.
Learn cooperation.	Be sweet.	Read only good books.

Be compassionate.	Be fragrant.	Don't hate others.
Be kind.	Avoid excesses everywhere.	Don't inflict injury.
Respect others.	Maintain decorum.	Don't use leather or plastic.
Aim at inner growth.	Live within limitations.	Be simple and think deep.

Vardhāpana: Janmadiwas Samskār: Birthday Celebrations

In India, the birth of a child is very sacred and enjoyed in many different ways. The birth of a son is compared to a *Deepa*, a light and the birth of a girl is claimed to be the arrival of Goddess *Laxmi* herself. The date of birth is calculated on the Lunar month of *Vikram Samvat*. In the case of dual *Tithi, Nakshatra* is given priority and in the case of *Adhimās* the *Shuddhamās* is taken as *Vardhāpana* or the date of birth.

The birthdays are celebrated in a very simple but pious and religious way. The *Vardhāpana Samskār* is to be celebrated every year. Indian birthday celebrations are very cultured, refined, interesting, healthy, that give long life and prosperity. The following Samskār is given according to *Dharmasindhu*. The 60th and the 80th birthday is celebrated in a grand way.

On the birthday of a person an earthen lamp should be *lighted* and kept burning for the next 24 hours.

In the morning the pasted seeds of *Til* (sesamum) or *Saraso* (mustard) *Ubatana* (unguent) is smeared on the whole body and massaged; and bath is taken in water mixed with sesamum seeds. New clothes are worn, blessings are taken from the parents, grandparents and other elders before starting the Poojā. Sitting on the worshipping mat one prays to gods, *gurus* and elders including the family deity. After that Prajāpati, Surya, Sri Ganesh, Mārkandeya, Vyāsa, Parashurāma, Aswathāmā, Bali, Prahalāda, Hanumāna, Vibhishana and six deities are worshipped. They include the eight Immortals and Sapt Rishis. They give pleasant and long life. At certain places Homa is also performed and *rakshāsutra* is tied at the wrist with the Mantra:

Yena baddho bali rāja dāna indram mahābalah;
Tenatwāma pratibandhyāmi rakshām achalam achalah.

Some things are strictly prohibited on the birthday: one should not ignore the elders; people should not be invited but each visitor should be provided with *Prasād*; hair cutting and nail cutting is prohibited on that day; one should not run from place to place; celibacy should be maintained; non-vegetarian food is prohibited; one should not be angry or fight against anyone and hot water should not be used for bathing.

For better prosperous and peaceful long life, one must follow the Indian way of celebrating birthdays.

❁❁❁

Samskārs for Inner Growth

Our ancestors longed for inner growth and inner refinement. Worldly wealth and worldly pleasures had little value for them. They not only performed sacrifices but their life itself was a sacrifice. They lived for others. They loved, respected and performed penance. It was another subtle and difficult way of inner growth. It is a wonder that they were attached and detached simultaneously. It is a rare phenomenon. It became possible because they gave Samskārs to their body and mind.

Samskārs for Everything

Our ancestors had Samskārs for everything. They tortured their body to make it strong, so that it could endure all. That way they got strength and remained healthy. They achieved balance with Nature and hence were able to live for quite a long time. So, they have numerous achievements to their credit. It is our weakness that we don't know all about them, about each of their achievement and we don't understand their process and the meaning behind their unique ways. We have reduced the number of Samskārs and yet are unable to perform them. We care only for physical facilities and physical pleasures. We have forgotten and discarded the soul and this has affected our life. We are neither healthy nor happy.

On the other hand, our ancestors kept inventing ways to keep the body healthy and the inner self happy. We are inventing ways and means to reduce the power and resources of Nature and ways and means to reduce physical activities. When we think of our ancestors and their ways of living life then everything seems to be miracle. It is a wonder that after the age of 55 they would leave the pleasures of a household and take *Vānaprastha* for greater development of the soul and better service to the society; and after the age of 75 they accepted *Sanyās* and lived totally in the open without a shed over head, with only two pieces of cloth on body and a stick to help in movement. That was all the wealth that they required and possessed. They kept on moving, teaching others and living on alms. The greatest thing about the alms was limitation imposed on them. They would ask for alms from only three houses. They won't go to the fourth house to beg even if they did not get anything to eat. They would spend that day without meal.

Aim of Samskārs

The aim of the Samskārs is to purify and strengthen the body, mind and speech. We can do it if we can get rid of the impurities related to them. *Manusmriti* was created particularly to achieve the aim of purifying the outer body and inner self of man. That is why *Manusmriti* is termed as 'a Scripture for all human beings'. Manu, himself, has directed men to purge body, mind and speech, in three qualities:

- *Uttam* (best)
- *Adham* (worst)
- *Madhyam* (general)

These three qualities determine the progress and prosperity as well as the achievement and salvation of each person:

Shubhāshubh phalam karmam mano wāg deha sambha-wam;
Karmajā gatayo nrinām uttam adham madhyamāh.

Manusmriti (12:3)

शुभाशुभ फलं कर्मं मनोवाग्देह संभवम्।
कर्मजा गतयो नृणामुत्तमधममध्यमाः॥

In this regard, he has listed the impurities of mind:

- To snatch the property of others; to think of bringing harm to others and to stick to false concepts are mental impurities and they destroy peace and wealth.
- To speak ill or to curse others or to say false things, or sycophancy or backbiting or to talk about unrelated things and discordant elements are the impurities of speech and destroy the character and mental equilibrium.
- To take the wealth or to capture the property of others in illegal way or forcibly, to show violence not prescribed by religion or scriptures and to get entangled with the wife of another person are physical impurities and bad deeds that destroy the reputation, wealth, health and mental ease.

So, in the eyes of all the scriptures only virtuous persons who have good Samskārs can save the knowledge, ecological balance, morality and make the life and society worth living.

Samskārs of the Body

Conscience is made to be the proof and judge during doubt and dilemma. This is possible when a person has purged his body, mind and speech. It is one and the greatest reason that for the purification of body, a particular god is called to strengthen a particular part of body. These are known as the Samskārs of the body, the parts of body or organs. They are:

- *Angnyās*
- *Shadangnyās*
- *Laghunyās*
- *Karnyās*
- *Brihannyās*

The idea is to become sublime and godly to worship God: *devo bhutwā yajed devam.* It is useless to worship God with a dirty body and corrupt mind.

Angnyās

In *Angnyās*, the *Mantras* are chanted and water is sprinkled on different parts of the body to purify them. It has deeper meanings and psychological and spiritual contents. With the sprinkling of water and chanting of *Mantras* that part is given the power and attributes of a particular god and thus it gets the physical and divine power of that god. In this way, with this process we give Samskārs to different parts of body. They become *Samskārita.* The following is the most popular *Mantra* for purification in which *bāhyābhantarah shuchih,* the purification of outer (*bāhya*) and inner (*abhyāntar*) is requested:

ॐ अपवित्रः पवित्रे वा सर्वावस्थां गतोऽपि वा ।
यः स्मरेत् पुण्डरीकाक्षं स बाह्याभ्यान्तरः शुचिः ॥

Aum apavitrah pavitro wā srvā awasthām gato api wā; Yeh smareta pundarikāksham sa bāhyābhyantarah shuchih.

Shatangnyās

The six Samskārs of the parts of body (*Shatangnyās*) include:

1. *Shikhābandhan* - It is not only the Samskār of the head but it also provides the brightness of Brahma, and skill and finesse to the mind.
2. *Mantrashravan* - Listening to *Mantras* is not only the Samskār of the ears but it also provides strength to words and sound.
3. *Darshan* – The meeting and looking at the elders, preceptor, teacher and saints etc are not only the Samskār of eyes but it also gives power of subtle analysis and deep thinking (*Sukshma* and *Paroksha Drishti*).
4. *Bhoga* – Eating *Prasāda* prescribed by the scriptures is not only the Samskār of the stomach but also a way to purify the blood and give energy to it.
5. *Sant-sevā* or *Deena-sevā* - Service to saints and poor is not only the Samskār of hands but it also gives immense power and skill to hands; the persons performing it easily become dextrous.
6. *Pradakshinā* – Taking rounds of a temple's corridor or visiting places of pilgrimage is not only the Samskār of legs but it adds to the inner power and confidence of the man doing these things: *Tanme manah shiva sankalpamastu.*

All these are usually performed just by sprinkling water on the parts or by touching the related organ as the centre of the head, eyes, ears, throat, chest, navel, thighs etc. ❋❋❋

Role of Women in Samskār

The best thing for a woman is to become a woman and remain like a woman – tender, smooth, soft-spoken, delicate, creative, *Annapurna*. If a woman becomes manlike, then she will not remain womanlike and won't get the pleasures and satisfaction that a woman should get from life. It will be a waste of life as well as of womanhood.

Samskārs and Kusamskārs for Women

Women are the balancing factors – very wise, very energetic, very alert, very sweet and very lively. They can make or mar a family. Howsoever alert and diligent men may be, the peace and progress of the family lies in the control of women. They are the leading powers and mentors. So if a woman has *Susamskārs*, she can give a height and status to a family. It makes no difference whether that family is rich or poor, but if a woman has *Kusamskārs* she will definitely and easily destroy the peace, pleasure, health and prestige of a family. It makes no difference even if it is a very rich family. So the *Susamskārs* and *Kusamskārs* of women are more important than that of the men or children. These are the *Susamskārs* and *Kusamskārs* of women:

***Susamskārs* of Women**	***Kusamskārs* of Women**
Saundarya (Outer and inner beauty)	*Kalah* (quarrelsome), *Karkashā*, (shrewd)
Lajjā (modesty)	*Nindā* (slanderous)
Vinamra (humble)	*Irshyā* (jealous)
Sanyam (restraint) *Tapa*,(penance)	*Bheda* (splitting nature)
Santosh (contentment)	*Moha* (infatuated)
Kshamā (forgiveness)	*Badalā* (vengeful)
Dheeratā (patience)	*Adhira* (impatient)
Gambhiratā (serious)	*Vāchāla* (talkative, garrulous)
Samatā (equality)	*Kusang* (bad company)
Sahishnutā (tolerance)	*Lobhi* (lustful, demanding)
Suniyojitā (capacity to manage well)	*Phoohar* (lewd, ludicrous)
Sanchayitā (cumulative)	*Vināshi* (destructive)
Sanyat (controlled, balanced)	*Dikhāwā* (showy, pomp)
Shramashilā (diligent)	*Ālasya* (sloth)
Nirabhimāni (egoless)	*Abhimāni* (egoist)
Mitavyayi (frugal)	*Phijoolkharcha* (extravagant)
Dayadra (compassionate)	*Krura* (cruel)
Shushrushā (nursing)	*Kupathya* (unhealthy food)
Sati (chaste)	*Vyabhichārini* (adulteress)

Bhakti (devotion)	*Dillagi* (merry, cutting jokes)
Sādagi (plain-living)	*Vilāsi* (luxuriant nature)
Milansār (mixing)	*Karawi* (bitter, harsh)
Prasannachit (pleasant nature)	*Vishāda* (aggrieved)

Women as Pivotal Point

From time immemorial, Indian women have been taking the initiative in performing the Samskārs. They have been responsible and have carried on their responsibilities well. Despite the growing modernity and tilt towards the western culture and way of life, Indian women have done justice to the faith shown in them by men. They are the authorities and they commandingly order the males to get the required Samskār performed. If a Samskār is not performed in a house it is because of the slackness and dilly-dallying attitude of the ladies of the family.

They have been the pivotal point, the central figure and the axis around which the complete family moves. They are the greatest force in Indian society although the credit often goes to men.

They have forced the men to perform the Samskār and in time, in the past, and still do it. They can show miraculous results. History shows that kingdoms and families have prospered because of the women and have perished because of them.

Women still hold the key. They can change the living style and lifestyle food and thinking, and bring all the positive changes to re-establish the Indian supremacy in almost every field. They have led men from the front and keeping themselves easily in the background, they have made them perform great task. Only they can make and keep the people *Samskāri* and on right path of morality and righteousness.

At almost every point of Samskār they sing special Samskār songs prepared meticulously well for the specific time, place and purpose. Through those songs they keep the place and environment alive and teach almost everything. In their free time too they sing the *Samskār Geet* for entertainment but it serves definite purpose. It enlivens the atmosphere and brings everything back to memory. It is their contribution that we have not as yet forgotten the Samskārs. The form may have changed but we have retained the content and are in a position to give them to the posterity to make better use of the celebrations and the strength, wisdom and prosperity that they give.

❋❋❋

Samskārs in Āyurveda

It is quite clear that Āyurveda is based on the purification of matter. Whether it is food material, medicinal plant, root, bark or leaf whether it is mineral or something from Nature or even poisonous, it must be processed first, cultured and made useful before taking. Only then they are worth eating, otherwise they may prove harmful.

Types of Purification

In Āyurveda, eight types of such purifications are discussed:

1. *Jal-sanikarsh* - In contact with or through water.
2. *Agni sanikarsh*- In contact with or through fire or heat.
3. *Shauch*- Through purification, for example sulphur is heated seven times and every time it is placed in cow-milk only then it is completely purified.
4. *Manthan* - Through churning.
5. *Desh*- Place. In Āyurveda three types of places have been discussed. They are forest, specialised and general. The quality of a thing depends on the place it is taken from.
6. *Kāla*- Time. For example, rice is usually hard to digest but one year old rice become easily digestible.

7. *Bhājana*- Pots and utensils in which something is stored make a lot of difference in the quality of the thing; the preparations from citrus fruits must be kept in pots of mud.
8. *Bhāwanā*- Repeated crushing for making a thing better, for example, pearl or oyster is crushed into powder then repeatedly rose-water is mixed with it and churned or crushed till it becomes dry.

The point of Āyurveda can be understood easily. If and when all matter must be cultured before use then why man is not made cultured before he/she takes the responsibility of running a household, and taking on other social responsibilities.

❁❁❁

SAMSKĀRS IN A NUTSHELL

The Samskārs are aimed at and must lead to a pleasant, healthy and happy life and salvation after death. If it is not so then there is something wrong with them or there are some *Kusamskārs*.

All the Samskārs combined together must give the following qualities discussed in the *Mahābhārat* (19:2-4) and must give salvation or freedom from the endless cycle of birth and rebirth.

सर्वमित्रः सर्वसहः शमे रक्तो जितेन्द्रियः ।
व्यपेतभयमन्युश्च आत्मवान् मुच्यते नरः ॥

Sarvamitrah sarvasahah shame rakto jitendriyah;
Vyapetabhayamanyushcha ātmawāna muchyate narah.

(The *Samskāri Purush* or *Stri* must become friend to all; endure everything and sustain through all calamities; have control over mind and senses; be fearless and without anger; exercise self restraint and be self-dependent; only then he/she can think of freedom or such men and women are free without a shred of doubt.)

आत्मवत् सर्वभूतेषु यश्चरेन्नियतः शुचिः ।
अमानी निरभीमानः सर्वतो मुक्त एव सः ॥

Ātmawat sarvabhuteshu yashcharenniyatah shuchih;
Amāni nirabhimānah sarvato muktah yewa sah.

(That man or woman who follows the scriptures, social customs and ethics; religious rites, rituals and tenets; and behaves well with all and treats others as a projection of the self; has no lust for fame or reward; is not conceited and has no ego problem; can think of freedom or such men and women are free without a shred of doubt.)

जीवितं मरणं चोभे सुखदुःखे तथैव च ।
लाभालाभे प्रियद्वेष्ये यः समः स च मुच्यते ॥

Jivitam maranam chobhe sukhdukhe tathaiwa cha;
Lābhālābhe priyadweshye yah samah sa cha muchyate.

(That man or woman who is detached and has no deep involvement in life and death, in pleasure or pain, in loss or gain, in happiness and sadness can think of freedom or such men and women are free without a shred of doubt.)

In a nutshell, it is the power, result and effect of Samskārs. It can be achieved by following the dictates of the scriptures. The essence of all the Samskārs that are performed is that a person is able to perform the following pious duties. If these duties are not performed then the *Yagyas* and the Samskārs are proved to be wastage. Such things have been summed up in the convocation address to the pupils that the teacher delivers after teaching *Veda-Wāngamaya* well. It is being quoted from the *Taittiriyopanishad* in three parts:

Part 1

संस्कृत	**Roman**	**Meaning**
सत्यं वद ।	*Satyam vada.*	Speak the truth.
धर्मं चर ।	*Dharamam chara.*	Follow the religion.
स्वाधयायान्मा प्रमदः ।	*Swādhyāyānmā pramadah.*	Never miss self-study.
आचार्याय प्रियं धनं आहृत्य प्रजातन्तुं मा व्यवच्छेसीः ।	*Āchāryāya priyam dhanamāhritya prajātantum mā vyawachchhesih.*	Give desired wealth to the teacher and then ensure continuity of life.
सत्यान्न प्रमदितव्यम् ।	*Satyānna pramaditavyam.*	Don't regress from truth.
धार्मान्न प्रमदितव्यम् ।	*Dharmānna pramaditavyam.*	Don't regress from religion.
कुशलान्न प्रमदितव्यम् ।	*Kushalānna pramaditavyam.*	Don't regress from virtuous deeds.
भूत्यै न प्रमदितव्यम् ।	*Bhootaiya na pramaditavyam.*	Never miss the opportunity for prosperity.
स्वाधयाय प्रवचनाभ्यां न प्रमदितव्यम्।	*Swādhyāya pravachanābhyām na pramaditavyam.*	Don't commit errors in study or teaching.
देवपितृकार्याभ्यां न प्रमदितव्यम् ।	*Deva pitri kāryābhyām na pramaditavyam.*	Don't forget to accomplish the duties towards God and parents.

Part 2

संस्कृत	Roman	Meaning
मातृदेवो भव ।	*Mātridevo bhawa.*	Treat mother as a goddess.
पितृदेवो भव ।	*Pitridevo bhawa.*	See a form of god in father.
आचार्यदेवो भव ।	*Āchāryadevo bhawa.*	Think the teacher to be god.
अतिथि देवो भव ।	*Atithi devo bhawa.*	Treat the guests, who have come without date or appointment or purpose, as god.
यान्यनवद्यानि कर्माणि ।	*Yānyanavadyāni karmāni.*	Perform only wholesome deeds.
तानि सेवितानि ।	*Tāni sevitāni.*	Only they should be performed.
नो इतराणि ।	*No etarāni.*	Don't miss it.
यान्यस्माकँ सुचरितानि ।	*Yānyasmākanga sucharitāni.*	Behave well whosoever elder or respectable comes to you.
तानि त्वयोपास्यानि ।	*Tāni twayopāsyāni.*	They should be served.
नो इतराणि ।	*No etarāni.*	There should not be any deviation.
ये के चास्मच्छ्रेयाँसो ब्राह्मणा ।	*Ye ke chāsmchchhreyāngaso brāhmanā.*	Whosoever preceptor or Brahmin comes to you
तेशां त्वया आसनेन प्रस्वसितव्यम् ।	*Teshām twayāāsanena praswasitavyam.*	give them seat and rest.
श्रद्धया देयम् ।	*Shraddhayā deyama.*	Donate with respect.

अश्रद्धयादेयम् ।	*Ashraddhādeyam.*	Don't give if lacks respect.
श्रिया देयम् ।	*Shriyā deyam.*	Give according to the status.
ह्रया देयम् ।	*Hriyā deyam.*	Give with humility.
भिया देयम् ।	*Bhiyā deyam.*	Give with fear.
संविदा देयम् ।	*Samvidā deyam.*	Give with wisdom.

Part 3

संस्कृत	Roman	Meaning
अथ यदि ते कर्मविचिकत्सा वा वृत्तविचिकित्सा वा स्यात् ।	*Atha yadi te karmavichikitsā wā vritvichikitsā wā syāt.*	If a doubt crops up in the mind about duty or wholesome deeds, then
ते तत्र ब्राह्मणाः सम्मर्षिनः ।	*Te tat brāhmanā sammarshinah.*	follow a Brāhmin with balance ideas and humble nature;
युत्ता आयुत्ताः ।	*Yuttā āyuttā.*	of virtuous deeds
अलूक्षा धर्मकामाः स्युः ।	*Alukshā dharmakāmāh syuh.*	whose only wish is religion;
यथा ते तत्र वर्तेरन् ।	*Yathā te tatra varteran.*	as he behaves under similar situation
तथा तत्र वर्तेथाः ।	*Tathā tatra vartethāh.*	you should behave in the same manner.
अथाभ्याख्यातेषु ।	*Athābhyākhyāteshu.*	If there is a doubt about someone's stigma or blemish then,

ते तत्र ब्राह्मणाः सम्मर्षिनः ।	*Te tat brvhmanā sammarshinah.*	follow a Brāhmin with balance ideas and humble nature;
युत्ता आयुत्ताः ।	*Yuttā āyuttā.*	of virtuous deeds
अलूक्षा धर्मकामाः स्युः ।	*Alukshā dharmakāmāh syuh.*	whose only wish is religion;
यथा ते तत्र वर्तेरन् ।	*Yathā te tatra varteran.*	as he behaves under similar situation
तथा तत्र वर्तेथाः ।	*Tathā tatra vartethāh.*	you should behave in the same manner.
एश आदेषः ।	*Yeshah ādeshah.*	It's the order.
एश उपदेषः ।	*Yeshah upadeshah.*	It's the teaching.
एशा वेदोपनिशत् ।	*Yeshā vedopanishat.*	It's the secret of scriptures.
एतदनुशासनम् ।	*Yetadanushāshanam.*	It's the discipline.
एवमुपासितव्यम् ।	*Yewamupāsitavyam.*	You should do it accordingly.
एवमु चैतदुपास्यम् ।	*Yewamu chaitadupāsyam.*	It should be done accordingly.

❁❁❁

Progress, Peace, Prosperity and Perfection through Samskārs

Samskārs give all types of cleanliness and purity that in turn give freshness and keep one rejuvenated, alert and active. That freshness helps one in thinking in a wider perspective, opens new vistas and looks at far beyond the petty things. It adds to vitality and increases zeal and stamina.

Strong Ladder

That ability to look far and wide is the real progress of the mind that looks easily at different ways, means and substitutes; performs the tasks skilfully and completes one's works easily and successfully. Thus, it is the strongest ladder to progress and prosperity. In this sense all the Samskārs are powerful means that give strength to mind and increase a person's ability to work and achieve targets very peacefully and with utmost perfection. If it comes to the life of a person then one can perform any task with ease and dexterity, and nothing is unachievable for him or her. This is the real gain from Samskārs apart from the greatest gain that all *Samskāri Purush* and *Stris* are respected by all: both *Samskārwāns* (who have Samskārs) and *Samskārvihins* (who do not possess any Samskārs).

In that way and in that sense, we get progress, peace, prosperity and perfection through Samskārs and one thing more must be added and that is fulfilment. Rest of the things that can be pointed out and talked about would be somehow related to these acquisitions.

Lighting the Lamp

Samskār is like lighting the lamp: giving light, heat and energy. Samskār is not like extinguishing a lamp; taking the heat out and turning something cold; no, Samskār can not and will never be negative. It is the accumulation of positive values. It is acquiring and emitting light. It is sweet. It gives sweetness and inwardly forces one to spread sweetness. It is the sweetness of words, speech, ideas and deeds and above all, of virtues. It is delight and delightful sweetness. It is fragrance. It gives fragrance. It sprays fragrance in all directions without inhibitions or prejudices.

Samskār is the knowledge and advantage of light, sweetness and fragrance. These are the qualities that we need for peace, progress, prosperity and pleasure. In that sense it gives bliss and beatitude, and final salvation is achieved. If people have the Samskārs then they need nothing else for they will get everything soon and in abundance for the satisfaction of physical needs and spiritual longings. All will be achieved and everything enjoyed. Be *Samskāri*, be satisfied and perfect.

Hari Aum Tatsat!

SECTION 2

Poojan Vidhi

Shatkarma (The Six Rituals)

Poojā is always performed before every Samskār. *Poojā* and *Poojan Vidhi* is made and kept simple to facilitate everyone to perform it easily. In every type of *Yagya, Anushthāna, Mangal-kārya,* common and similar *Shuddhi, Awāhan, Swastivāchana, Punyāhavāchan, Mantrochāra* and *Mantras* are used. Before the *Anushthāna, Shatkarma* (six rituals) are performed. They are: *Pavitrikaran; Āchamana; Shikhābandhana; Prānāyāma; Nyās* and *Prithvi-Poojan.*

Pavitrikaran

In *Pavitrikaran,* water is taken in the left palm and covered with the right palm. The following *Mantra* is chanted in that position. After that the water is sprinkled on the body with right hand fingers.

Aum apavitrah pavitro wā sarvāwasthām gato apivā;
Yah smareta pundarikāksham sa bāhyābhyāntarah shuchih.

ॐ अपवित्रः पवित्रो वा सर्वावस्थां गतोऽपिवा।
यः स्मरेत् पुण्डरीकाक्षं स बाह्याभ्यन्तरः शुचिः॥

Āchamana

It is the act of purifying mind, speech and deeds. Thrice water is taken preferably in *āchamani*, in mango-leaf or in right palm and poured in mouth. While doing so the following *Mantras* are chanted:

1. First time - Aum amritopastaranamasi swāhāh.

ॐ अमृतोपस्तरणमसि स्वाहाः।

2. The second time - Aum amritāpidhānamasi swāhāh.

ॐ अमृतापिधानमसि स्वाहाः।

3. The third time - Aum satyam yashah shrirmayi shri shryatām swāhāh.

ॐ सत्यं यशः श्रीमयि श्री श्रयतां स्वाहाः।

Shikhābandhana

It is performed for getting connected to the cosmic electro-magnetic flow. It is jokingly compared to antenna but it's not a joke. It is a very sensitive place. The knot of the topknot of hair at the centre on the head is tied; if there is no topknot then the central place is touched. It is believed that the thumb-size Brahma is inside there. In fact, that is the place that controls our action. The following *Mantra* is chanted:

Chida rupini mahāmāye dipye tejah samanwite; Tishtha devi shikhā madhye tejovriddhim kurushwa me.

चिद् रूपिणि महामाये दिप्ये तेजः समन्विते।
तिष्ठ देवि शिखा मध्ये तेजो वृद्धिं कुरूश्व मे।

Prānāyāma

It is performed for activating the five main *Prāna vāyus* and five sub-*Prāna vāyus* (life-forces). It is done to acquire access to the sublime life-element. In *Prānāyāma*, *Puraka* (the act of breathing in); *Kumbhaka* (keeping breath inside as much as possible) and *Rechaka* (breathing out) are performed. During the practice session of the three actions, the following *Mantra* is chanted:

Aum bhuh Aum bhuwah Aum swah Aum mahah Aum janah Aum tapah Aum satyam. Tatsaviturvarenyam bhargodevasya dheemahi dhiyo yo nah prachodayat. Aum āpo jyotih raso amritam Aum Brahma bhurbhwah swarom.

ॐ भूः ॐ भुवः ॐ स्वः ॐ महः ॐ जनः ॐ तपः ॐ सत्यम्। तत्सवितुर्वरेण्यं भर्गोदेवस्य धीमहि धियो यो नः प्रचोदयात्। ॐ आपो ज्योतिः रसोऽमृतं ॐ ब्रह्म भुर्भुवः स्वरोम्।

Nyāsa

It is done to give excellence to all the sense organs. It is done both for purifying them and for making them alert and keeping them conscious. Water is taken in the left palm and after touching the related parts the following *Mantras* are chanted:

Aum wāng me asyeastu. (Touch mouth)

ॐ वाङ् मे अस्येऽस्तु।

Aum nasorme prānoastu. (Touch nostrils)

ॐ नसोर्मे प्राणोऽस्तु।

Aum akshanorme chakshurastu. (Touch eyes)

ॐ अक्ष्णोर्मे चक्षुरस्तु।

Aum karnorme shrotamastu. (Touch ears)

ॐ कर्णोमे श्रोत्रमस्तु।

Aum wāhworme balamastu. (Touch arms)

ॐ वाहवोर्मे बलमस्तु।

Aum uorme ojoastu. (Touch thighs)

ॐ उओर्मे ओजोऽस्तु।

Aum aristāni me angāni tanustanwā me sah santu.

ॐ अरिष्टानि मेऽगांनि तनूस्तन्वा मे सहसंतु।

(Sprinkle water on the whole body)

Prithvi-Poojan

The Earth makes life possible, helps in sustaining life and hence she is the mother. We owe everything to her, so, in a way, the Earth is the first one to be worshipped, even before Shri Ganesh. The Earth should be offered incense, *akshat* (unbroken rice), flowers, water and showed the lamp; and the following *Mantra* should be chanted:

Aum prithvi twayā dhritā lokā devi twam vishnunā dhritā.

Twam cha dhārana mām devi pavitram kuru cha āsanam.

ॐ पृथिवी व्यया धृता लोका देवि त्वं विष्णुना धृता।
त्वां च धारण मां देवि पवित्रं कुरू चासनम्।।

Only after completing these *Shatkarmas* one should proceed ahead to perform the real *Anushthāna* or Samskār for which the ceremony is arranged beginning with *Samkalp*, the resolution to perform that *Poojan* or Samskār.

❋❋❋

Shodashopachāra (The Sixteen Steps)

After the *kalash* is placed at the centre and Ganesh *Poojan* is performed, the other gods and goddesses are worshipped. In worshipping them *Shodashopachāra* is performed beginning with Shri Ganesh. *Shodashopachāra* includes calling *āwāhana*; and offering the following fifteen things: *Āsana; Pādya; Arghya; Āchamana; Snāna; Vastra; Upavita; Gandh; Akshat; Pushpa; Dhupa; Deepa; Naivedya; Tāmbul* and *Dakshinā*. If one is not able to perform the sixteen steps, then one can perform only ten, known as *Dashopachāra*; if one is unable to perform those ten steps then he/she can opt for the five steps known as *Panchopachāra*; which are the parts of *Shodashopachāra*. The following are the *Panchopachāra*.

Panchopachāra

The *Panchopachāra* includes the offering of five things: *Gandha* (fragrance); *Pushpa* (flowers); *Dhoopa* (incense); *Deep* (lamp) and *Naivedya* (oblation).

While offering *Panchopachāra* one should chant the following *Mantras*:

ॐ लं पृथिव्यात्मकं गन्धां समर्पयामि ।
Aum lang prithvyātamakam gandham samarpayāmi.

ॐ हं आकाशात्मकं पुष्पं समर्पयामि ।
Aum hring ākāshātmakam pushpam samarpayāmi.

ॐ यं वायात्मकं धूपं समर्पयामि ।
Aum yam wāyātmakam dhoopam samarpayāmi.

ॐ रं तेजसात्मकं दीपं समर्पयामि ।
Aum rang tejasātmakam deepam samarpayāmi.

ॐ वं अमृतात्मकं नैवेद्यं समर्पयामि ।
Aum wam amritātmakam naivedyam samarpayāmi.

Dashopachāra

The *Dashopachāra* includes the offering of ten things: *Pādya* (washing the feet); *Arghya* (libation in honour); *Āchaman* (rinsing of mouth ceremoniously); *Snāna* (bath); *Vastra* (cloth) and the five of *Panchopachāra – Gandha, Pushpa, Dhoopa. Deep* and *Naivedya.* The first five *Mantras* are:

ॐ वं पाद्यं समर्पयामि ।
Aum wam pādyam samarpayāmi.

ॐ वं अर्घ्यं समर्पयामि ।
Aum wam arghyam samarpayāmi.

ॐ वं आचमनं समर्पयामि ।
Aum wam āchamanam samarpayāmi.

ॐ वं स्नानं समर्पयामि ।
Aum wam snānam samarpayāmi.

ॐ वं वस्त्रं समर्पयामि ।
Aum wam vastram samarpayāmi.

The rest of the *Mantras* are as given above in *Panchopachāra*.

Shodashopachāra

The *Shodashopachāra* includes the offering of sixteen things: *Āwāhan* (invocation); *Āsana* (a seat); *Upavit* (sacred thread); *Akshat* (sacred rice); *Tāmbulādi* (betel etc); *Dakshinā* (presents); and ten other things of *Dashopachāra*: *Pādya, Arghya, Āchaman, Snāna, Vastra, Gandha, Pushpa, Dhoopa, Deep, Naivedya*. The first six *Mantras* are:

ॐ सर्वेभ्यो देवेभ्यो नमः । आवाहयामि स्थापयामि ।

Aum sarvebhyo devebhyo namah. Āwāhayāmi sthāpayāmi.

ॐ वं आसनं समर्पयामि ।

Aum wam āsanam samarpayāmi.

ॐ वं यज्ञोपवितं समर्पयामि ।

Aum wam yagyopavitam samarpayāmi.

ॐ वं अक्षतान् समर्पयामि ।

Aum wam akshtāna samarpayāmi.

ॐ वं ताम्बुल पुंगीफलानि समर्पयामि ।

Aum wam tāmbul pungiphalāni samarpayāmi.

ॐ वं दक्षिणां समर्पयामि ।

Aum wam dakshinām samarpayāmi.

The rest of the *Mantras* are given as per the *Panchopachāra* and *Dashopachāra*.

❁❁❁

Swasti-Vāchan (Recitation of Auspicious Mantra)

After *Panchopachāra* or *Dashopachāra* or *Shodashopachāra* and again at the end of the *Anusthāna*, one must pray while prostrating or with folded hands, chanting the following *Mantra* that asks for boons for the self and *sarva*, all else:

Namah sarvahitārthāya jagadādhār hetawe.
Sāshtāngo ayam pranāmaste prayatnena mayā kritah.

नमः सर्वहितार्थाय जगदाधार हेतवे।
साष्टांगोऽयं प्रणामस्ते प्रयत्नेन मयाकृतः॥

While worshipping during a *Poojā* or *Samskār*, the recitation of the following *Stuti* is completed without fail and recommended to all:

Aum ganānām twā ganapati ang hawāmahe priyānām twā priyapati ang hawāmahe nidhinām twā nidhipati ang hawāmahe vaso mama āham jāni garbhadhama twamajāsi garbhadham.

Swasti-Vāchan

Every *Anusthāna* or *Samskār* is closed with *Swasti-Vāchana* or blessings and *Prasād. Swasti-Vāchan* is an important thing and recited without fail:

Aum swasti nah indro briddhashrawāh swasti nah pushā vishwavedā swasti na tākasharyo aeishtanemih swasti no brihaspatih dadhātu.

During *Swasti-Vāchan*, at many places *Kalashsthāpana* is completed by putting it on grain for decorating it and placing mango leaves etc.

1. Aum mahidyauh prithvi archan imam yagyam mimikshatām. Pipritām nobharimabhih.
2. Aum aushadhayah samvadanta somena sah rāgyā. Yasmai krinoti brāhmanastam. Aum rajanpārayāmasi.
3. Aum ājighra kalasham mahyā twā vishanti vandawah. Punah urjā nivarttāh wasānah sahasram dhukshaworudhārā payaswati punah mā vishatādrayih.
4. Aum imam mey varuna shrudhi hawamādya cha mridaya. Twāma wasyurāčhake.
5. Aum gandha dwārām durādharshā nitya pushtām karishinim. Ishwarim sarva bhutānām tāmi ahopahwayeshriyam. Aum yā aushadhih purvājātā daivebhya striyugampurā. Manainu babhrunāmah. Aum shatah dhāmāni sapta cha.
6. Aum kāndāt kāndāt prarohanti purusham parushpari. Avāno durve pratanu sahasrena shatena cha.
7. Aum ashwathewo nishadanam parne wauvasatishkritā. Gobhājat kilāsatha yatsnawatha purusham.

8. Aum syānā prithvinobhawānriksharāni veshani. Yachchhānah sharmasa prathāh.
9. Aum yā phalāniryā aphalām apushpāyāshaha pushpini. Brihaspati prasutā snāno munchhantwa Aum hasah.
10. Aum paripājapatih kavih agnih havyānkramit. Dadhatnānidāshshe.
11. Aum hiranya garbhah samvartatāgre bhuyasya jātah patireka āsit. Sadādhāra prithvi dyāmutemākasmai devāya havishā vidhema.

❁❁❁

Āshirvāda Mantra (Blessings)

There is a very long procedure of blessings by the *Brahmins* present at a *Yagya* but the following are the often-repeated *Mantras*

- *Ahrishchate laxmishcha pahorātre pārshwe nakshatrāni rupam ashwinau vyāttam. Ishanannis hānāmummaishāna sarva loka maishāna.*
- *Aum shataminnu sharado ayanti devā yatrānashcha kājah santanunām. Putrā so yatra pitaro bhawanti mānomakshyāririshatā yugah antoh.*
- *Manasah kāmamākutim vāchah satyam shimahi. Pashunā ang rupamannasya raso yashah shri shri shrayatāmmayi.*
- *Prajāpatih lokapālo dhātābrahmā cha devarāt.*
- *Bhaganāna shāshwato nityah sano rakshat sarvatah.*
- *Āyushmate Swastih!*
- *Āyushmate Swastih!!*
- *Āyushmate Swastih!!!*

❁❁❁

Shodasha Mātrikā Poojan (*Worshipping Mothers*)

In India, mothers are given preference over everything else. So, in almost every Yagya there is a provision to worship and show respect by Mātri Poojā and Mātrikā Poojan. Usually, both are performed at a time. Since the parents of a batuka or bride or groom perform it so the grand old lady, not the oldest but the eldest one is worshipped as a deity. It is the recognition that because of her all others, were born, got life and are living.

Traditionally and symbolically, we worship sixteen other mothers whose names are given in the chart. It is suggested that when many poojans are to be performed then *Shantipāth, Ganapati Poojan, Swasti Vāchan, Panchdhārā* and *Mātrikā Poojan* should be performed at a time. There is no need to perform them separately:

Ganeshah kriyamānānām matribhyah poojanam sakrit;
Sakrideva bharechchhrāddhamādaun prithagādishu;
Kudaya lagnā vasādhārāh panchdhārāh tenatu;
Kāryet sapt wādhārā nātinichānachochchhritāh.

गणेशः क्रियमाणानां मातृभ्यः पूजनं सकृत्।
सकृदेव भवेच्छ्राद्धमादौन पृथगादिषु॥
कुडयलग्नावसार्धारा: पंचधारा: तेनतु।
कारयेत्सप्तवाधारा नातिनीचानचोच्छ्रिता:॥

The *Mātrikā* are collectively worshipped on the pattern of *Shodashopachāra*. Add the following to the *samkalp*:

Adya shubha punya tithi (mention the tithi and purpose behind the poojan) *karmā gatayā ganapati sahita gāryādi shodasha mātrikā poojanam aham karishye.*

Sixteen squared *Mandal* (chart) is prepared as given below. Either red rice or wheat or oat is put in each of them. Each of the mothers are called by touching their respective place and chanting the *āwāhan* mantra.

Kula Devatā 16	*Lok Mātarah 12*	*Devasenā 8*	*Medhā 4*
Tushtih 15	*Mātarah 11*	*Jayā 7*	*Shachi 3*
Pushtih 14	*Swāhā 10*	*Vijayā 6*	*Padma 2*
Dhritih 13	*Swadhā 9*	*Sāvitri 5*	*Gauri Ganesh 1*

Āwāhan Mantras

- *Aum ganapataye namah. Ganapatim āhayāmi sthāpayāmi.*
- *Aum gaurai namah. Gaurim āhayāmi sthāpayāmi.*
- *Aum padmāyai namah. Padmā āhayāmi sthāpayāmi.*
- *Aum shachai namah. Shachim āhayāmi sthāpayāmi.*
- *Aum medhāi namah. Medhām āhayāmi*

sthāpayāmi.

- *Aum sāvitrai namah. Sāvitrim āhayāmi sthāpayāmi.*
- *Aum vijayāyai namah. Vijayām āhayāmi sthāpayāmi.*
- *Aum jayāyai namah. jayām āhayāmi sthāpayāmi.*
- *Aum devasenāyai namah. Devasenām āhayāmi sthāpayāmi.*
- *Aum swadhāyai namah. Swadhām āhayāmi sthāpayāmi.*
- *Aum dhrityai namah. Dhritim āhayāmi sthāpayāmi.*
- *Aum pushtyai namah. Pushtim āhayāmi sthāpayāmi.*
- *Aum tushtyai namah. Tushtim āhayāmi sthāpayāmi.*
- *Aum ātmakula devatāi namah. Ātmakula devatām āhayāmi sthāpayāmi.*
- *Aum mātribhyo namah. Mātāh āhayāmi sthāpayāmi.*
- *Aum loka matribhyo namah. Loka mātribhyo āhayāmi sthāpayāmi.*

Pratishthā Mantra

Aum manojutih jushatām ājyah asya brihaspatih yagyabhimam tanotu. Arishtam yagya ang samimam dadhātu vishwedevā saihamādayantāpo pratishathah.

Hari Aum Tatsat!

❁❁❁

SECTION 3

Sixteen Samskãrs

Samskār-1

Garbhādhān Samskār (Conception)

Garbhādhān (conception) is the first process for the birth of a human child. It is the first among the sixteen Samskārs. It has been universally accepted as the first duty after entering the *Grihastha Āshram*, to a life of a householder. It is the pious duty of everyone to raise family for the continuity of life, as we all know that each person is mortal. There is no family life if one fails to have at least one male and one female child. Some people may prefer male children, as they know that it is their physical and social need. But the presence of both male and female is essential. Separately, they are incomplete; united together they become a complete unit. Whether male or female, a childless parent leads a tense and meaningless life.

Garbhādhān is performed for better and healthy children who are free from physical deformity. The Manusmriti says that all the cultured and refined persons who have got another birth by different Samskārs must perform Garbhādhān Samskār so that they can get better life here and hereafter:

Vaidikai karmabhih punyah nishekādi dwijanmanām. Karyah sharira samskārah pāwan pretya cheha cha.

वैदिकै कर्मभिः पुण्यर्निषेकादि द्विजैन्मनाम्।
कार्यः शरीर संस्कारः पावन प्रेत्य चेह च॥

(It is worth mentioning here that the parents lead a hell of a life if and when even a single son or daughter goes astray.)

Preparations and Precautions

Preparations and precautions start from the time of marriage and continue even after the birth of every child. The newly married couple waits for this Samskār. In this way, it keeps the waywardness of the couple under control along with ensuring the health and brightness of the future child.

Since the day of their marriage, the groom and the bride are physically and mentally prepared for physical union and birth of children. *Garbhādhān* makes them firm, physically strong and mentally ready to face the pain and rigours of giving birth to a child and then fostering the child with care. It is achieved because *Garbhādhān* helps in overcoming the defects in the foetus because it aims at purifying womb and strengthening the couple. During the Samskār, most of the physical defects and psychological problems are taken care of.

Garbhādhān is the most important Samskār because the refinement and inner power of the child to take birth depends on it. It is a reciprocal game between the couple hence their physical health and mental state makes a lot of difference. Indifferent relation or tense union will naturally make the child abnormal. Since we have moved away from this process, particularly in the 20th century, we are not getting balanced and healthy offsprings. The number of abnormal births can easily be determined by the growth of such hospitals, care-centres, doctors and psychiatrists. So, it is essential to be conscious and pious, healthy and happy, balanced and normal before going for union with the intention to bear a child.

Eligibility

Garbhādhān is performed on the wish of the married couples who are willing to have children. Unwilling couples should not go for it. Only a married couple is eligible for *Garbhādhān*. Unmarried male and female are not allowed. It can't be performed between them. Their children are not accepted. They are declared illegal and illegitimate. *Manusmriti* says:

Apatyalābhādyā tu stri bhartā ramati vartate.
Seha nindāmawāpnoti patilokāchcha heeyate.

अपत्यलाभाद्या तु स्त्री भर्ता रमति वर्तते।
सेहनिन्दामवाप्नोति पतिलोकाच्च हीयते॥

(The lady that transgresses the social barrier and indulges in sex with another person is condemned in this life and defiled in the life afterwards.)

So, while keeping oneself under strict discipline and showing true sincerity towards the wife or the husband, one can opt for *Garbhādhān*. A simple failure of a few minutes destroys virtually and literally everything in life. Samskārs give strength to live together even under worst conditions. Only those couples are praised and are happy who lead such an honest life of faith and interdependence. This is the real strength of a household. No tempest can break them apart.

Time

Garbhādhān should be performed from the 5th day onwards till the 16th day from the start of the menstrual period.

According to Manusmriti, one must avoid the first four nights beginning with menstruation. Sixteen nights from thereon are called Ritukāla and is the right time for copulation. Manu suggests avoiding the 11th and the 13th nights along with the first four nights. He has predicted that after copulation during even nights (6th, 8th, 10th 12^{th,} 14th and 16th), a son is born but during odd nights (5^{th,} 7th, 9th, and 15th) a daughter is born. The person who indulges in sex only during the prescribed eight days is like a Brahmachāri, though a householder. This odd and even may have something to do with the XY-factors of genetics.

Manusmriti says:

Rituh swābhāwikah strinām rātrayah shodash smritāh.
Chaturbhih ritaraih sārddhamahobhih sadwigarhitah.

ऋतुः स्वाभाविक स्त्रीणां रात्रयः षोडश स्मृताः।
चतुर्भिः रितरैः सार्धमहोभिः सद्विगर्हितः॥

(The first four nights after menstruation are not good. After that sixteen nights are good for conception.)

Age

A girl gets the needed maturity only after the age of 16 years or after a minimum of 18 menstrual cycles.

Before that, a girl is not physically or psychologically fit enough to carry, to give healthy maturity and to foster the embryo. There will either be miscarriage, affecting the health of the girl or the child thus born will be weak or physically impaired. In the same way, the semen of a boy of less than 25 years is not strong enough as it lacks most of the strong proteins and cell-making powers to create a healthy embryo or to turn it into a healthy child. So, the sages of ancient India and later on the doctors and surgeons including Charak, Chyavan and Sushrut fixed the minimum age for *Garbhādhan* to be 16 years for girls and 25 years for boys. Though of different age yet they possess equal maturity. However, they preferred the age of 20 for girls and 30 for boys.

The *Rishis* were absolutely right in prescribing the age of marriage and the time to give birth to children. It is very scientific. Modern science is trying to verify them but they are so deep rooted in the study of physiology and psychology and the cosmic effect on different persons at different places and time, that they may take a few centuries to verify most of them. It is a happy sign that they are making speedy progress and the West is turning fast towards ancient ways, culture, Samskārs and rituals invented and perfected by the Indians.

It is said that *Garbhādhān* is no longer in vogue in India. This is not true. The concept is there, the process of the ritual and its name has changed.

There were some moral and ethical difficulties before the elders of the family when *Garbhādhān Samskār* was performed. It grew more during Muslim rule when most of the girls were married before the age of puberty. So, as a substitute to it they invented another social custom, confined only to the ladies, the bride and the groom. It is very popular and performed at the time of every marriage. It is known as *Kohabar*, when the bride and groom are made to meet alone in a room for the first time. Songs are sung and some rituals are performed at that time. These rituals vary from place to place.

Garbhādhān Vidhi

On the fixed day the couple must remain fresh and happy. There should be no negative feelings like anxiety or anger or jealousy. They must be in a pleasant mood. It would help them in many ways. It is very clearly stated that if they are not happy, they cannot give pleasure and satisfy one another and they won't get healthy children:

Yadi hi stri na rocheta pumāns na promodayet.
Apramodātpunah punsah prajanam na pravartate.

यदि हि स्त्री न रोचेत पुमांस न प्रमोदयेत्।
अप्रमोदात्पुनः पुंसः प्रजनं न प्रवर्तते॥

(If the lady is not happy or unable to give pleasure to husband or if the husband is not pleased, then they won't get children or good children.

On the fixed day, during noon hours, the couple should perform *Ganesh-Poojan* with the following *Mantra*:

Aum ganānāntwā ganapati ganghwā mahe priyānantwā priyapati ganghwā mahe nidhinantwā nidhipati ganghwā vaso mam āhamjajānigarbhadhamā twamajāsi garbhadham.

Along with this *Mantra* they should perform *Shadmātrikā Poojan*; and during the *Poojan* drink

Swagandhā Rasa or *Durvā Rasa* through the right nostril. Then they should salute together the source of energy, *Surya* (sun), with the following *Mantras*:

1. Aum ādityam garbham payasām samangadhi sahastrasya pratimām viswarupam.
   Parivringadhiharsāmābhimangasthāhshatāyusham krinuhi cheeyamānah.
2. Suryo no diwaspātu wāto antarikshāt.
   Agnirnah pārthiwebhyah.
3. Joshā savitarasya te harah shatam sawān arhati.
   Pāhi no didyutuh patantyāh.
4. Chakshurno devah savitā chakshur uta parvatah.
   Chakshurdhātā dadhātu nah.
5. Chakshurno dhehi chakshushe chakshurvikhaiya tanubhyah.
   Sam chedam vi cha pashyema.
6. Susandrishangtwā vayam prati pashyewma surya.
   Vi pashyewma nrichakshasah.

They should salute all the elders present there and take their blessings.

On the fixed day, before the evening, the lady concerned should take bath, wear new clothes, ornaments and garlands of fragrant flowers. She should come and sit at the place fixed for *Pooja,* facing east. Other married ladies who have children should offer her wheat, oats and coconut. The husband should chant the following *Mantra*:

Aum yeh bhaliniryām afalā apushpā yāshya pushpini.
Brihaspati prasatā stā nomunchantan anga hansah.

ॐ यः भलिनीर्यां अफला अपुष्पा याश्य पुष्पिणी।
वृहस्पति प्रसता स्ता नोमुञ्चन्तन ꣳ हंसः।।

The husband should take the resolve like the following:

Mamāsyah patnyāh pratham Samskarane nātra janishyamāna garbhānam veejagarbha samudabhawaino nirākarnārtha garbhādhānakhyam samskār kamām aham karishye.

Late Night Ritual

In the second part of the night, the couple should enter the decorated room for the purpose, clad in white dress. The wife will lie down flat on a soft bed. The husband should sit facing east and perform *Upastha sparsha kriyā,* touch her navel with his right hand while reciting the following *Mantra*:

Aum pooshā bhagang savitā mein dadātu rudrah kalpayatu lalāmagum.

ॐ पूशा भगंग सवित मेन् ददातु रूद्रह कल्पयतु ललामगम्

Aum vishnuyor nikalpayatu twashtā rupāni pingashatu.
Āsinchita prajāpatirdhātā garbha dadhātu te.

ॐ विष्णुर्यो निकल्पयतु त्वष्टा रूपाणि पिंशतु।
आसिंचित प्रजापतिर्धाता गर्भ दधातु ते।।

(May your vagina be made potent for conception and may the Lord bestow His grace upon you so that the foetus grows happily and does not abort before ten months)

He should touch the *Upastha* with three fingers. The following three other *Mantras* should also be chanted:

1. Aum garbhadehi shitiwāli! Garbhadehi prithushtuke!
   Garbha te aswinau devāvadhattām pushkarstrahau.

2. Aum tejom vaishwānarodadyādatha brahmānuMantrayed.
   Brahmā garvhadadhātu te.
3. Aum gāyetrena twā chhandsāmanthāmi.
   Traishtubhena twā chhandsāmanthāmi.
   Jāgatena twā chhandsāmanthāmi.

Then they should have intercourse. Afterwards when the lady sits up, the husband should place his right hand on her right shoulder and touching her heart he should say:

Aum reto mutram vijahāti yoni pravishedindriyam.

Garbho jarāyunāvrita ulam jahāti janmanā ritesatyam indriyam vipān ang shukramandhas aindrasyendriyemidpayo amritam madhu.

The following *Mantra* should also be chanted:

Aum yattesumise hridya diwi chandramasi shritam.

Vedāham tanmām tadwidyātpashyema sharadah shatam.

Jivema sharadah shatam ang shanuyāma sharadah shatam.

❁❁❁

Samskār-2

Punswan Samskār (Fertilisation)

Punswan Samskār is performed three months after conception for life-being and safety. It is explained as a Samskār for begetting a son as Āshwālana points out in his *Grihyasutra* that the process through which a male child takes life is called *Punswan Samskār*. However, in reality, it is calling the life force to descend on the Earth and enter the womb of the lady to give life to the foetus. In fact, it is done for the balanced physical and mental growth of the child in the womb. It was also done as a precautionary measure to avoid abortion. To give birth to a child has always been like a rebirth for the mother.

This Samskār is very important for the mental growth of a child. The *Shāshtras* say that to correctly bear the responsibility of the birth of a child, one must make preparations to welcome the child. So, it is a sort of pre-natal welcome:

Hridaye pitarau gyātā purnadāyitwam uttamam.
Janamanah santate kuryāte vyavasthā swāgatāya cha.

हृदये पितरौ ज्ञाता पूर्णदायित्वं उत्तमम्।
जन्मन: संतते कुर्यात् व्यवस्था स्वागताय च।।

Meaning and Objectives

The word *Punswan* is derived from the words - *Punsya* (prowess) and *Avanah* (descent from above on to the Earth). It is basically performed for a son, as it is difficult to get a son and all the more difficult for a male child to survive. There are some inherent weaknesses that are not in a girl child. A girl child has some inherent advantages and can survive under difficult circumstances, also in which a male child won't. So, more care is taken for a male child.

The resolve that is taken at the time of performing this ritual shows different things, such as - to overcome any defects in the ovum or foetus; to conceive a male child, to destroy the demons that devour flesh and blood, and to worship Mahālaxmi, the presiding deity for *Saubhāgya* (continuance of bestowal of opulence). Some scholars say that it should be performed only when there is the need or wish to get a male child; others express the view that it has nothing to do with male and female, it is about life-force, health and brightness of the child, hence it should be performed by everyone.

The claim of modern science that the male and female children depend on the semen and sperm is not true. Had it been so, then males would not have breasts to feed as child. The difference is that female breasts develop but male breasts do not. The presence of breast in all male mammals, both human and non-human declares the modern scientific theory to be wrong. Both male and female embryo is the same. The growth into male and female foetuses depends on the secretion of related hormones first from the mother's glands and later on from the child. The hormones and its effects are established facts. The *Rishis* had their perfect theory and expressed it symbolically which we are unable to understand but their ways were far more healthier than the modern ways that is creating a growing army of handicapped and turning the males into effeminate and females into amazons.

Precautions

There is a condition also. It says that the lady who leads a sincere and pious life during pregnancy gets a brighter child:

Devatā brāhman aparāh shauchāchār hiteratāh.
Mahāgunān prasuyate vipiritāstu nirgunān.

देवता ब्राह्मण पराः शौचाचार हितेरताः।
महागुणान् प्रसूयते विपरीतास्तु निर्गुणान्॥

So, the *Rishis* have issued some precautions for the pregnant women to follow. The following are those important precautions:

- The pregnant lady should not ride a horse or a camel or similar means of transport.
- She should not ascend stairs or go for mountaineering.
- She must not practice exercise, running or moving on bullock-carts.
- She should not be sad and the flow of blood from the body must be checked immediately.
- She should neither sleep during the day nor remain awake during the night.

- She should not eat too hot, too cold, very sour, very sweet or any other hard food which is tough for digestion.
- She should not go for swimming or walk on uneven ground. She should neither climb a tree nor cross a river.
- She should remain clean and maintain purity; and take *Chandan* and *Kesar* (preferably massage as paste on body) in different forms with different things.
- She should keep fragrant flowers close to her and write letters expressing healthy and optimistic ideas.
- The husband of the pregnant woman is not allowed to go on a long (sea) journey, take part in funerals, take a haircut or cut the nails during this period. He should not create dispute or participate in war etc. He should not get a new house constructed. It is to keep him close to his wife so that he can take care of her and her child.

Time

One thing must be made clear that though Punswan Samskār is performed by the wife or the would-be mother of a child, it is not related to her. The Samskār is related to the conceived child. So, in this Samskār, Guru-asta, Shukra-asta, Mal-mās, and other Yogas (celestial combinations) are not considered. It can be performed on any auspicious day. It is deemed to be the best during Punarvasu, Pushya,

Hasta, Mrigshirā, Moola, and Shrāvan Nakshatras. Pārsakar Grihyasutra clearly states that it is the best day when the moon is under male Nakshatras: *Yadahah punsā nakshatran chandrā.*

Punswan Vidhi

Cleanliness and piety is the basic and essential requirement in every Samskār, so it need not be mentioned every time.

The Punswan is prepared with the juice of the rootlets of Nyagrodha banyan tree. Banyan, Brāmni Buti, Somalatā, and Giloya are the trees that prevent Pitta (bile juice) and help in overcoming defects in the ovum; enhance the Oja Guna (the divine energy) and help in secretion of needed and appropriate hormones. It is believed that the cumulative effect of all the rituals and herbs creates masculine components in the embryo. In the opinion of other scholars, equal parts of all the components are mixed and pasted as powder then passed through a muslin cloth (Pisa-chhā kar) and kept separately. Special Kheer (rice-pudding) is also prepared. The Punswan so prepared is rejuvenated with the following two Mantras and afterwards poured into the left nostril of the lady concerned. The appropriate place will be mentioned later on. Before that the Mantras for rejuvenation (*Utakramana*) are essential:

Mantra- 1

Aum hiranyagarbhah samwartatāgre bhutasya jātah pat-ireka āsit.

Sadādhāra prithvi dyāmuteshām kasmai devāya havishā vidhema.

ॐ हिरण्यगर्भः समवर्तताग्रे भूतस्य जातः प्रतिरेक आसीत्।
सदाधार पृथिवी द्यामुतेषां कस्मै देवाय हविषा विधेम॥

Mantra- 2

Aum adabhyah sambhritah prithvyai rasāchcha viswakarmanah samwartatāgre.

Tasya twastā vidadhadrapameti tāmatyarsya devatwam ājānamagre.

ॐ अदभ्यः सम्भृतः पृथिव्यै रसाच्च विश्वकर्मणः समवर्ततागे्र।
तस्य त्वष्टा विदधद्रपमेति तामर्त्यस्य देवत्वं आजानमग्रे॥

The Ritual

- The initial step of *Punswan* is *Shodashmātrikā Poojan* and *Homa* (sacrificial fire).
- After that the woman should cup her hands and hold them around her knees. On her right hand, curd prepared from the milk of a cow that has a he-calf (not she-calf); a cob of barley with its head facing east and two black grams are placed by it symbolising male sex organs. The woman should say: *Punswan grihityāmi* (I'm taking the punswan) and partake it. Then take *Āchamana* (clean water from her right palm). It is repeated twice.
- Then the *Punswan* prepared with crushed rootlets is poured in the left nostril of the lady by her husband. The above quoted two *Mantras* are also chanted at that time. Then, water with a coconut in an earthen plate is placed below the navel of the lady. At certain places it is placed in the lap of the lady. It should be preferably placed below the navel as the touch of the earthen pot with water and coconut revitalises and enriches the inner organs of the lady. The husband touches her abdomen with the tip of the ring finger and recites the following *Mantra* known as *Aum Suparnoasi*:

Aum suparnoasi gurutwāma stribrite shirogātram chakshur brihadarath antare pakshau.

Stoma ātmā chandang syamāni yaju ang shi nāma.

Sāma te tanurwāmadevyam yagyāyaygiyam puchcham dhishnayāh shaphāh.

Suparnoasi gurutmān divam gachchha swah pata.

- The special *Kheer* prepared earlier (with milk, rice, sugar and various dry fruits) is given as *Āhuti* to *Agni*, the sacrificial fire. Five *Āhuties* should be given with the following *Mantra* to be repeated every time:

Aum dhātā dadhātu dashushe prāchi jeevātumakshitām.

Vayam devasya dheemahi sumati wājiniwatah swāhāh.

Idam dhātre na mam.

- The husband gives a part of the *Kheer* covered with another utensil and a flower at the top to the lady while chanting the following *Mantra*:

Aum payah prithvivyām payah aushadhishu payo divyantikshe payo dhā payaswatih pradishah santu mahyam.

- After giving the *Kheer* the husband should place his right palm on the head of the lady and chant the following *Mantra*:

Aum yatte suseeme hridaye hitawantah prajāpatau.

Manye aham mām tadwidwām samāham pautrāmadyanniyām.

ॐ यत्ते सुसीमे हृदये हितवन्तः प्रजापतौ।
मन्येहं मां तद्विद्वां समाहं पौत्रामद्यन्नियाम्॥

The end of the Samskār is marked by the blessings by all the elders present there. The lady should eat the *Kheer* first when she is ready to take her meal after the *Mātrikāvisarjana* and when the *Brahmins* have finished their meals. After that she can eat her meal.

Punswan and Modernity

Only in the countryside *Punswan Samskār* is alive and that too in changed form, particularly in singing songs and in giving herbs and herbal preparations fried in clarified butter, to the pregnant woman.

But this Samskār is fast dying or has completely died out in the towns and cities where the doctors are consulted for everything and all the gynaecologists suggest ultra-sound to know about the growth of the foetus, and mostly to know the gender. The idea is that female foetus is to be aborted. This is affecting the girls and boys ratio. The very purpose of the birth of a healthy child is defeated. The practice of checking the gender of the foetus should be stopped with immediate effect and all should turn towards providing healthy environment, healthy food and herbal preparations for a healthy child. The herbs have no side effect. This is an alarming situation and in place of trying to be modern, the couples and guardians should be wise.

❁❁❁

Samskār-3

Seemantonnayan Samskār (Prosperity)

The general meaning of *Seemantonnayan Samskār* is upgradation of limitations but the real meaning is the maximum prosperity or the prosperity of the extreme quality. People wrongly believe that it is the combing ceremony in which the husband combs the hair of his wife. That is a part of the ritual. It is done in such a way that the 7th and the highest chakra, the *Sahasrār Chakra* is activated for the all-round development of the child in the womb. It gives confidence, solace, love and respect for caring family members, responsibility and attraction towards the child growing inside.

Seemantonnayan Samskār is as important as *Punsawan*. It is mostly done a month before the delivery for safe and secure birth of the child but it can also be done in the 4th or 6th month of pregnancy for the utmost development of the foetus. A son is needed, no doubt, but the son must be healthy, strong and free from all sorts of deformities. Moreover, the girl who is to become a mother for the first time must have confidence that everything will be all right otherwise she may succumb to intense pain.

Because of growing deforestation and unnecessary uprooting of the herbal plants for the construction of aerodromes, railway tracks, four to six-lane highways, factories and markets, it has become very difficult to collect the materials needed for this Samskār. Till some fifty years ago, all such things were available in every part of the country in abundance.

Time

Just as in *Punswan* a lunar asterism with the masculine gender is necessary, in *Seemantonnayan*. Most of the people prefer to perform it on the even numbered after conception: the 4th, 6th, or 8th.

Pārskar says: *Pratham garbhamāse shashte ashtame wā* (Either sixth or eighth month after conception).

Āswālayan suggests under the *Punsā* constellation of a moonlit fortnight. He opts for the fourth month.

Seemantonnayan Vidhi

After getting ready in every way the couple should sit on a pious *Āsana* (mat) near an 18-inch square *Vedi* (altar). The husband should select a *Brahmā* from among the *Pandits* who shall preside over the ritual. When that ritual is over then after performing *Āchaman* and *Prānāyāma* the husband should take the *Samkalp* (resolve) loudly. After completing the usual '*Hari aum vishnurvishnu...* etc. the following *Mantra* should be added:

Asyāh mama bhāryāyā garbhāwayawe abhyastejo briddhayartham kshetragarbhayo samskārārth pratigarbh samud bhawano nirwahan pourasasaram shri parameswar prityartham seemantonnayan samskāram karishye. Tatra nirbighnam samāpanārtham ganapatim poojanam swastipunywāhanam mātrikāpoojanam samkalpātmakam nāndi shrāddham cha karishye.

Homa

The *Homa* is performed with the prescribed articles and in detail. The following *Mantras* should be chanted:

- *Aum prajāpataye swāhah.*
- *Idam prajāpataye namama iti manasā.*
- *Aum indrāya swāhah.*
- *Imam indrāya namama. Ityādhārau.*
- *Aum agnaye swāhah. Idam agnaye namama.*
- *Aum somāya swāhah. Idam somāya namam.*
- *Aum bhuh swāhah. Idam agnaye namama.*
- *Aum bhuwah swāhah, Idam wāyawe namama.*
- *Aum swah swāhah. Idam suryāsta namama.*

The *Homa* would come to an end with the following *Mantra*:

Aumdevagātumavidogātumavitwāgātumita.Manasaspat imam deva yagyam Aum swāhā. Wātedhā swāhā. Idam wātāya namama.

Then the pregnant lady should sit on a smooth plank of devadaru tree. The husband should comb her hair with a branch of *Gular* with thirteen boughs or the boughs can be tied to the branch, 3 *Pinjali* of *Kusha*, white spine of porcupine tied with yellow thread and a conical nail of banyan tree. He should keep on reciting the following

Mantras and combing it. When it is completed he should bind the hair at the back as a plait:

- *Aum bhuh viniyāmi*
- *Aum bhuwah viniyāmi*
- *Aum swah viniyāmi*

He should tie five *Gulars* in the plait with the following *Mantra*:

Aum ayammurjāwato briksha urjiva phalinibhava.

Two Veena players should sing the following *Mantra* during that period:

Aum soma yewa nirāje māsānushih prajāh.
Avimukta chakra āsiram stiretubhyam asau.

ॐ सोम एव नीराजे मासानुषीः प्रजाः।
अविमुक्त चक्रऽआसीरं स्तीरेतुभ्यम् असौ।

The last word *'Asau'* can be replaced by the name of the river in the close vicinity. The pregnant woman should pronounce the name of the river.

The Samskār comes to an end when *Brahmins* are fed and departed and the *Visarjana* is completed. Then, the *Bhasma* from the *Vedi* is taken and anointed with the following *Mantras* to others as well as to the couple:

- *Aum trayāyusham jamadagne.* (Anoint at the forehead)
- *Aum kashyapasya trayāyusham.* (Anoint throat)
- *Aum yadadeveshu trayāyusham.* (Right arm)
- *Aum tanno astu trayāyusham.* (Anoint heart)

❁❁❁

Samskār-4

Jātkarma Samskār (Birth Ceremony)

Jātkarma liberates the father from all the four debts:

- Debt to the deities
- Debt to the sages
- Debt to the ancestors
- Debt to the society

It ensures the continuation of life on the Earth. Though a man has to die but it is expected that his son will also perform his duties to free him from such debts, because from birth till death we depend on deities, sages, family members and society for survival.

The Process

Jātkarma is less of a ceremony and more of a process performed at the time of the birth to be sure that all necessary precautions have been taken; that both the mother and the child are healthy, that the child is cleaned well and has started taking the feed. Jātkarma is a long process that begins before the delivery pains of the woman begin and continues for a short time after the birth.

Jātkarma is performed at the time of the birth of a child as *Jātkarma* denotes the action and steps taken at the time of birth. It includes both the precautionary measures and that of the actual birth. Some people by mistake take *Jātkarma* to be a ritual performed after the birth of a child. It is, in fact, performed to eliminate the defects in the foetus, to help the mother deliver a child easily and to clean the child just after birth, particularly if it has taken some amniotic fluid found in the womb during the process of birth; and to ensure that the child can take liquid food.

Time

That is the correct time for Jātkarma when the period of pregnancy as well as the period of delivery pain is over; when the umbilical cord (*nāla*) is cut; when the child is born and when it starts taking mother's milk.

The umbilical cord or the *nāla* should be cut off within 16 to 32 *ghati* i.e. within 6 to 12 hours; and the *Jātkarma Samskār* should be completed within that period but definitely before cutting the umbilical cord. *Manusmriti* says:

Prāng nābhinardhanātpu so jātkarma vidhiyate.
Mantraiwatprāshanamchāsyahiranyamadhusarpishām.

प्राङ् नाभिनर्धनात्पु सो जातकर्म विधीयते।
मन्त्रैवत्प्राशनं चास्य हिरण्यमधु सर्पिषाम्॥

The Rituals

Ganesh Poojan; Swasti-punyāhwāchan; Sodash-Mātrikā Poojan; Āyushya Mantra Jāpa; Nāndi Shrāddha; Medhā Janana; Āyushyakaran; Janmabhumi-

abhimantran, Shishu-Abhimarshan; Jananya Abhimantrana and *Standwaya-Prakshālan* are the rituals that are performed in *Jātkarma*. After giving the right (not the left) breast to the mouth of the newly born child, place a *kalash* full of water. Then, cutting of umbilical cord and keeping *Agni* (fire) in the room are done. It is essential to give *Homa* every morning and evening with rice-chaff (*bhusi*), broken rice and mustard seeds. The *Kalash*, *Agni* and *Homa* will continue for ten days without break. It is said in the following lines:

Jate putram sachalam bhawati janayato mātri nāndiyamedhā;

Yushye twewam japah syānjanana bhuwamamum Mantra yen mātaranchā;

Savyam prakshālya wāmam stanamudakyutam chāta prachichhadya nālam;

Sutyagni sthāpaya hutwā dwitayamanudinam vinshati dwe dwādra shāham.

Jātkarma Vidhi: Before Birth

When the pain starts the husband should massage the body of the wife with a light hand and chant the following Mantra:

Aum yejatu dashamāsyo garbho jarāyuna sah.

Yathāyam wāyurejati yathā samudra yejati.

Yewāyam dashmāsyo astrajjarāyunā sah.

After finishing the massage he should chant the following *Mantra* near her:

Aum avaitu prishinshevala shune jarāywattawe naiyā mā

sena peewarim na kasmishachanāyatanamawajarāyu padyatāmiti.

If the pain increases and the child is not delivered within two hours then the husband should take 31 pieces of the top of *Durvā* grass and place it in 4 ounces of oil and move it around the body of the wife in the sequence of *Pradakshinā*, reciting the following *Mantra* 108 times:

Aum himawatyuttare pārswe shawari nāma yakshini. Tasyā nupur shabdena vishalyāsyātu garbhini swāhā.

ॐ हिमवत्युत्तरे पार्श्वे शवरी नाम यक्षिणी।
तस्या नूपुर शब्देन विशल्यास्यातु गर्भिणी स्वाहा।।

Some of the oil should be given to the lady to drink and rest of it should be massaged on her abdomen.

Jātkarma Vidhi: After Birth

After taking bath and changing into clean clothes smear fragrance and saffron; put annotation on the forehead; sit at the *Āsana* and perform *Pranāyāma*. After performing the rituals of the beginning add the following *Mantra* to the resolve (*samkalp*):

Mamāsyātmajasyagarbhawāsjanit sakal dosha nibritituh asasarmāyurmedhā abhibridhaye beejagarbha samud bhawaino nirbahanārtha shri parmaeswar pityartham jātkarma samskār karishye. Tatra nirbighnārtham ganapati poojanam swastipunyāhwāchanam mātrikāpoojanam āyushya Mantrajapam nāndishrāssham cha hemnaiva karishye.

Medhājanan

Accordingly all the rituals are performed up to *Medhājanan, the first feeding with ghee and madhu.* Then *Medhājana* is performed:

- Take gold at the tip of the ring finger
- Dip it into honey and refined butter (of cow-milk)
- Steadily let the child lick it.

It is repeated four times. Every time one of the following *Mantras* is chanted in sequence:

1. *Aum bhusatwayi dadhāmi.*
2. *Aum bhuwa satwayi dadhāmi.*
3. *Aum swa satwayi dadhāmi.*
4. *Aum bhurbhuwah swah sarva twayi dadhāmi.*

Ayushyakaran

Ayushykaran is the external help given to the child so that he starts breathing normally through nose which he was doing through umblical cord. To perform *Ayushyakaran* bring your mouth close to either right ear or the navel of the child and patiently and correctly repeat the following *Mantra* thrice:

1. *Aum agnih āyushamāntasa vanaspatibhih āyushamāntasa tenatwā āyushamantam karomi.*
2. *Aum soma āyushamāntasa aushadhibhih āyushamāntasa tenatwā āyushāmantam karomi.*
3. *Aum brahmāyushamattad brāhmanah āyushmaktenatwā āyushāmantam karomi.*
4. *Aum devā āyushamante amritena āyushamantenatwā āyushāmantam karomi.*
5. *Aum rishaya āyushamantaste vratah āyushamatastenatwā āyushāmantam karomi.*

6. *Aum pitara āyushamantaste swadhāmih āyushamantenatwā āyushāmantam karomi.*
7. *Aum yagya āyushamantas dakshinabhih āyushamantatenatwā āyushāmantam karomi.*
8. *Aum samudra āyushamantasa sravantibhih āyushamastenatwā āyushāmantam karomi.*
9. *Aum trayāyusham jamadagneh kashyapasya trayāyusham. Yad deveshu trayāyusham tanno astu trayāyusham.*

Then repeat the last one thrice. Then the father should touch the child and chant the following *Mantra*:

Aum asmā bhava parashurabhava hiranyamsru bhava.

Ātmā wai putranāmāmasi sa jivema sharadah shatam.

After getting the right breast washed, he should give the nipple to the mouth of the child and chant the following *Mantra*:

Aum imang stanam urjjaswantam dhayāpām prapeenamagne sharirasya madhye.

Utasanjushaswa madhumatam arnavantasama mudriyang sadamāvishaswa.

After that the pitcher with water should be placed near the head side of her bed and the fire at the gate.

Even if the child is a daughter, all the above rituals are performed with right earnest because the scriptures make no difference between a son and a daughter. One must feel pleasure of the similar intensity and one must do everything for the growth and development of son and daughter in equal measure:

Kanyā suputrayoastulyam vātsalyam cha bhawet sadā.

Tulya ānandam vijāniyād dwayormanasi prāptyoh.

Sukh shāntih vyavasthām cha suvidhā yārddhyarapi.

Samutakarsha vikāsābhyām dhyānam yatnam samam bhawet.

कन्या सुपुत्रयोस्तुल्यं वात्सल्यं च भवेत्सदा।
तुल्यानन्दं विजानीयाद् द्वयोर्मनसि प्राप्तयोः।।
सुख शान्तेर्व्यवस्थां च सुविधा यार्द्धयरपि।
समुत्कर्ष विकासाभ्यां ध्यानं यत्नं समं भवेत्।।

The *Jātkarma Samskār* comes to an end with *Visarjana* and blessings.

❋❋❋

Samskār-5

Nāmkaran Samskār (Naming Ceremony)

Nāmkaran Samskār is a very important and popular Samskār and it is happily performed less religiously and more ceremoniously for the pleasure of all. At the time of this Samskār, the tension of the childbirth is over and hence it's held as a pleasurable ceremony.

In modern times, it is usually seen that *Jātkarma Samskār* is also included in it and both are performed at the same time. It is so because now mostly the deliveries take place in a clinic or hospital and many a times after Caesarian operation. In many cases, the mother and the child are released from the hospital after eight days, so, *Jātkarma Samskār* cannot be performed and it remains due. So it is but natural to perform both of them at the same time.

Palanārohan Samskār

At some places, this Samskār is called *Palanārohan Samskār* i.e. putting the child into a cradle. But at other places the ladies put the child into the cradle on the next day amidst music, song, dance and pleasantries. Surrounded by ladies in colourful dress, the head of the child must be in the south.

There is yet another thing that is performed during or after this ceremony. Often it is found that the mother's milk is not enough. To compensate for it, cow's milk is given. For the first time, the cow's milk should be given through *Shankh* (conch) and afterwards through *Seep* (oyster). The child should be in the lap of the mother with the head in the south and higher in comparison to the body. While the mother gives the milk through conch, the father should chant the following *Mantra*:

Aum āpyāya swasametute viswatah somavrishinayam.

Bhawāwājeshusangathe.

Before all these rites and rituals, three *Brāhmins* must be fed and adequate *Dakshinā* should be offered.

Time and Objective

Naming (*Nāmkaran*) ceremony is held eleven days after the birth of the child to give an individual identity for longevity and prosperity in worldly life to the newborn child. It is performed when the *Sutikā* (period for the mother and the child, of remaining confined under intensive care) is over. It is also known as *Shuddhikaran* (purification) and because the period of *Sutikā* varies in different families so it is invariably performed accordingly and as per the convenience of the family. The elderly women prefer an auspicious day for it therefore, the 11th day is not a fixed day.

In the absence of the father, the grandfather or uncle can perform this ceremony. One must avoid *Samkrānti, Amāwasyā, Grahan, Bhadrā, Vyatipāt* and *Vaidhriti Yoga* and the day of *Shrāddha.*

In certain families the *Nāmkaran Samskār* of only a male child is performed and a girl child is neglected. This not correct. We must remember that the girls are more needed for the continuation of life and their nature will determine the prosperity, peace and pleasure of both the families – parental as well as marital. It is difficult to say when and why such discrimination between the boys and girls entered in the minds of the people though the scriptures are unanimous about performing each Samskār for both of them. The sex of a child is not known during the Samskārs that are performed before the birth but barring the *Yagyopavit Samskār* no other Samskār is exclusively for sons only. What *Manusmriti* says makes it clear that the *Nāmkaran Samskār* of a girl child must also be performed. Manu is particularly keen on giving the sweetest, musical and soothing name for girls:

Strinām sukhodyam akruram vispashtārtha manoharam.
Mangalyam deerghavarnāntam āshirvāda abhidhānwat.

स्त्रीणां सुखोद्यं अंक्रूरं विस्पष्टार्थ मनोहरम्।
मंगल्यं दीर्घवर्णान्तं आशीर्वादाभिधानवत्।।

Nāmkaran Vidhi

The father should be ready in every way. He should sit down with his face towards east and perform *Prānāyāma.* The mother should sit in the south with the child. Then after initial *Poojā* and *Samkalp* the following *Samkalp* should be added:

Mamāsya shiauh beejagarbha samud bhawaino apmārjanāpura abhibriddhyārtham shri parameshwar prityartham nāmkaranam karishye. Tatrā nirbighnārthāya ganpatipoojanam swasti punyāhwāchanam cha karishye.

Then he should spread rice in a bronze dish and write the agreed name in it with a gold stick and say:

Mamāsya shishorhawāyushya prātyartham nnāmdevatā poojanam aham karishye.

And, pray to the God of Name:

Aum manojur justāma ajyasya brihaspatih yagyamimam tanoti aristam yagyangmimam dadhātu viswedevāya ih mādayāntām ompratishthah. --------- *nām supratishthitam astu.*

(At the blanks add the agreed name of the child.)

The following *Mantra should* also be chanted:

Aum shrishachate laxmishcha patnyāwa ahorātre pārshwe nakashatrāni rupam aswinā vyāttam ishnannishānamum ishāna savalokamma ishāna. Nāma devatābhyo namah.

After performing the *Shodashopachāra,* the father should say into the right ear of the child.

Hey kumār! Twam mamkuldevatāsya bhakto asi. Hey kumār! Twam māsānāmnā --------- *asi.*

Some prefer it to be repeated four times but one time is enough.

The others along with the *Brāhmin* should say the following as an acceptance to the name:

"--------- *nāma suprathistham astu.*

(Give the name of the child at both the blank spaces in the above *Mantras*.)

The parents, along with the child, bow to the elders and the elders should bless the couple and the child. With the *Visarjana* the ceremony comes to an end.

Selection of Name

The following things should be considered while deciding the name for a male or female child:

- The most important point is to choose a meaningful and distinctive name. It may project wishes and aspiration and show the ability to fulfil.
- Names can be taken from the names of gods; months and their synonyms; *Nakshatras* or a general name can be thought over, considered and selected.
- There has been a system of choosing a name for *Brahmins* that showed welfare and good omen; for *Kshatriya* that showed strength; for *Vaishyas* that showed wealth and for the *Shudras* that showed service. It is still being followed.
- Nowadays, there is a general way of giving name. Someone suggests a name for the child or someone declares that such and such will be the name of the child and that name is accepted. The suggestion may come from a family member or from a friend or a senior citizen.
- The ancient wise men suggested eight ways to select names:
  - (i) A name should have two to four varnas.
  - (ii) A name should end in *Krit Pratyaya.*
  - (iii) A name should be of *Taddhighosha Varna.*
  - (iv) It should have *ya, ra, la, wa Varna* in the middle.

(v) It must end in *Deergha* sound or accented syllable.

(vi) It must possess a part of the name of the ancestors.

(vii) Whatever it is, it must be attractive, virtuous.

(viii) A name should not incorporate the names or a part of the names of *Asuras*.

- According to *Nāmasamkirtan Yoga,* the first letter should be chosen from the following nineteen varnas: *ga, gha, anga, ja, jha, yan, d, dh, n, da, dha, na, ba, bha, ma, ya, ra, la, wa.* The first two letters of each five classes (*varga*) should be left out of consideration. The logic given is that they are *Prithvi Tatwa* and *Jala Tatwa* and represent the darker side, *Tama Vriti.*
- According to the same source the last letter should be either a *Deergha* sound, accented syllable or *Visarga*, 'h' sound as they represent the *Shiva-tatwa*, the morality and creativity while the *Hraswa* or unaccented syllables represent *Shakti* or energy.
- A boy's name should consist of *Varnas* in pair with two or four or six; the names of girls should contain *Varnas* in odd number *viz.* 3, 5, 7; while 11 is the best.
- Double letters symbolise *Purush Tatwa*, masculine element, so one must avoid double letters in the name of a girl; particularly, the initial letter should never be a double letter.
- Two-lettered names give fame; four-lettered names make spiritual as the four-lettered words invariably represent the four objectives of human life (*Chāra Purushārtha*): *Dharma* (righteousness); *Artha* (wealth); Kāma (desire) and *Moksha* (Salvation).

- There are five ways or general principles of selecting names according to the lunar asterism i.e. *Nakshatranām*; according to the month of birth i.e. *Māsānāma;* according to the family deity i.e. *Devatānāma;* according to the Zodiac sign i.e. *Rāshināma* and the worldly name *Samsārikanāma.* One must decide the general principles then search for the name accordingly.
- Bad, dirty, low or negative names (*Kutasita Nāma*) are given to the surviving child of the couple whose children have died after birth.
- In many tribes, there is a tradition of giving the child the name of a dead ancestor.

Names According to the Months

No.	Month	Synonym	Male	Female
1.	*Chaitra*	Krishna	Krishna Kumār	Krishnā
2.	*Vaishākh*	Anant	Anant Nath	Ananti
3.	*Jyeshtha*	Achyuta	Achyutānand	Achyutā Devi
4.	*Āshādh*	Chakrau	Chakradhar	Chakrāntā
5.	*Shrāvana*	Baikuntha	Baikuntha Nātha	Baikunthā
6.	*Bhādrapada*	Janārdan	Janārdan Gupta	Janārdani
7.	*Āshwina*	Upendra	Upendra	Upendrāni
8.	*Kārtika*	Yagya	Yagyadeva	Yagya Devi
9.	*Mārgshirsha*	Vāsudeva	Vāsudeva	Vasudevi
10.	*Paush*	Hari	Harihar	Haritimā
11.	*Māgha*	Yogish	Yogishwar	Yogishā
12.	*Phālguna*	Pundarikāksha	Pundarāi	Pundarikā

Names According to the Signs of Zodiac

No.	Rāshi	Zodiac	Initial Letter or Sound
1.	*Mesh*	Aries	*chu, che, cho, la, lee, lu, le, lo, ā.*

2.	*Vrish*	Taurus	*e, u, a, o, wā, vi, woo, wey, wo.*
3.	*Mithun*	Gemini	*kā, ki, ku, gha, ang, chha ke ko, hā.*
4.	*Karka*	Cancer	*hi, hoo, hey, ho, dā, di, doo, dey, doe.*
5.	*Singh*	Leo	*mā, mee, moo, mo, tā, tee, too, tey.m*
6.	*Kanyā*	Virgo	*to, pā, pi, poo, shā. Nā, thā, pey, poe.*
7.	*Tulā*	Libra	*rā, ri, ru, rey, to, tā, ti, tu, te.*
8.	*Vrishchika*	Scorpio	*to, nā, nee, nu, ney, no, yā, yi, yu.*
9.	*Dhanu*	Sagittarius	*ye, yo, bhā, bhee, bhu, dhā, phā, dhā, bhey.*
10.	*Makar*	Capricorn	*bho, jā, jee, ju, khee, khu, khe, gā, goe.*
11.	*Kumbh*	Aquarius	*gu, gey, goe, see, sau, su, se, dā.*
12.	*Meena*	Pisces	*dee, doo, tha, jha, ta, de, do, chā, chi.*

❁❁❁

Samskār-6

NISHKRAMANA SAMSKĀR (FIRST CEREMONIOUS OUTING)

Nishkramana Samskār is performed after the child is three months old. The child is taken out into the open to face the wind and sunshine, so that the sustaining power of the child can grow and that others may recognise the child and protect the child. This request for the protection is clear when the parents and other members give the child into the care and protection of the Sun, the Moon, *Dasho Dikapāla* (the guardians of the ten directions) and the sky. The meaning is that the child now goes under the protection of the world and the society.

As a part of Nishkramana Samskār and a month after it, the child is made to look at fire, a cow, and the moon; and making the child sit on land (*Bhumyupaweshana Vidhāna*) on auspicious days. In the last rite, the child is first made to sit on wheat and then on land.

Time

Nishkramana Samskār is usually performed three months after the day of birth or the lunar asterism at birth or another auspicious day. It is performed when the child is to be taken out in the open and out of the house for the first time. Before that a child is kept under intensive care and constant watch of the mother and the ladies of the house. Nowadays, this Samskār is being performed on the very day of *Nāmkaran* for the obvious reason that the parents work and they may have to take the child out any time.

Nishkramana Vidhi

When the father is ready in every respect and the child too is ready after taking bath and in new clothes, then the father should sit at proper *Āsana* and the mother places the child in his lap with the child's head in the south. The father should take resolve (*Samkalp*). After the initial *Samkalp* he should add the following *Mantras* as its vital part:

Mamāsya kishore āyuh vriddhi vyavahār siddhih twena shri parmeshwar preetyartham grihā nishkramana karishye. Tadangatwena ganapatipoojanam swastipunya āwāhanam cha karishye.

(I'm performing the *Nishkramana Samskār* to win over the favour and grace of the God so, as to increase my child's lifespan and Shri Laxmi may shower her blessing in the form of wealth; and to overcome all the ills. For it I'm worshipping Lord Ganesh and chanting *Punya Āwāhana Mantra.*)

Then in correct sequence all *Samkalps* and *Poojas* are performed. The father should take the child out and show him the sun first and chant the following *Mantra*:

Aum tachchakshuh devahitam purastāt
sukramuchcharat.

Pashyema sharadah shatam! Jivema sharadah shatam!
Shrinuyāma sharadah shatam!
Prawāma sharadah shatamadināh!
Shyāma sharadah shatambhushcha sharadah shatāt!

After that he should take the child to a temple and then to a family of some well-wisher in the close vicinity. If there is a shop nearby then the child should be taken to the shop as well.

After returning home, the father should give the child to the mother. The married ladies should welcome the child in various ways ending the ritual with annotation of *Bhasma* or consecrated rice. After that, place the child on the cradle.

The same day, during the early evening, the father should show the child the moon also. At that time he should chant the following *Mantra*:

Chandrārkayodigishānām dishām cha varunasya cha.
Nikshepārtham idam dadyi te twām rakshantu sarvadā.
Pramattam wā prasuptam wā diwālātram yathā piwā.
Rakshantu satatam te twām devāh shakrapurogamā.

चन्द्रार्कयोदिगीशानां दिशां च वरूणस्य च।
निक्षेपार्थं इदं दद्यि ते त्वां रक्षन्तु सर्वदा।
प्रमत्तं वा प्रसुप्तं वा दिवालात्रं यथा पिवा।
रक्षन्तु सततं ते त्वां देवाः शक्र पुरोगमा॥

(I'm putting this child into the shelter of *Chandra, Surya, Dikpāla, Dishā* and *Varuna* for protecting him all the time. O Child! In danger or in sleep or during the day or night all the gods and Indra will always protect you.) ❁

Samskār-7

Annaprāshana Samskār (Giving First Cereal Food)

Annaprāshana is ceremoniously giving a child his first cereal food (Anna) when he is six months old.

Taittariya Upanishad declares: *Prāno wai annama* (The life element is cereal.)

The above statement makes the inseparable relation of cereals and life element clear. That is why everyone is directed not to waste cereals or ignore them for they are *Vrat* (penance): *Annam na parichakshit, tad vratam*. Life sustains and mind develops with *Anna*. Life can't sustain without *Anna*:

Annasya sukshma bhāgena vikāso bhawet.
Ato nyāyadarshanam kuryāchchāmalam satkriyādibhih.

अन्नस्य सूक्ष्म भागेन् विकासो भवेत्।
अतो न्यायादर्शनं कुर्याच्चामलं सत्क्रियादिभिः॥

(The mind develops with the essence of the cereals that we take. Hence, earn cereals through rightful means and purify it with the best and only wholesome deeds.)

This advice is given because *Vaidyas* and *Āyurveda* claim that impure *Anna* creates anxiety and gives rise to diseases. People who eat impure *Anna* fall ill, grow weak and die early. So, our food intake must be pure and must be earned through rightful and ethical means. Each impure food intake will create some sort of disorder in body:

Āhāra shuddhau sattwashuddhih sattwa shuddhau dhruvā smritih.

Smriti labhye sarva granthinām vipramokshah.

आहारशुद्धौ सत्वशुद्धिः सत्वशुद्धौ ध्रुवा स्मृतिः।
स्मृति लभ्ये सर्व ग्रंथीनां विप्रमोक्षः॥

(If the food is pure, the inner self remains pure and mind becomes stronger; if mind and inner self are pure then memory becomes intense and strong; and when the memory is sharp and strong then all the glands, the *chakras* open up and spiritual union and salvation becomes easier.)

Taittiriya Upanishad declares *Anna* to be *Brahma* and also medicine. It says that all the living beings on this Earth are born out of *Anna* in the form of semen, sperm, embryo, foetus getting the essence of grain through umbilical cord before getting life and taking birth and at the end are metamorphosed into *Anna* in the form of burnt dead body or dilapidated body, changing into the food for plants and finally becoming a part of the fruit or the grain. It is the endless cycle that began with the beginning and may end with the end of this world or there may not be any end at all. Since, the plants and the grains are the oldest creation, and give the energy in different form and ways, so all of them are medicines. Those who accept *Anna* as *Brahma* get united to *Brahma*.

- That is the reason why agriculture, the process of producing *Anna,* is treated as the best profession:

  Annādwai prajāh prajāyante.
  Yāh kāshcha prithiang shritāh.
  Atho ante naiwa jeevanti.
  Athai na dapipiyantya anantah.
  Annang hi bhutānām jyeshtham.
  Tasmāt sarvau aushadhayam uchyate.
  Sarva vata annam āpnuwanti
  Ye annam Brahmopāsate.

- That is the reason that in different scriptures including the *Smritis Anna* is accepted as *Brahma* and given a very high status. The wastage of *Anna* is forbidden.
- That is the reason that the scriptures ordered to use the *Anna* carefully with love, respect and honour according to the rules framed for their use:

Matwānam Brahma hityetat prema shraddhāwarena cha.
Hanāsiuchchhista binā kuryād upayogam vidhānatah.

मत्वानं ब्रह्म हि त्येतत् प्रेम श्रद्धावरेण च ।
हनासीच्चिछष्ट बिना कुर्याद् उपयोगं विधानतः॥

The Need and Time of Annaprāshana

After the above noted comments, it is needless to state the reason why *Annaprāshana* was declared to be a Samskār and the rules were framed for it. It was the importance of *Anna* that the *Rishis* fixed rules for its first use by a human being. Moreover, *Anna* is different from the liquid food that the child had been taking after birth. Therefore, special and particular care had to be taken before giving grains to a child and the new mother needed instructions in detail. That was another reason that *Annaprāshana* was declared as another Samskār. If the mother and other family members take it seriously and show love and respect to *Anna* there are the chances that the children of the family will copy them and start showing similar love, respect and honour; and learn the art and technique of handling grain with care without wasting it.

The *Rishis* were careful in asking the parents to select the *Anna* according to their liking and wish. They had the belief that the *Anna* given at the time of *Annaprāshana* or for the first time to a child will have its lasting effect and the child would imbibe the quality of that *Anna*. So, they suggested that whatever the parents wanted to make their child, they should select that type of *Anna* for the *Prāshana*:

Swasantatau cha purusho gunanichchheda yāhrishān.
Tathānna chayan kritwā kāryet prāshanam tadā.

स्वसन्ततौ च पुरूषो गुणनिच्छेद याहृशान्।
तथान्न चयन कृत्वा कारयेत्प्राशनं तदा।।

It is apparent then that the type and quality of the *Anna* will be the type and quality of the person taking it. It is already accepted that our food intake makes lasting influence on us. It is very easily felt in the nature and habit of vegetarians and non-vegetarians; in herbivores, carnivores and omnivores. The *Rishis* and *Āchāryas* made it crystal clear that the best *Anna* is that which has been honestly produced, procured and prepared: *Nyāyād arjanam kuryād cha amalam sakriyādibhih.*

All the texts and *Āchāryas* including Sushruta, are unanimous about the time that *Annaprāshana* should be performed in the sixth month. In the first five months ,the digestive system of the child is not very strong to be able to digest the grains.

But Manu is clearer in this respect: *Shashtena prāshanam māsi yadweshta mangalam kule.* (*Annaprāsha* should be performed in the sixth month or at the time that suits the family or which is the most auspicious for the family.)

Annaprāshana Vidhi

After completing all the needed rituals for piety and freshness like taking bath in clean water with auspicious and purifying elements and grains (*Mangal Dravya*) etc and after wearing only two new clothes and preparing the child in the same way and annotating with fragrance and fragrant pastes; the father should sit on the pious seat, take *Āchamana* and perform *Prānāyāma*. After chanting the early parts of the *Samkalp*, he should add the following *Mantras*:

Mamāsya shishomātrigarbhi putaprāshana shuddhyartham annādya brahma āwarchasa tejai driya āyur balam lakshana siddhi beejagarbham samud bhava kalmash āpa mārjane shri parameshwar preetyartham annaprāshana akhyam karma aham karishye. Tatra nirbighnārtha ganapati poojanam swasti punya āhwāchana mātrikā poojanam nāndi shrāddham cha karishye.

He should perform all the *Poojan* accordingly. Then *Vedikā* (altar) should be constructed and *Agni* should be placed in it. Now select the *Brahmā* and perform the other rituals as directed and prepare the *'Chāru-pāka'* and perform the *Āhuti* with the *Mantras* given earlier. Then perform the extraordinary *Ahuties* with the following *Mantras*:

Aum devi wāchamjanyanta devāstām viswarupāh pashawo vandati.

Sā no mandresh murjaduhānā dhenuh wāgasmān upaitushtutaitu swāhā.

Idam wāche namam.

Aum devi wāchamityādiMantram pathitwā.

Aum wājo no adya prasuwāti dānam wājo devām ritubhih kalpayāti.

Wājo hi mā sarvaveeram jajān viswā āshā wājapatih jajeya ang swāhā.

Idam wāche wājāya namam.

And, offer four sthalipāka āhuties with the following Mantras:

Aum prānena annam asheeya swāhā. Idam prānāya namam.

Aum apānena gandhān asheeya swāhā. Idam apānāya namam.

Aum chakshushā rupāny asheeya swāhā. Idam chakshushe namam.

Aum shrotrena yasho asheeya swāhā. Idam shrotāya namam.

Perform another *Āhuti* called *Swistakrita Āhuti* with the refined butter taken out from *Chāru*. Chant the following Mantra:

Aum agnaye swistakrite swāhā. Idam agnaye swistakrite namam.

Then perform the three *Āhuties* to *Mahāvyāhrities* with the *Mantras* as given earlier. The last *Āhuti* should be given to *Prajāpati* with the following *Mantra*:

Aum prajāpataye swāhā. Idam prajāpataye namam.

At this juncture the *Annaprāshana* should be performed in the presence of all. The child should be brought ready after bath and in new clothes, fragrant and with ornaments, and made to sit with the father in his lap. Every thing cooked either at the *Yagyasthal* or inside the kitchen should be brought. The father should feed the child slowly and patiently; preferably from a silver plate with silver spoon while chanting the following *Mantra* with each morsel:

Aum annapate annasya no dehyana namiwasya shushminah.

Prapradātāram tārisha aurjagno dehi dwipade chatushpade.

ॐ अन्नपते ऽन्नस्य नो देहयन नमीवस्य शुष्मिणः।
प्रप्रदातारं तारिष ऽऊर्जंग्नो देहि द्विपदे चतुष्पदे॥

After giving three, five or nine morsels and finishing *Annaprāshana,* the father should perform *Āchamana* and clean the mouth of the child.

Then different articles should be placed before the child like books, weapons, instruments, toys, grain, mercantile, art and sculpture. Whatever the child touches first shows his genuine inclination towards that thing and it is presumed that he may earn his living through that. If he refuses to touch anything then he may take a new path.

The father should rise, collect the needed materials and perform the *Poornāhuti* with the following Mantra:

Aum murdhānam divo ararti prithvyā vaiswānar amrit ājātam agnim.

Kaviang smrājam atithim janānām āsanna pātram janyanta devāh swāhā.

Then, he should put *Bhasma* on his own forehead and that of the child in the given sequence while chanting the *Mantras* given earlier.

Tulā-Dāna

Before closing the ceremony *Tulā-dāna*, weighing the child with grain, once, five times or nine times which is then donated to *Brāhmins* or poor, should be done with the following *Mantra*:

Aum tejo asi shukram amritam āyushyā āyurme pāhi.

Devasya twā savituh yasawe aswinoh bāhubhyām pushno hastābhyām ādade.

The *Visarjana* should be completed and a part of the *Kheer* should be distributed as the *Prasāda* among the people present there to mark the completion of the ceremony.

Samskār-8

Chudākarma Samskār (Cutting Hair)

Chudākarma Samskār is known by many different names as: *Chaulakarma; Mundana Samskār; Keshānt, Keshachhedan* and *Shamshru* etc.

Besides longevity, strength and radiance, this *Samskār* is performed to facilitate the cosmic electromagnetic waves to enter in controlled proportion through the *Brahmarandhra* to *Sahasrār Chakra* because a small portion of hair is cut one by one from all the four sides of the head before the whole head is shaved off. A bit of hair is left at the centre to work as an antenna. The mind is the centre of all the actions and ideas; and all the orders: instant or delayed; of attack and in defence; of creativity and criticism; of action and rest. Chudākarma Samskār activates, enriches and refines the mind. If the head is not cleaned and washed regularly, there are chances that the person may go mad and remain retarded. The mind will not grow in a balanced way. It is the *Oja*, the divine energy that is given through this Samskār.

The meaning behind cutting off the hair that came with birth is very clear. It is to eliminate the animal qualities from the life and mind of the child. That is the reason that each *Dwija* (*Vaishya, Kshatriya* and *Brāhmin*) must perform it. Some people wrongly think that *Dwija* stands for *Brāhmin* alone. In fact, *Dwija* stands for all those who have tried to take another birth by reforming themselves or their children by giving better Samskārs to them, thereby refining their sense and sensibility.

Chudākarma is one such Samskār that erases the animal instincts and replaces them with human quality and nature. It makes a child humane, purges character, strengthens the mind, and helps the child to acquire better knowledge and grow wise:

Kalyānāya cha lokānām prayogo buddhi gyānyoh.
Sāphalyam mānwiyasya jivansyeha nishchitam.

कल्याणाय च लोकानां प्रायोगो बुद्धि ज्ञानयोः।
साफल्यं मानवीस्य जीवनस्येह निश्चितम्॥

(Whatever is done for knowledge, wisdom and betterment of the character is useful for social welfare and guarantees success in life.)

Time

Although, some people perform *Chudākarma* after one year but it is always advisable to perform it after three years when the child has grown a bit and is getting wise everyday. He has the needed strength to bear the divine illumination that a one-year-old child can't.

Āshwālāyana Grihyasutra says: *Tritiye varshe chaulam.*

Pāraskar Grihyasutra also expresses the same view: *Sāwant sarikasya chudākaranam.*

Despite this clear instruction, *Chudākarma* is performed after a year, after three years and also after five years. Some people perform the *Yagyopavit* along with it. At certain places there is the tradition of performing the *Chudākarma* after sixteen years. Many people go to places of pilgrimage for *Chudākarma*. Although, it is clearly stated in *Manusmriti* that among the *Dwija* the *Chudākarma Samskār* of each one should be performed after one year or three years, the *Shrutis* say:

Chudākarma dwijātinām sarveshām yewa janmatah.
Prathame shabde tritiye wā kartavyam shruti cha odanāt.

Chudākarma Samskār Vidhi

After being ready in traditional and religious way to perform the Samskār, and after sitting at the designated pious place (it is for both the parents and the child), the following religious rites are to be performed in that order: *Āchamana*; *Prānāyāma; Stuti-Prārthanā; Swastivāchanam; Shāntikaranam; Yagyakundnirmāna; Samkalpa; Brahmā-Chayan; Homa (Hawan, Āhuti); Punyāhwāchan; Ganesh-Poojan; Mātrikāpoojan* and *Nāndishrāddha.* In the *Samkalp* (the resolve) after the preliminaries, add the following *Mantra*:

Asya kumārasya bijagarbham samudabhava kalmashnirākaranain bala āyuh varcho abhibriddhih vyavahārsiddhyartham shri parmaeshwar preetyartham chudākarma karishye. Tatra nirbighnārth ganapati poojanam swasti punyāhwāchanam matrikāpujanam karishye.

(I am performing the *Chudākarma Samskār* in order to win the grace of the Lord so as to acquire pure food for attaining longevity, to add *Oja* and strength; and also to neutralise the sins generated during the period in the womb. Along with it, I am worshipping Shri Ganesh, sixteen *Mātrikās* and chanting *Punyāhwāchan* and also performing *Nāndi Shrāddha*.)

After the rites are performed as stated above. Actual *Chudākarma* begins with the division of the hair in four parts and tying them up separately. It is done after finishing the *Homas* of every type as directed earlier.

Cold and hot water are mixed together with churned curd while chanting the following *Mantra*:

Aum ushnena wāya udakene hyaditi keshānyap.

With this mixture, the plait of the right side (out of the already bifurcated four plaits) is tied with the following *Mantra*:

Aum savitā prasutā daivyā dāpa ung dantu te tanum. Deergha āyutwāya balāya barchase.

Then add three *Kushās* to their roots bifurcating them in three parts with the Mantra:

Aum aushdhaye trāyaswa.

While taking the shaving razor (*Ustarā*) of iron with its handle of brass, chant the following *Mantra*:

Aum shivo nāmāsi swadhitiste pitā namaste astu mā māhiangsih.

Then, while cutting that bunch of hair recite the following *Mantra*:

Aum nibartayāmyāyu annādyāya prajananāya rāyasya poshāya suprajāswatwāya suviryāya.

While cutting the other bunches recite the following *Mantra*:

Aum yenāwanatsavitā kshurena somasya rāgyo varunasya vidwāna.

Tena brāhmano vapatedam asyāyusyam jaradashtih yathāsat.

ॐ येनावनत्सविताक्षुरेण सोमस्य राज्ञो वरूणस्य विद्वान।
तेन ब्रह्मणो वपतेदमस्यायुष्यं जरदष्टिः यथासत्॥

Then sit down and place the hair on oxen's dung or in a pot with *Shami* leaves. Again after standing up, in the way previously done, place three *Kushās* in the left plait and divide it into three parts with a *Kusha* in each and cut it with the following *Mantra*:

Aum trayāyusham jamadagne kashyapasya trayāyusham.

Yad deveshu trayāyusham tanno astu trayāyusham.

ॐ त्र्यायुषं जमदग्ने कश्यपस्य त्र्यायुषम्।
यद् देवेषु त्र्यायुषं तन्नो अस्तु त्र्यायुषम्॥

Repeat the same process with the remaining two plaits but cut them without chanting the *Mantra*. All the hair so cut should be placed at the same place as directed earlier. If a part of it flies away then collect it with the help of the dung and place with other. While cutting the plait of north repeat the same procedure and cut the first part with the following *Mantra*. The other two bunches are to be cut without *Mantra*.

Aum yena bhurishcharā divam jyoshcha pashchāddhi suryam.

Tena te vapāmi brahmnā jivātawe jivanāya sushlokāya swastaye.

When the bunch cutting is finished, and the hair placed at proper place then move the razor thrice all over the head. While moving it the first time chant the following *Mantra* but repeat the act twice more without *Mantra*:

Aum yatksharena majjayatā supeshashā wapatwā wā wapati keshāmshichhadhim shiro mā syāyuh pramoshi.

Now wet the head again with the mixture of cold and hot water and churned curd. Then, give the razor to the barber and say: *Aum akshinawan pariwap*

The father should instruct the barber to shave the head carefully after leaving a thin plait of hair at the centre. The mother should collect all the hair in a new cloth and place on the dung and then return back to her place to perform *Purnāhuti*. The following is the *Mantra* for *Purnāhuti*:

Aum murdhānam divā arti prithvyā vaishwānar amrit ājātam agnim.

Kavi ang samrājama tithi jinnānāmāsanna pātram janayant devah swāhā.

The hair should be collected in the new cloth along with the oxen dung and bury it after digging a ditch near the cowshed or at the bank of a pond or river.

After that, the *Bhasma* is to be anointed to both the father and the child as done in other Samskārs.

The Samskār comes to an end with *Visarjan*, salutation, blessings, *Prasād* and feast to *Brāhmins* and others.

❁❁❁

Samskār-9

Karnabedha Samskār (Ear Piercing)

In the present time ears are pierced of both: the boys and girls for wearing ornaments. Earlier on, it had two definite purposes: one was to avoid paralytic attack and the other was to give a sense of security to the child. Other than these, it helps in listening clearly.

Chakrapāni adds another advantage that it checks bad planetary influences: *Karnabedhe bālo na grahaih abhibhuyate* (The planets do not affect one whose ears have been pierced.)

Sushrut says: *Rakshābhushan nimitta bālasya karno vidhyate* (It is for security and wearing ornaments that the ears are pierced)

Time

Karnabedha should be performed only after three years of age; on any *Shubh Muhurt* (auspicious day and time). It should be performed only in morning hours during moonlit fortnight and preferably in *Pushya, Mrigisharā, Chitrā,*

Shrāvana and *Revati Nakshatras*: *Jyotish Shāstra* insists on getting auspicious day and time fixed for the *Samskār*.

Karnabedha Vidhi

After getting ready in every respect, the father of the child (in the absence of father, grand father or uncle can perform it) and the child should sit at already arranged place. After performing initial *Poojā* the father should add the following to the *Samkalp*(resolve):

Asyakumārasyaāyuhabhibriddhivyavahārsiddhihetawa shri parmeshwar preetyartham karnabedham karishye. Tadangatwenanirbighnārthganapatipoojanamkarishye.

Then he should perform rest of the *Poojā* and perform salutation to gods and offer sweets to the child. The child should preferably sit in the lap of his mother and given sweets and toys to play.

Separate *Mantras* for each ear are chanted into the ears a little before the actual piercing. It is as a precaution. There are chances that the child will cry and disrupt the proceedings of the *Poojā*. Hence the following *Mantra* is chanted towards the right ear and the next *Mantra* towards the left ear:

Mantra for the Right Ear

Aum bhadra karnebhih sharnuyāma devā bhadram pashyemāksha abhirya jatrāh sthirai rangaih tushduvān tanubhih abyashemahi devahitam yadāyu.

Mantra for the Left Ear

Aum vakshanti vedāganigatim karnapriyangv sakhāya parish swajānā.

Yosheva shingate vitatādhindhwa anjjā eyam ang samane pāryanti.

The right ear of the boys should be pierced first but the left ear of the girls should be pierced first. It should be performed only by an expert man or woman:

Tasmād bhishak kushalah karna vidhyed vichakshanah.
Shishorharsha pramatasya dharmakāmārtha siddhaye.

तस्माद् भिषक् कुशलः कर्णं विध्येद् विचक्षणः।
शिशोर्हर्ष प्रमत्तस्य धर्मकामार्थ सिद्धये॥

A ring or a stick should be inserted in the ear hole to save it from getting closed. To avoid septic and pain, precautions are taken and for a week a drop of hot mustard oil is applied every morning and evening.

With the *Visarjan*, *Prasād*, salutation and blessings the *Samskār* comes to an end.

Samskār-10

UPANAYAN SAMSKĀR (INVESTITURE WITH SACRED THREAD)

Upanayan is known as *Brahmacharyavratdhārana* hence it is also called *Vratbandha*. The *Munja* is tied either to the waist or worn as *Janeva* so it is called *Munjadhāran*; and because sacred thread called *Janeva* is worn from that day so it is also called *Yagyopavit Samskār*.

The boy who is being given the Samskār is called a *Batuka*, *Munjamani* or a *Brahmachāri*. The one whose *Upnayan Samskār* has already been performed is called *Upanit*.

Upanayan is that Samskār that gives inner vision. The word Upanayan is formed of two words: Up (near or sub) and Nayan (the eye and to take towards). Our eyes take us towards something. Upanayan Samskār is, therefore, our sub-eye that takes us towards the teacher, knowledge and wisdom. Hence it is the rite that facilitates us with the power to get knowledge. In the scriptures it has been praised thus in the following Shloka:

Yagyopavitam paramam pavitam prajāpateh yat sahajam purastāt.

Āyushyam agrayam pratimuncha shubhram yagyopavitam balamastu tejah.

यज्ञोपवीतं परमं पवित्रं प्रजापतेः यतसहजं पुरस्तात्।
आयुष्यं अग्रयं प्रतिमुञ्च शुभ्रं यज्ञोपवीतं बलमस्तु तेजः॥

(Yagyopavit is completely pious. The Prajāpati has imagined it in a very natural form. It adds value and longevity; it gives power and energy, and Oja and brightness.)

Upanayan Samskār is like the foundation stone of human life, of the four pursuits of a human being namely *Dharma, Artha, Kāma* and *Moksha*. It is the preparation to know the social, moral, worldly, and spiritual responsibilities and to fulfil them. It is the entry into the life of *Āshrams* as with it begins the first *Brahmacharya Āshrama*.

The moment one enters into *Brahmacharya Āshrama,* one is bound by restrictions of vowed religious, social and moral restrictions and observances, the *Vratas* and hence it is also known as *Vratbandha*. The restrictions start from this point. Before that a child enjoys his childhood free from everything; leading a completely non-restricted life as there is no restrictions on a child's behaviour.

Because of the restrictions imposed and the vows that one has to observe, the *Upanayan Samskār* is treated as the rebirth. In this rebirth Savitā is the mother and his teacher is the father. Though loosely worn, yet the *Janeva* binds him with many things because for the first time he qualifies to chant the *Gāyatri Mantra* and that *Mantra* is taught during this *Samskār*. So, the *Janeva* is treated as a link between a man and *Gāyatri Mantra*. For becoming a *Dwija* (for the rebirth) this *Upanayan Samskār* is a must. It is claimed in the following *Shloka*:

Āchārya upnaymāno brahmchārinam kanute grabhmantah.

Tan rātrististra udare bibharti tan jāta drashtum abhisanyanti devāh.

आचार्य उपनयमानो ब्रह्मचारिणं कणुते गर्भमन्तः।
तं रात्रीस्तिस्त्र उदरे विभर्ति तं जात द्रष्टुं अभिसंयंति देवाः॥

(The birth from the womb of a mother is ordinary but the birth from the knowledge as *Brahmchāri* during *Upanayan* is the real one)

A hyperbolical praise is also given in the following *Shloka*:

Koti janma arjitam pāpam gyān-agyān kritam cha yat.

Yagyopavit mātrena palāyante na sansayah.

कोटि जन्मार्जितं पापं ज्ञान-अज्ञान कृतं च यत्।
यज्ञोपवीत मात्रेण पलायन्ते न संशयः॥

(Known-unknown sins and vices of millions of life are eradicated with only taking the *Janeva* after proper *Samskār*.)

Time

All *Dwija* (*Vaishya*, *Kshatriya* and *Brahmins*) are qualified for this Samskār but there is the restriction of age. *Āshwālayan Grihyasutra* says:

- *Yagyopavit Samskār* of the *Brahmins* should be performed at the age of nine.

- *Yagyopavit Samskār* of the *Kshatriya* should be performed at the age of eleven.
- *Yagyopavit Samskār* of the *Vaishyas* should be performed at the age of twelve.

In practice, nowadays, most of the *Kshatriyas* and the *Vaishyas* are given this Samskār at the time of marriage. As a result most of them are not getting good education. A proper and higher education remains beyond their reach although they are spending a lot on education. They must realise that higher education comes with inner vision, strong character and quality but never with money. Often they give excuses that their sons have to come into business so higher education is not essential for them. It is wrong. Higher and deep knowledge is a must for prosperity. That is one reason that most of the men and women spend their whole life in only *Artha* and *Kāma* and badly fail at the fronts of *Dharma* and *Moksha*. Most of them spend a rich, luxurious life devoid of pleasure and contentment.

Manusmriti holds and expresses a different view about the age and time of *Upanayan Samskār*:

Garbhāshthame abde kurvita brāhmanasya upanayanam;
Garbhād ekādashe rāgyoh garbhātu dwādasho vishah.
Brahma varchasa kāmasya kāryam viprasya panchame.
Ragyoh balārthinah shashte vaishasya ahārthino ashtame.
Āshodashād brāhmanasya sāvitri nāti vartate.
Ādwā vishāt kshatra bandhorā chaturvinshateh vishah.

गर्भाष्टमेऽब्दे कुर्वीत ब्राह्मणस्य उपनयनम्।
गर्भाद एकादशे राज्ञो गर्भातु द्वादशे विशः॥
ब्रह्मवर्चस कामस्य कार्यं विप्रस्य पंचमे।
राज्ञो बलार्थिनः षष्ठे वैश्यस्य एहार्थिनो अष्टमे॥

आषोडशाद् ब्राह्मणस्य सावित्री नाति वर्तते।
आद्वा विंशात् क्षत्र बन्धोरा चतुर्विंशतेः विशः॥

(A *Brahmin* should perform the Sacred Thread Ceremony at the age of five to get divine splendour; a *Kshatriya* in the 6th year for strength and courage and a *Vaishya* in the 8th year for wealth. For the *Brahmins* it can be performed in the 8th year or up to 16th year; in the case of *Kshatriyas* in the 11th year or up to 22nd year; and in the case of *Vaishyas* in the 12th year or up to 24th years of age.)

Some *Achāryas* have gone to the extent to fix the seasons for *Upanayan Samskār* as spring season for the *Brahmins*; summer season for the *Kshatriyas* and winter season for the *Vaishyas*.

The following chart will make many things clear at a glance:

No.	Subject	*Brahmin*	*Kshatriya*	*Vaishya*
1.	Minimum age	5	6	8
2.	Maximum age	16	22	24
3.	Season	Spring	Summer	Winter
4.	*Mekhalā*	Cotton	Hemp	Wool
5.	Colour of cloth	Saffron	Red	Yellow
6.	Animal skin	*Mriga*	*Ruru*	Goat
7.	*Danda* (Stick)	*Dhāka/Bilva*	*Bargad*	*Gular*
8.	Size of *Danda*	Up to hair	Up to forehead	Up to nose
9.	*Phalāhar*	Milk	*Yawāgu*	*Shrikhand*
10.	Sacred Thread	Cotton	Cotton	Cotton
11.	*Bhikshātan*	*Bhawati bhikshām dehi.*	*Bhikshām bhawati dehi.*	*Bhikshām dehi bhawati.*
12.	*Dātuna*	12 inches	10 inches	8 inches

There was a time when all the wealth was confined and kept with the *Vaishyas*, all the power and valour with *Kshatriyas* and all the wisdom with the *Brāhmins* while all the skill was given to the *Shudras* who were experts in performing the most difficult tasks with ease and pleasure. The times have changed. All the four *Varnas* are accumulating wealth, all are trying to be fighters; wise and skilled in everything. Hence, there is neither depth nor stature in their wisdom, skill and wealth, nor there is cohesion in the society. Interdependence and almost blind faith on one another has been brutally erased. Doubt is prevailing in the society and everyone is forced to live in fear and uncertainty. It is the real reason behind the lack of pleasure and happiness in the life of modern man.

Upanayan Vidhi

The boy should have *Vrat* on *Phalāhār* which is almost like fasting for a day or for three days earlier. When everything and everyone is ready for the ritual, the father should sit in the *Yagya Mandap*, specially prepared for the purpose; his wife would sit in the south and his son in the south to his mother. With *Pavitri* in hand the father should perform *Āchaman* and *Prānāyāma* before taking the resolution. After the preliminaries of the *Samkalp*, he should add the following:

Krichchhratrayātmak prāyāshchita pratyāmnāya gonishkrayee bhuta yathā shakti rajat dravya dāna purvakam dwādash sahastram Gāyatri japamaham brāhmanena kāryishye.

The father should only say *Karishye* in the end of the above *Mantra* if he is willing to do the *Japa* himself.

The *Batuka* (from here onwards the boy would be called *Batuka*) should also take the *Samkalp*. After the preliminaries of the *Samkalp* (resolve) he should add the following *Mantra*:

Mama kāmachāra kāmavāda kāmabhakshanādi dosha parihārārtham krichchhratrayātmak prāyāshchita pratyāmnāya gonishkrayee bhuta yathā shakti rajat dravya dāna purvakam dwādash sahastram Gāyatri japamaham karishye.

After taking the *Mantra* during the rite, he should start the *Japa* of the *Mantra* from the next day. One thousand *Japa* will have its effect on his memory.

Then the father should restart the *Samkalp* afresh and after the preliminaries he should add the following *Mantra*:

Asya kumārasya dwijatwā siddhi dwārā Vedādhyayanadhikār siddhyartham shri parameshwar preetyartham cha upanayanam shwarvo wā karishye.

- At certain places these rites are completed a day before the *Mandap* is ready. But these are repeated again the next day.
- At other places, *Satyanārāyana Vrat Kathā* is told a day before the *Upanayan Samskār*. A *Mangal Kalash*, an auspicious Earthen or brass vessel is placed with the *Shodasha Upachāra.*
- At some places, the boy eats for the last time with his mother.
- At other places eight mothers and eight boys at the verge of the *Upavit* are fed.

These are local variations. The ladies perform the rites and rituals in their own way as is in vogue in the family or the region. The relatives, particularly *Mausā*, *Māmā*, and *Behanoi* play important roles. These are not given here because of the variations in the versions.

Then *Ganapatipoojanam*, *Punyāhwāchan*, *Matrikāpoojan*, *Grahayoga* and *Nāndi Shrāddha* should be performed. A bit away from the *Poojā Mandap* the *Achārya* should get a *Vedikā* prepared. When it is ready then *Batuka* should be called and sit in the south of the *Āchārya* but in the west of the *Vedikā*. All *Brāhmins* present there should bless him with *'Abrannityam'* then the *Acharya* would ask the *Batuka* to say:

- *Brahmacharyamāgam*
- *Brahmacharyasāni*

Then *Batuka* would be given *Kati-sutra*, *Kaupina* (loin-cloth) etc to wear amidst the chanting of the following *Mantra* by the *Āchārya*. All the clothes needed by the *Batuka* should be given at that very time with this *Mantra*:

Aum yenedrāya brihaspatih wāsah paryadadhād amritam.

Tenatwā paridadhāmyāyu she deerghāyu twāya balāya barchase.

ॐ येनेद्राय वृहस्पतिर्वासः पर्यदधाद अमृतम्।
तेनत्वा परिदधाम्यायु षे दीर्घायु त्वाय बलाय वर्चसे।।

The *Batuka* should wear *Mekhalā* (according to the *Varna*) of equal number of *Parwars* (wrappings) and *Gāntha* (knots). While tying it around the waist of the *Batuka*, the *Āchārya* should chant the following *Mantra*:

Aum eyam duruktam pariwādhamānā varna pavitram punatima āgat.

Prāṇāpānābhyām balam ādadhānā swaso devā subhagā mekhaleyam.

ॐ इयं दुरूक्तं परिवाधमाना वर्ण पवित्रं पुनतीम आगत्।
प्राण अपानाभ्यां बलं आदधाना स्वसोदेवा सुभगा मेखलेयम्॥

The *Brahmins* should give a pair of *Janeva* each and the *Batuka* should take the following *Samkalp* and give *Dāna* to the *Brahmins* accordingly:

Aum tatsaddyāt ----- gotro ----- aham swakiya Upanayan karma vishayaka satsamskār prātyarthamidam bhāndāstātryam sayagyopavitam sadakshinam nānānāma gotrabheyo brāhmanebhya sampradade.

(in the blank spaces name and *gotra* of *Batuka* should be given)

Then the *Āchārya* should start and perform *Upanayan* as stated below. First he should sprinkle water on the *Upavit* with the following *Mantras*:

1. Aum āpo hishtāmayo bhuwastāna urje dadhātana. Maheranāya chakshase.
2. Aum yowah shivatamoh rasastasya bhājayatehanah. Ushtiriva mātarah.
3. Aum tasmā arangamāmawo yasyakshayāyajinwatha. Āpo janayathāchanah.

With the following three Mantras he should move the thumb on the Upavit:

1. Aum Brahamaja gyānam prathamam purastād dwisomatah suruchovena āwah. Subudhnyā upamā asya vishthāh satasyoni masatashcha vivah.
2. Aum idam vishnuh vichakrame tredhā nidadhe padam. Samudhasya pā nag sure.
3. Aum namaste rudra manyava utota ishawe namah bāhubhyām ute namah.

He should arrange the nine threads of Upavit and embellish it with nine gods and chant one of the following *Mantras* with each one:

1. Omkār prathame tantau vinasyāmi.
2. Agnim dwitiye tantau vinasyāmi.
3. nāgān tritiye tantau vinasyāmi.
4. Somam chaturthe tantau vinasyāmi.
5. Indram pancham tantau vinasyāmi.
6. prajāpatim shashtam vinasyāmi.
7. Vāyum saptam tantau vinasyāmi.
8. Suryam ashtam tantau vinasyāmi.
9. Viswedevāna navam tantau vinasyāmi.

He should chant *Gāyatri Mantra* ten times while looking at the *Upavit*:

Aum bhurbhwah swah tat saviturvarenyam bhargo devasya dheemahi dhiyo yo nah prachodayāt.

And while showing it towards the sun he should chant the following *Mantra*:

Aum upayāma grihito asi sāvitro asi cha na udhāshcha nodhā asi cha no mayi dhehi. Jinva yagyam jinva yagyapatim bhagāya devāya twā savitre.

The *Āchārya* should himself give the *Yagyopavit* to the *Batuka* and chant the following *Mantra*:

Aum yagyopavitam paramam pavitram prajāpateh yat sahajam purastāt. Āyushyam agrayam pratimuncha shubhram yagyopavitam balamastu tejah yagyopavitam asi yagyasya twā yagyopavite nopanhyāmi.

The *Batuka* should also chant the *Mantra*; and raising the right arm wear the *Yagyopavit* from the left shoulder.

He should be given new clothes and the *Āchārya* should chant the following *Mantra* while he wears them:

Aum yuvā suvāsāh parivit āgatsa ushreyān bhawati jāyamānah.

Tandhi rāsah kavaunnayānti swādhayo manasā devayantah.

ॐ युवा सुवासाः परिवीत आगत्स उश्रेयान् भवति जायमानः।
तन्धीरासः कवउन्न भान्ति स्वाध्यो मनसा देवयन्तः॥

The *Batuka* should be given deerskin with the following *Mantra*:

Aum mitrāsya chakshuh adharunam baliyastejo yashaswi sthavirang samiddham.

Anāhansyam vasanam jarishnu paridam wājya jinam dadheaham.

ॐ मित्रास्य चक्षुः अधरूणं बलीयस्तेजो यशस्वि स्थविरꣳसमिद्धम्।
अनाहनस्यं वसनं जरिष्णु परीदं वाज्य जिनं दधेऽहम्।

The Batuka should be given *Danda* (staff) with the following *Mantra*:

Aum yo me dandah parāpata dwaihāyaso adhibhumyām.

Tamaham pukarādad āyushe brahmane brahmavarchasāya.

Then the *Achārya* should fill the *Anjuli* (the cupped palm) of the *Batuka* thrice with water while chanting the following *Mantras* one at a time:

1. Aum āpohrishtāmayi bhuwastāna urje dadhātana. Maheranāya chakshase.
2. Aum yovah shivatamoh stasya bhājayeteh na ushtiriva mātarah.

3. Aum tasmā arangmāmao yasya kshayāya jinwatha. Āpo janayathāchana.

Every time the *Batuka* should offer that water with the *Āchārya* saying: *Suryam deekshaswa.* Then he should look at the sun and chant the following *Mantra*:

Aum tad chakshuh devahitam purastātchhukram uchchareta. Pashyema sharadah shatang jivema sharadah shatang shrinuyāma sharadah shatam pravrawāma sharadah shatamdeenām shyām sharada shatam bhuyashcha sharadah shatāt.

The *Āchārya* should place his hand at his heart from over the right shoulder and chant the following *Mantra*:

Aum mama vrate te hridayam dadhāmi mama chittam anuchittam te astu. Mama wāchamekanājuswa brihaspatishtrawā niyunuktu mahyam.

The *Āchārya* should ask for the name thrice and the *Batuka* should reply each time saying his name with the surname in the following way:

.....(Sharmāham) bho/ ..... (Vermāham) bho/ ...... (Guptoaham) bho etc.

Then the *Āchārya* should ask:

Kasya brahmachāryasi?

The *Batuka's* simple answer would be:

Bhakt.

Then the *Batuka* will stand facing each direction one by one and the *Āchārya* will chant the following four *Mantras*, one for each direction as given with the text:

East: *Aum prajāpatate twā paridadāmi.*

South: *Aum devāya twā savitre paridadāmi.*

West: *Aum adabhyastwa aushadhibhyah paridadāmi.*

North: *Aum dhyāwā prithvibhyām twā paridadāmi.*

The *Batuka* should look below with folded hands, and the *Āchārya* should chant: *Aum vishwe bhyashtwā bhutebhyah paridadāmi*; then *Batuka* should look up and the *Āchārya* will chant: *Aum sarvebhyashtwā bhutebhyah paridadāmi.*

The *Batuka* would come to the north of the *Achārya*, sit relaxed, take flower, sandal, betel and clothes and choose and worship a *Brahmā* for the *Yagya* with the following *Mantra*. His offerings would be accepted by the *Brahmin* as *Brahmā* with:

Aum vritoasmi:

Aum adya kartavya upanaya homa karmāna kritākritābekshanarupa brahmakarma karttum ...... gotra ....āham brāhamanamebhih pushp chandan tāmbul wāso abhibrahmatwena twāmaham vrine.

The *Brāhmin* or *Brahmā* should take a round of the fire and then sit down at his place. The father should say: *Asmin karmani twam me brahmā bhava.*

The *Brāhmin* should accept by saying: *Bhawāmi.*

With the help of *Brahmā*, the *Batuka* should prepare the *Ahuti* as directed by the scriptures and perform the following five *Ahuties*:

1. Aum tawanno agne varunasya vidwān devasya hedo ayavayāsisishthāh. Yajishtho wahni tamah

shoshachāno viswādweshā ang si pramu mugdhya smat swāhā. Idam agni varunābhyām namam.

2. Aum sa tawanno agne awamo bhawoti nedishtho asyā usaso vyushtau. Awayakshwa no varunang rarāro wihi mridik ang suhawonayedhi swāhā. Idam agni varunābhyām namam.
3. Aum ayāsh cha agne asyanabhishasti pāshcha satyam itwa mayā asi. Ayā no yagyam wahāsyayā no dhehi bheshajang swāhā. Idam agnaye ayase namam.
4. Aum ye te shatatam varun ye sahastramyagiyāh pāshā vitatā mahāntah. Tebhirno adyā savitota vishanuh vishwe munchantu marutah swarkāh swāhā. Idam varunāya savitre vishnave vishwebhyo devebhyo marudbhyah swarkebhyashcha namam.
5. Aum uduttamam varunam pāshamasmad bādham vimasyam ang shrayāya. Ath āwayam ādityam vrate tawānāgas aditaye swāhā. Idam varunāya namam.

After completing all the *Āhuties* the *Batuka* should wash his hand and offer *Dakshinā* to the *Brahmā* with the following *Mantra*:

Aum adyau tasminna panayena homa karmani kritākritā vekshana rupa brahmakarma pratishthārtham idam purna pātram prajāpati daivatam ----- gotrāya ----- ane brahmne brāhmnāya dakshinām tubhyam aham sampradade.

The *Brahmin* should accept it with: *Aum swasti.*

He should sprinkle water over his head with: *Aum sumitriyā na āpa aushadhayah santu* and pour water in *Ishāna Kona* with: *Aum durmitriyā astasmai santu yoasmān dweshthi yam cha vayam dwishmah.*

Then after collecting the *Kushās* in the sequence they were spread, he should put them into celestial fire as *Homa* with the following *Mantra*:

Aumdevāgātuvidogātumvitwāgātumita.Manaspayibham devayagyaangswāhāvātedhāhswāhā.Idamvātāyanamam.

The Teachings by Āchārya

The *Āchārya*, then teaches the *Batuka* in the following way and the *Batuka* should answer positively. It has been given below as dialogue with the meaning.

Āchārya: Brahmachāryam asi. (You are *Brahmachāri.* It means, you are now authorised to study the *Vedas*.)

Batuka: Bhawāni. (It should be so.)

Āchārya: Aposhāna. (You should wash your mouth.)

Batuka: Ashāni. (I will do that.)

Āchārya: Karma kuru. (Perform duties. It includes morning and evening prayers, study of *Vedas* and begging.)

Batuka: Kariwāna. (I will do.)

Āchārya: Mā diwā sushupthā. (You should not sleep during the day.)

Batuka: Na swapāna. (I will not sleep.)

Āchārya: Bācham yachchha. (Remain silent while eating.)

Batuka: Yachchhāni. (I will remain silent.)

Āchārya: Adhyayanam sampadāya. (Complete your study.)

Batuka: Sampadayāni. (I will complete.)

Āchārya: Samidham ādehi. (You will perform offerings to *Agni*.)

Batuka: Ādadhāni. (I will.)

Āchārya: Apo ashāna. (Wash your mouth after every meal.)

Batuka: Ashāni. (I will.)

When the teaching is over the *Batuka* should touch both the feet of the *Āchārya* with reverence and should sit in the south of the *Agni* facing east. The *Āchārya* must be close to the *Batuka* looking towards north of the *Agni*. At that time he should teach him the *Gāyatri Mantra*.

Teaching Gāyatri

Just before the teaching of *Gāyatri*, rice is spread in a bronze dish and the complete *Gāyatri Mantra* is written with a pen-like stick of gold, silver or bronze whichever is available. Then the *Batuka* takes a resolve with the following *Mantra*:

Aum adya mam brahma barchas vedādhyayan adhikār siddhartham Gayatraya upadeshāng vihitam Gāyatri Sāvitri Saraswati poojan purvakam chrya poojan karishye.

(For the brilliance of *Brahma* and for the completion of the study of *Vedas* and as a part of it I, like the worshipping of *Gāyatri*, *Sāvitri* and *Saraswati*, worship my teacher.)

Immediately after it he should worship the three deities and then the *Achārya* with the two *Mantras*:

1. *Aum Manojutirjushatām*
2. *Shrishachate*

Though, the popular *Gāyatri Mantra* is the same but there are as many as 24 types of *Gāyatri Mantras*. It is taught in three different ways to the *Batukas* of the three *Varnas*. Both the *Āchārya* and the *Batuka* chant *Gāyatri* one by one. It is taught in three steps by repeating it in different ways. The *Achārya* says a part of it and the *Batuka* repeats it.

The Gāyatri for Brāhmins

- The first teaching is done with *Pranava* and *Vyāhrities* in the following way:

Aum bhurbhuwah swah; tatsaviturvarenyam.

Aum bhurbhuwah swah; bhargodevasya dheemahi.

Aum bhurbhuwah swah; dhiyo yonah prachodayāt.

- The second teaching is done with half *Richā* and *Vyāhrities*:

Aum bhurbhuwah swah; tatsaviturvarenyam; bhargodevasya dheemahi.

Aum bhurbhuwah swah; dhiyo yonah prachodayāt.

- In the third teaching, the complete *Mantra* is taught:

Aum bhurbhuwah swah; tatsaviturvarenyam bhargodevasya dheemahi.

Dhiyo yonah prachodayāt.

The *Gāyatri* for *Kshatriyas*

The Gāyatri for *Kshatriya* is in *Trishtupa Chhand* whose *Rishi* is Brihaspati and the *Devatā* is Savitā:

Aum deva savitah prasuva yagyam prasuva yagyapati bhagāya.

Divyo gandharva ketupuh ketanah punātu vāchaspatih wācham nah swadatu.

The Gāyatri for Vaishyas

The Gāyatri for *Vaishyas* is in *Jagati Chhand* whose *Rishi* is Prajāpati and *Devatā* is Savitā:

Aum viswarupāni pratinchatekavih prāsavit bhadra dwipade chatushpade.

Vinākamkhyat savitāvavarenyo anuprayānamushasovir ājati.

This separate teaching is for spirituality for *Brāhmins*, strength for Kshatriyas and wealth for *Vaishyas*. If any of them wish to opt for spirituality, the first *Gāyatri Mantra* in three steps should be taught to them.

Brahmacharya and Related Duties

Usually, at this very point the *Brahmacharya Vrat* and related duties are explained to the *Batuka*. It is all stated in *Manusmriti*:

Varjaye madhumānsam cha gandha mālyam rasān striyah.

Shuktā niyāni sarvāni prāni nāmchaiva hinsanam.

Abhya ang manjanam chakshaksho rupāna cha chhatra dhāranam.

Kāma krodham cha lobham cha nartanam geet vādanam.

Dyutam cha janavādam cha parivādam tyathā anritam.

Strinām cha prekshanā lambham upaghātam parasya cha.

Eka shayita sarvatra naretah skandayet kwachid.
Kāmāddhi skandaya aneto hinasti vratam ātmanah.

वर्जये मधु मांसं च गन्ध माल्यं रसान् स्त्रियः।
शुक्ता नियानि सर्वाणि प्राणिनां चैव हिंसनम्।।
अभ्यंगमज्जन चक्षक्षोरूपान छत्र धारणम्।
कामक्रोधं च लोभं च नर्तनं गीतवादनम्।।
द्यूतं च जनवादं च परिवादं तथाऽनृतम्।
स्त्रीणां च प्रेक्षणालम्भमुपघातं परस्यच।।
एक शयीत सर्वत्र नरेतः स्कन्दयेत्क्वचित्।
कामाद्धि स्कन्द्यनेतो हिनस्ति व्रतं आत्मनः।।

A *Brahmachāri* has to lead a life of purity as a teetotaller and as a pure vegetarian. He should never touch wine, woman, meat, fragrant matters, intoxicating things, flowers, garlands, any of the six *rasas* (juices), stale and junk food. He should not kill a living being, enter a river or reservoir for bathing, and should not take an umbrella for protection against sunrays or rain. He should be free from sex, anger, lust, songs and dance and musical instruments. Gambling, spreading rumours and scandals, eulogy or praise of others, lies, touching or looking at women, or beating another human or non-human being is strictly prohibited for him. He has to sleep alone and has to save *Shukra* (semen) for greater energy and concentration and endurance. He would need them for fulfilling the greater desires, wishes and ambitions. When semen is lost, the penance is lost. Any sort of luxury is not for him. He would get them when he is strong and able enough, and enters the *Grihastha Āshrama* (domestic life).

He has to take water in a big vessel and take bath with a smaller vessel. He has to wear only a *Kopin* that should never be torn or dirty, and a *Danda*. If and when the *Yagyopavit* gets torn, he should take it off and offer to some reservoir with *Mantra* and take a new one with *Mantra*.

Since, the *Brahmachāri* has to be with the *Āchārya*, far away from home and as the *Āchārya* alone is not able to look after each student so the students have to take care of themselves. That is the reason that all the works where there could be some danger to life, are strictly prohibited for a *Brahmachāri*. For that particular reason he is not allowed to enter a pond, a lake or a river or to climb a tree etc.

Samidādhān

Samida Ādhāna, after pronounced together as Samidadhān is the offering of the fuels to *Agni*. This should be performed just after teaching the *Gāyatri Mantra*. It is one of the difficult daily rituals that were perhaps performed at regular intervals. It was to be performed throughout the life of *Brahmacharya*. Basically, it is for concentration and physical fitness; and perhaps for absorbing heat but that is not very clear. It is offering for specific purpose. It is not sacrifice although most of the people call it so. Offerings to *Agni* in a *Yagya* should not be called sacrifice.

The *Batuka* or *Brahmachāri* sits in the south of the *Āchārya* and the west of the fire. He takes pieces of dry dung (*Upla*) in right hand, dips them in refined butter (*ghee*) and offers to *Agni* and chants the following five *Mantras*:

1. Aum agne sushravasu shravasam mā kuru swāhā.
2. Aum yā twam agne sushravah sushravā asi swāhā.
3. Aum yewam wā ang sushrawah saushravasam kuru swāhā.
4. Aum yathā twam agne devānām yagyasya rishidhā asi swāhā.
5. Aum yewam aham manusyānām vedasya nirdhipo bhuyāsam swāhā.

He should sprinkle water from a pot around the fire starting from *Ishāna Kona* and completing the round. He should take three *Samidās*, dip in refined butter and offer to *Agni* with the following *Mantras* that are to be repeated every time one performs *Hawan* with *Samidā*:

- *Aum agnaye samidham āhārsh brihate jātavedase yathā twam agne samidhā samidhyasa yewa mahim āyushā medhayā varchasā prajayā pashubhih brahma varchasena samindhe jivaputro mam āchāryo medhā vyaha sānya nirākrarishnyuh yashaswi tejaswi brahma varchasya ānando bhuyāsam.*
- *Aum yeshāte agne samittayāvarddha swachāchā apyāya swavarddhi dheemahi cha vayam āchāpya asi mahi swāhā.*

The earlier process of placing dry cow dung with refined butter and chanting five *Mantras* should be repeated and water sprinkled as stated earlier. The *Batuka* should take the heat on hand (warm his hand on the fire) without chanting a *Mantra*; and touch the face and other parts of head with the following *Mantras*:

Aum tanupā agne asi tanwa me pāhi.

Aum āyurdā agne sthāyuh meydehi.

Aum wachaudā agne asi varcho meydehi.

Aum agne yanme tanwā unantanma āpana.

Aum medhā mey devah savitā ādudhātu.

Aum medhām mey devi saraswati ādudhātu.

Aum medhām mey aswinau devabādhattām pushkarastrajau.

With heated left hand he should touch the whole body (the parts of body are indicated after every *Mantra*) and chant the following *Mantras*:

- *Aum angāni cha ma āpyāyantām.* (All parts)
- *Aum wāk cha ma āpyāyantām.* (Mouth)
- *Aum prānav cha ma āpyāyantām.* (Nose)
- *Aum chakshushcha ma āpyāyantām.* (Eyes)
- *Aum shrotramcha ma āpyāyantām.* (Ears)
- *Aum yashobalam cha ma āpyāyantām.* (Both arms)

Then he should anoint the four parts with *Bhasma* with the *Mantras* indicated and given earlier.

[There is a variation in *Sāndhya Vandanā* (evening prayer.) At many places, it is called *Brahmāndya* (cosmic) *Sāndhya* and is performed only with the *Gāyatri Mantra*.]

Abhivādana

With respect and devotion, the *Batuka* should salute *Vaishwāner* with the first *Mantra*; *Surya* with the second *Mantra* and the *Achārya* with the third *Mantra*:

1. ------- gotrah ------ pravarah ------- (Sharmā/Vermā/ Gupta) aham Vaishwāner twām abhiwādaye.
2. ------- gotrah ------ pravarah ------- (Sharmā/Vermā/ Gupta) aham Suryadeeva twām abhiwādaye.
3. ------- gotrah ------ pravarah ------- (Sharmā/Vermā/ Gupta) aham bho abhiwādaye.

The *Āchārya* and other *Brahmins* should bless him with *'Ayushamāna bhava'* or other such blessings. Then the *Batuka* should bow before all other elders and take their blessings.

Bhikshā Charana

The next step after salutation is *Bhikshātana*. After taking a *Bhikshā Pātra* he should go for *Bhikshātana*. It is actually dummy *Bhikshātana* only to teach him the way he has to perform it later in life. So, he can confine it to three or six or twelve ladies because during his actual *Bhikshātana* he will have to meet mostly ladies during the day, as the men will be away on work. The ladies should not refuse. Raw or uncooked grains should not be given as the *Brahmachāries* have no way to cook their food. The wording of the call of *Bhikshātana* is the same but the word order has been changed for each *Varna*. It is given below:

- *Brahmin: Bhawati bhikshām dehi.*
- *Kshatriya: Bhikshām bhawati dehi.*
- *Vaishya: Bhikshām dehi bhawati.*

The *Batuka* should take the first alms from the mother or the elder sister or the sister of the mother (*mausi*) if the mother is not alive or present. After taking the alms he should say *'Aum Swasti'* and bring it to the *Āchārya*.

When the *Achāya* says *'Bhaiksha bhungakshwa'* only then he should eat from it.

After taking his food, he should stand still and silent till the evening. He can sit only with the specific order of the *Achārya*. But this is not done at all the places. In the evening he should perform *Samida Ādhāna* again and salute the *Āchārya, Brāhmins* and elders (including the elder ladies) again. The *Āchārya* should bless him with the Mantra: *Ābrahmana, brahmavarchswi bhava.*

The others should also bless him.

He should worship the *Achārya*, offer him food, flowers, fragrance and take his blessings.

After *Visarjana* the *Brāhmins* (a minimum of four but as many as one is able to) should be fed. With the *Prasāda* and feast the *Upanayan Samskār* comes to an end.

At many places, the *Bhikshātana* is kept in the *Mandap* and that too for a month and a quarter. The *Brahmachāri* eats something from it first everyday, only then he takes anything else.

❁❁❁

Samskār-11

VEDĀRAMBHA SAMSKĀR (STARTING STUDIES)

Initiation into Study (*Vedārambh*) to start study of the *Vedas* and *Vedānga* is an important Samskār in our life. It is the Samskār of greatness and sublimity. Through this Samskār, we get all the knowledge and wisdom. Our queries are answered and each problem is solved. It is like giving immense and indefatigable power to mind and get knowledge, wisdom and skill to perform every task. It gives prosperity, name, fame, wealth, and economical, political and spiritual power. It makes us better. So, everyone must perform it. One thing is sure that luxury is not in there while one is studying. One must remember the saying:

Sukhārthinah wā tyajet vidyā vidyārthinah wā tyajet sukham;

Sukhārthinah kuto vidyā vidyārthinah kuto sukham.

सुखार्थिनः वा त्यजेत् विद्या विद्यार्थिनः वा त्यजेत् सुखम्।
सुखार्थिनः कुतो विद्या विद्यार्थिनः कुतो सुखम्॥

(One who wants knowledge should forget luxury and pleasure, or one who wants luxury and pleasure should forget knowledge because a person who wants pleasure and luxury cannot get knowledge and a person who wants knowledge cannot get pleasure and luxury.)

Vedādhyayan is considered to be the greatest among the *Brahma Yagyas*. It gives the ample reward of many *Yagyas* combined together. That is the reason that the *Āchāryas* have called it *Brahma Yagya*. The *Vedas* as well as other parts of the *Vedas*, from the *Samhitās* to *Vedānta*, all the *Shrutis* and *Smritis*; including the *Upvedas; Sutra Granthas; Upanishadas; Āranyaka; Brāhman Granthas; Shākhās; Prtisākhya; Nibandha; Itihās; Purāna; Vyākaran; Darshan Granthas; Āgam Granthas; Chhand; Vedānga; Kalp; Jyotisha; Āyurveda,* and *Nitishāshtras* must be read with concentration, dedication and devotion. Those who read and learn them are easily metamorphosed into a power house for enlightening others and a storehouse of knowledge to illuminate all lives. They get everything. They need nothing else and nothing more. It is incomparable wealth.

Time

Vedārambha Samskār is performed after *Upanayan Samskār*. At many places it is performed along with *Upanayan Samskār* and at other places as the last part of *Upanayan Samskār*. The reason may be that both the *Samskārs* are performed in the presence and the guidance of the *Achārya*, the teacher who has to teach him. But it is better to perform it separately for it creates a deep and lasting effect on the mind.

In the modern race for technical knowledge and technical studies everyone has forgotten these books that are full of knowledge. No one should be given technical educationbeforecompletingthegeneralstudies.InBachelor exam, in recent times, a paper of general studies has been added but one must accept that a paper of general studies is one thing and 'complete general studies' is a different thing. If and when one takes technical knowledge after knowing the general things, he/she is a mature person. This knowledge and maturity will definitely help the society in achieving values and in living without making everything polluted and without wasting important life-giving and life-saving elements.

If one knows some technical things and has no knowledge of life, then it is sure wastage of life. It is said that to read the *Vedas* and scriptures without applying them into life is like wasting time and energy:

Vedādhyayanam sarva dharma shāshtrāsya chaiva hi.
Ajānato arth tad vyartham tushānām kandanam yathā.

वेदाध्ययनं सर्व धर्मशास्त्रस्य चैव हि।
अजानतो अर्थ तद् व्यर्थं तुषाणां कण्डनं यथा।।

For *Vedārambha Samskār* a day should be fixed earlier. It can be performed on that very day or after three days. In both these cases auspicious day is not needed. It should be decided which branch of the *Vedas* one has to study because the *Vedas* and other scriptures are usually taught one by one and according to the parentage and tradition of the family. The person who leaves out the branch of his parentage is said to be of divisive branch. Other branches are learnt after getting mastery over the one that has come down as family tradition. As *Maharishi Vasishtha* has said:

Paramparāyā gato yeshām veda saprirawahanah.

Yachchha shākhā karma kurvita tat shākhā adhyayanam yathā.

परम्पराया गतो येषां वेद सपरिर्वहणः।
यच्छ शाखा कर्म कुर्वीत तत् शाखाऽध्ययनं तथा।

Vedārambha Vidhi

When the Samskār is to be performed, the *Achārya* should be ready in all respect and sit at the *Yagyasthal.* After the preliminaries, take the *Samkalp* and add the following to it:

Rig Veda vratādesham wā Yajur Veda vratādesham aham karishye.

(I order the disciple to study either the *Rig Veda* or the *Yajur Veda.*)

The branch of learning should be mentioned clearly. Then he should perform the *Panchabhu Samskār* (five different worships) as described earlier and call the disciple. The disciple will sit in the north of the *Achārya* and in the west of the celestial or sacrificial fire, facing east. A *Brahmā* should be nominated and general *Āhuties* are to be performed.

Before starting the teaching of the *Rig Veda,* two *Āhuties* of *Antariksha* (Space) and *Vāyu* (Air) should be given with the following *Mantras*:

- Space: *Aum antarikshāya swāhā. Idam antarikshāya namam.*
- Air: *Aum vāyave swāhā. Idam vāyave namam.*

Then nine *Āhuties* of *Brahmā* should be offered with the following *Mantras*. It is to be noted that two *Āhuties* are separately given for different *Vedas,* and after those two special *Āhuties* these nine *Āhuties* of *Brahma* are repeated. So at the end of these nine *Āhuties* the *Mantras* for the special *Āhuties* are given. Only two *Āhuties* with the concerned *Veda* are to be performed and not all the six. If all the four *Veda Samhitās* are to be studied then two *Āhuties* are given for each but the nine *Āhuties* of *Brahma* will be repeated at the end of the fourth *Veda* and not after every *Veda*:

Nine *Ahutis* of *Brahma*

- *Aum brahmane swāhā. Idam brahmane namam.*
- *Aum chhandobhyah swāhā. Idam chhandobhya namam.*
- *Aum prajāpataye swāhā. Idam prajāpataye namam.*
- *Aum devebhyah swāhā. Idam devebhyah namam.*
- *Aum rishibhyah swāhā. Idam rishibhyah namam.*
- *Aum shraddhāyai swāhā. Idam shraddhāyai namam.*
- *Aum medhāya swāhā. Idam medhāya namam.*
- *Aum indrāya swāhā. Idam indrāya namam.*
- *Aum sadāsaspataye swāhā. Idam sadāsaspataye namam.*

For the Rig Veda

- *Aum anumataye swāhā. Idam anumataye namam.*
- *Aum agnaye swāhā. Idam agnaye namam.*

For the Sāma Veda

- *Aum diwe swāhā. Idam diwe namam.*
- *Aum suryāya swāhā. Idam suryāya namam.*

For the Atharva Veda

- *Aum digabhyah swāhā. Idam digabhyah namam.*

- *Aum chandramase swāhā. Idam chandramase namam.*

Then three *Āhuties* of *Mahāvyāhrities* and five *Āhuties* of *Prāyaschita* (atonement) and *Swishtikrit* should be given as stated earlier. The chosen *Brahmā* is to be given *Dakshinā* after *Samkalp*. Then *Brahmā* should sprinkle water, collect *Kusha* and put it to *Agni* while chanting the related *Mantras*.

The Study of the Vedas

The study of the *Vedas* should be completed only at the feet of the *Āchārya* as it needs explanations as many imperceptible and symbolical expressions are there in it. *Manusmriti* (2:70-71) is very clear about it:

Adhweshya mānastwā cha anto yathā shāshtram udang mukhah.

Brahmānjali krito adhyāpayo laghubāsā jitendriyah.

Brahmārambhye awasāne cha pādau grāhyo guroh sadā.

Sahastya hastāwadhyeyam sa hi brahmānjali smrit.

अध्वेष्य माणस्त्वा च अन्तो यथाशास्त्रं उदंग मुखः।
ब्रह्माञ्जलिकृतो अध्याप्यो लघुवासा जितेन्द्रियः।।
ब्रह्मारभ्येऽवसाने च पादौ ग्राहयो गुरोः सदा।
सहत्य हस्तावध्येयं स हि ब्रह्माञ्जलि स्मृत।।

(One who wishes to get knowledge must sit in the north of the teacher with folded hands in all readiness and in neat and tidy clothes; and controlling the sense-organs with great concentration, he should study the *Vedas*. He must touch both the feet of the *Guru* before and after studying.)

Vyatya stayāninā kāryam upasangrahanam guroh. Savyena savya sprishtavyo dakshinena cha dakshinah.

व्यत्यस्तयाणिना कार्यमुपसंग्रहणं गुरोः।
सव्येन सव्य स्पृष्टव्यो दक्षिणेन च दक्षिणः॥

(The disciple should touch the feet of the *Guru* by making a cross of his own hands and touching his left feet with his left palm and right feet with right palm.)

Aum must be pronounced from the navel everyday before starting and after finishing the study of *Vedas*. It increases the memory power in the beginning and adds to the power to retain at the end. Hence, if it is not pronounced in the beginning he won't be able to memorise it and if not pronounced at the end he would lose the very knowledge of *Vedas*. While reading the *Rig Veda* he should muster up maximum concentration and while chanting the *Sāma Veda* he should move the hands and fingers as directed by the *Guru*. At the start chant the *Gāyatri Mantra* after taking the following *Samkalp*:

Aum adya shubh puny tithau brahma varchas prāpti kāmanāyā vedasaraswati poojanam aham karishye.

The disciple should then worship the *Veda Grantha* with the following two *Mantras* for the *Veda* and *Saraswati* and perform their *Shodashopachāra Poojan*:

1. Aum vedo asiyenatwam devaveda devebhyo vedo abhawaste namahyam vedo bhuyāh.
2. Aum shrishchate laxmishchapatnyā wahorātre parshwe nakshatrāni rupam ishwa nauvyādyam. Ishna nishānam ummaishāna sarvalokam ishāna.

After the *Shodashopachāra Poojan* of the *Veda* and *Saraswati*, the disciple should touch the feet of the *Guru* and sit there with folded hands and the teacher should start teaching with *Pranava Aum* and *Gāyatri* and then start the actual teaching of the *Veda.*

Samāpana

When the study of the *Veda* is over, both the *Āchārya* and the disciple should say "*Aum Swasti*". They should stand up and the *Ācharya* should give him *Shruvā* (ladle) along with *Ghee* (refined butter), flowers and fruits and ask him to perform the *Āhuti* with the following *Mantra*:

Aum murdhānam divo arati prithvyā vaishwānar amrita āgyātam agnim. Kavi ang samrājam atithim janānām āsannāpātrāyam janayantah devāh swāhā.

The *Ācharya* should anoint himself first and then the disciple with *Bhasma* as stated earlier. Then with *Visarjana* and *Prasāda* the *Vedārambha Samskār* will be over.

❁❁❁

Samskār-12

SAMĀVARTAN SAMSKĀR (CONVOCATION)

Mahānāmni Vrat, Mahāvrat, Upanishad Vrat and *Keshānt Karma* (also known as *Godān Vrat*) are parts of the study and are done under the guidance of the *Āchārya* when one or the other *Veda Adhyayana* is completed. All of them are important in their individual respect but *Keshānt Karma* is also treated as a part of *Samāvartan Samskār*. In this Samskār, the *Brahmachāri* gets his head shaved off along with the moustache, beard, the hair of the armpits. Either the head is completely shaved or a *Shikhā* (tuft of hair) is left at the centre. It is performed only after the 16th year of age when the *Brahmachāri* has attained a degree of maturity.

Some associate it with *Chudākarma* but it is different although the rites of Samskār are quite similar. The only difference is that the *Āchārya* performs it in place of the father and declares in the *Samkalp*:

Aum asya brahmachārinah keshānt karmāham karishye.

It is performed when the sun is in *Uttarāyan* (in the northern hemisphere). All the preparations and early *Poojans* are done like that of the *Chudākarma* and *Brahmā* is also selected like that. The prayers and the *Āhuties* are performed in the same way. The barber divides the hair and shaves the hair in the same way.

Samāvartan Samskār (Convocation) is also known as the end of study or the end of celibacy or *Brahmacharya*. After this *Samskār*, the *Brahmachāri* returns home. It marks the end of his stay with the *Āchārya*.

On an auspicious day and time, in the *Yagya Mandap*, all the preparations are made for the general rites and rituals. When the *Āchārya* with his wife and the disciple are ready, they come there. Preliminaries are performed and in the *Samkalp* the *Samāvartan Samskār* is mentioned.

Ganapati Poojan and other rituals are completed. *Brahmā* is selected with the *Samkalp*. He accepts it by saying: *Vrittoasmi*.

He makes all the preparations for the *Homa* and when the *Vedi* is ready then he places *Agni* according to the instructions of the scriptures.

Along with general articles, special articles for this *Samskār* are also placed there. They include: *Samāvarjana Kusha;* three *Samidā* of *Dhāka;* dry dung; *Samidā;* green *Kusha;* eight earthen pots filled with water; *Dhoti; Dātuna* of *Gular;* curd; *Til*; water for bathing; *Ubtan*; *Chandan*; *Janeva*; two sets of new cloths; turban; *Anjan*; mirror; new umbrella; new shoes; a pot with 256 fists of rice measured by the *Āchārya*; and *Dravya* for *Dāna*.

The disciple should perform the preliminaries of *Āhuties*. When everything is ready then he performs the following *Āhuties*:

- *Ājya Āhuti*
- *Ādhār Āhuti*
- *Phāga Āhuti*
- Nine *Āhuties* of *Brahma*
- Two *Āhuties* of each *Veda*
- Nine *Āhuties* of *Brahma* to be given again
- The *Āhuties* of *Mahāvyahrities*
- *Swishtakrit Āhuties*; *Prayāshchita Āhuties*
- *Prajāpati Āhuties*.

After finishing them, he should give *Dakshinā* to the *Brahmā* and he should accept it by saying: *Aum swasti* and sprinkle water as directed earlier.

Then the disciple should perform *Samida Ādhāna* and *Angsparsh* as directed earlier with all the given *Mantras*. Then he should anoint with *Bhasma* with the *Mantras*. Just after anointing with *Bhasma* he should salute the *Guru* introducing himself. It is like taking permission from the *Āchārya*. He should say:

Aum ----- gotra ---- (Sharmā/Vermā/Gupta) aham abhivādaye. And the *Achārya* would bless him:

Ayushmāna bhava.

The Ritual

Actual *Samāvartan Samskār* begins from here.

The disciple spreads *Kusha* in the north of the celestial fire and places all the eight earthen pots filled with water. He should take water from the first pot with the following *Mantra*:

Aum ye apswantaragnāyah pravishtā gohya upagohyo mayukho manohāskhalo virujasta nudushur indriyahān vijahāmi gorochanasta mahi. Grihanāmi.

It is known as the *Abhisheka Mantra*. It will not change while taking water from each of the pots. But each time he showers himself with the water taken from each pot (the first four) then he should chant the following *Mantras* respectively:

First Abhisheka Mantra

Aum tena māma abhishinchāmishrai yashase brahmane brahma varchasām.

Second Abhisheka Mantra

Aum yena shriyam krinutā yenāvamrishitā ang sunān yenākshyā vabhyasinchātām yadwā tadaswinā yashah.

Third Abhisheka Mantra

Aum āpohishthā mayobhuwastāna urje dadhātana. Maheranāya chakshase.

Fourth Abhisheka Mantra

Aum tasmā arang māmvo yasya kshāya jinwatha. Āpojanayathā cha na.

The water from the rest of the pots is to be taken with the *Abhisheka Mantra* given above but showered without any *Mantra*.

Now, he should take off the *Mekhalā* with the following *Mantra*:

Aum yad uttamam varna pāshamasmad vādham vimadhyam shrathāya.

Athāvayam āditya vrate tawānāgaso aditaye shyāma.

Surya Upasthāna

Without chanting any *Mantra* he should put off the *Danda* and the deer skin; and without chanting a *Mantra* he should wear all the new cloths. After putting the *Angvastram* on the shoulders he should look towards the sun and chant the following *Surya Upasthāna Mantra*:

Aum udyanbhrājavishnuh indromarudbhih syāt prātah yāwabhih sthādrishanirasi dashasanim mākurvā vinimāgamaya. Udyanbhrājavishnuh indromarudbhih syād diwāyāwabhih sthāchchhata sanirasi shatsanim mākurwādidenmāgamaya. Uttanbhrājam vishnuh indro marudibhah sthātsāyam yāwabhih sthāt sasasranirasi sahasrasani mākurwādidenmāgamaya.

He should eat some *Til* and curd without chanting *Mantra* and get the tuft of hair and the nails cut by a barber and perform *Āchamana*. He should brush his teeth with a *Dātuna* of *gular* amidst the following *Mantra*:

Aum annādyāya vyuhadhwa somo rājā ayamāgamat. Sameymukhampramārkshayateyashasāchabhagenacha.

ॐ अन्नाद्याय व्यूहध्व सोमो राजाऽयमागमत्।
स मे मुखं प्रमाक्ष्र्यते यशसा च भगेन च।

After throwing the *Dātuna* he should clean his mouth and perform *Āchamana*. Then he should smear the body with *Ubtan* (a paste of fried mustard seed) with fragrant matter like saffron and then take bath with hot water. As a *Brahmachāri* is making use of the make-up articles for the first time so it is a sort of training to him by the *Achārya* and in his presence as to where and in what proportion and how such things are to be used. He should pestle and smear sandal and saffron on nose, eyes and ears with these *Mantras*:

- *Aum prānāpānau mey tarpaya.*
- *Aum chakshuh mey tarpaya.*
- *Aum shrotram mey tarpaya.*

Then he should sit down on three *Kushas* doubled for the purpose and with *Til* and water he should offer *Tarpan* to the ancestors saying:

Aum pitarah shundhadhwam.

He should again smear sandal and saffron to nose, eyes and ears but with the following *Mantra*:

- *Aum suchakshā aham akshobhyām.*
- *Aum bhuyāsa ang suvarchā mukhena.*
- *Aum sushrat karnābhyām bhuyāsam.*

He should wear white cloth that has not been washed by a washer man with the following *Mantra*:

Aum papidhāraye yashodhāsyai deerghā yutwāya jara-dashti asmi.

Shatam cha jivāmi sharadah puruchirāyah poshamb-hisam vyayishye.

ॐ पपिधारये यशोधास्यै दीर्घायुत्वाय जरदष्टि अस्मि।
शतं च जीवामि शरदः पुरुचीरायः पोषमभिसं व्ययिष्ये॥

He should put up two *Upavit* or *Janeva* one by one with the following two *Mantras*:

1. Aum yagyo pavitam paramam pavitram prajāpatyeh sahajam purastāt.
   Āyushyamagraham pratimuncha shubhram yagyopavitam balamastu tejah.

2. Yagyo pavitam asi yagyasya twā yagyo pavite na upanahyāmi.

After performing *Āchamana* he should take *Angvastram* with the following *Mantra*:

Aum yashasā mā dyāwā prithvi yashasendrā brihaspati.

Yansho bhagashcha vidadyāsho mā pratipadyatām.

ॐ यक्षसा मा द्यावा पृथिवी यशसेन्द्रा बृहस्पती।
यंशो भगश्च विदद्याशो मा प्रतिपद्यताम्॥

He should take the garland with the following first *Mantra* and wear around his neck with the second *Mantra* given below:

1. Aum āharajjamadagnih shraddhāyai medhāyai kāmāya indriyāya.
   Aham prati grahnāmi yashasā cha bhagena cha.
2. Aum adyasho apasarasām indrashchakāra vipulam prithu.
   Tena sangranthitāh sumanasah āwadhnāmi yasho mayi.

Pāga Dhārana

After the above ritual, he should bind the turban on his head with the following *Mantra*:

Aum yuvā suvāsāh pariveeta āgātsau shraiyān bhawati jāyamānah.

Tam dheerāsah kavaya unnayanti swādhyo manasā devayantah.

ॐ युवा सुवासाः परिवीत आगात्स उथैयान्भवति जायमानः।
तं धीरासः कवय उन्नयन्ति स्वाध्यो मनसा देवयन्तः॥

He should first wear the earring in the right ear and then in the left ear with the following *Mantra*:

Aum alankaranam asi yo alankaranam bhuyāt.

He should take *Anjan* with the first *Mantra* and put it first in the left eye and then to the right eye with the second *Mantra*:

1. Aum vritra syāsi kaneenakash chakshuh dā asi chakshuh mey dehi.
2. Aum rochishnuh asi.

He should take the umbrella with the following *Mantra*:

Aum brihaspateshchhadirasi pāmmajo māmantar dehi.

He should wear the shoes first in the left leg then the right leg with the following *Mantra*:

Aum pratishte astho viswatomā pātam.

As the last item he should take the staff of bamboo with the following *Mantra*:

Aum vishwebhyo mānāshtrābhya asparipāhi sarvatah.

It is important that whenever a new thing is taken or a new cloth worn the *Mantra* should be chanted, but not while taking or wearing old and used things or cloths.

Then the *Āchārya* should also stand up and touch the flowers, fruits and *Shravā* kept in the right hand of the disciple who performs the *Purnāhuti* with the following *Mantra*:

Aum murddhāna divo arati prithvyām vaishwānar amrit ājātam agnim.

Kavi ang samrājam atithim janānāma sannapatram janyanta devāh swāhā.

ॐ मुर्द्धानं दिवो अरतिं पृथिव्यां वैश्वानर अमृत आजातं अग्निम्।
कविं ॐ सम्राजं अतिथिं जनानामा सन्नपत्रं जनयन्त देवाः स्वाहा॥

Both of them should sit down and the *Achārya* should first anoint himself with *Bhasma* and then anoint the disciple with *Bhasma* while chanting the *Mantras* given earlier for the purpose.

The disciple has now become a *Snātaka*. He should first touch the feet of his *Āchārya* then all the elders present there and take their blessings. Then with *Visarjana*, *Dakshinā* and feast the *Samāvartan Samskār* comes to an end.

❁❁❁

Samskār-13

Vivāh Samskār (Marriage)

Marriage (*Vivāh*) is *Pānigrahan Samskār*, the *Parinayotsava*, the bringing in of a *Parinitā* or the *Badhu* or the bride from her parents' home to one's own home for life. It is such a lasting union that some say that the bride comes on *Pālaki* (palanquin) to her husband's house and goes out on *Chitā* (pyre) to the funeral. It is *Parinaya* because it marks the beginning of their love life. They can make it a loving life, keep it a lovely life and enjoy the bliss.

All the Samskārs are really very important but the *Vivāh Samskār* is the most important Samskār for it marks the end of the days of preparations for bearing the responsibilities of life. It marks the beginning of real life of a man and woman filled with work, responsibilities, achievements, procreation, independence, accumulation, tests, fulfilment, contentment, and everything else. It is the most important part of life also because it is the busiest part of life. It is because of its greatest need and importance that *Vivāh Samskār* is arranged on a huge scale, and celebrated ceremoniously by everyone.

Sharing Life

Marriage is a physical, social and spiritual need. One can pay back the debts to the parents, to the society and to the Creator with one's own good deeds. The union of a man and a woman satisfies the physical longings as well as procreates for the continuance of life. It is a life of give and take, of dependence on each other, of sharing the pleasures and pains of life and of sustaining through difficult moments by helping one another. That house is a home that shows hope, faith, control and cooperation. There should be a healthy competition between the couple of helping each other for greater prosperity, better life, higher gain and maximum pleasure:

Samutkarsh nikāsārtham anyoanyasya cha dwāwapi.
Kalyān ānandayoh syātām spardhāsheelo prasārane.

समुत्कर्ष निकासार्थं अन्योन्यस्य च द्वावपि।
कल्याण आनन्दयोः स्यातां स्पर्धाशीलो प्रसारणे।।

The permanence of love and faith between the couple is the success of a married life. The very aim of union is to serve the family, the society, country and life at large. The couple should give everything to achieve this end with their brilliance, even at the cost of personal inconveniences, problems and pains:

Dāmpatya jivana uddeshyo mahān sevāmayah tathā.
Samāja desh vishwabhyo divyātmānam samarpayet.

दाम्पत्य जीवन उद्दश्यो महान् सेवामयः तथा।
समाज देश विश्वेभ्यो दिव्यात्मानं समर्पयेत्।।

The progeny depends upon the relationship of the couple. The progeny will be good only if the couple is attached to one another and is righteous and dutiful. *Dharma* (righteousness), *Artha* (wealth) and *Kāma* (desire and sex) are the three pursuits to be followed by a couple with an aim to achieve the fourth pursuit i.e. *Moksha* (salvation). All these are to be shared by them: *Dharma prajā sampatih prayojanam dāra sangrahasya.* (It is the aim of a marriage to collect wealth, good deeds and religiosity and only then they can be happy.)

The *Vivāh Samskār* advises the newly-wed couple to reduce self-centredness and opt for the deeds and emotions that are useful in making a society good and worth living. It is the most responsible phase of life. All the relations are decided at the time of marriage. The marriage changes the meaning of different relationships and the best thing is that all the relations are maintained.

Discipline

Marriage controls the impetuous behaviour of the bride and the groom, who are now the woman and the man. They control one another and encourage for doing the best under different situations. They are both the masters and guides of one another. Erratic behaviour, whims and fancies are controlled. Marriage teaches them discipline. They learn to face the hard realities of life. It is rightly said that in marriage ceremony not only, the bride and groom are united but two families and two societies are united. So, marriage should not be taken lightly and should not be thought to give only pleasure. Contradiction is the rule of Nature. Pleasure always comes with pain. The greatest example is the pleasure of a new mother who takes a lot of pain in giving birth to a child but forgets everything the moment she sets her eyes on the beautiful face of her child.

Procreation

The most important aim of marriage is to procreate. We are indebted to God and to our ancestors for they fostered us with great care, took all the pains and kept us healthy and happy. We can be free from that debt to the ancestors by fostering our own child with matching skill and care. That is why at many places the scriptures mention that the aim of marriage is to liberate oneself from the debt of God and one's ancestors.

This is a very important reason that the moment people enter the *Grihasthāshram* their own *Samskārs* are over and they start performing the *Samskārs* of their children.

Types of Marriages

There are eight types of marriages stated in our sciptures. They are:

1. Brāhma Vivāh

When a gentle, humble, wise, ideal, diligent, healthy and impressive groom, who is a good match for the daughter, is selected and the marriage is performed, it is called *Brāhma Vivāh*. They seem to be made for each other and form a nice pair. Such selection was neither easier in ancient time nor it is in modern time but in India almost all parents try for a suitable match and each girl dreams like that. It is the purest of all marriages and the most progressive one as the parents select a groom keeping the best for their daughter in mind. The groom side neither asks nor gives anything as a precondition to the marriage. The father of the daughter, however, may give *Dāna*, *Dahej*, *Dakshinā* and *Upahār* according to his social status.

2. Daiva Vivāh

When a father chooses and offers his daughter with wealth and ornaments to one of the wise sages, it is called *Daiva Vivāh*, for it happens by chance and during a *Yagya*.

3. Ārsha Vivāh

Without any exchange of material things when a marriage and its rituals are performed according to the scriptures, it is called *Ārsha Vivāh*. It is good in social, religious and spiritual aspects and hence it is a very happy and blissful marriage.

4. Prājāpati Vivāh

A groom asks for the hand of one's daughter in marriage and the father lays the condition that they would lead a life of righteousness and follow religious path and live happily together, and the marriage is performed. It is called *Prājāpati Vivāh* because there is a social and religious agreement and the concerned persons have accepted each other.

5. Āsura Vivāh

By giving a lot of wealth to the father and family of the bride or to the bride and marrying her is called *Āsura Vivāh* as it is almost like buying the bride.

6. Gāndharva Vivāh

A boy and a girl meet and like each other. They agree to live as a married couple. When they perform marriage at a lonely place or in a lonely temple only by garlanding one another, is known as *Gāndharva Vivāh*. It was once very popular among the *Gandharvas*, so it got this name.

7. Rākshas Vivāh

To forcibly take away the girl after beating her family members and to marry her is known as *Rākshas Vivāh*. It is a demonic marriage in which there is no human value.

8. Paishācha Vivāh

Forcibly making physical relation with a sleeping girl or insane or immature or unconscious girl is called a *Paishācha Vivāh* for the clear reason that such degenerated deeds can be performed only by a person with demonic attributes.

Beside these eight types, there are some other types of marriages too. They are:

Swayamvar and Pana Vivāh: It was the most popular and widely accepted form of marriage at one time. In it the prospective grooms were invited and the girl was given the right to choose a person as spouse. In Indian context, the most famous *Swayamvar* was that of Prithvirāja and Sanyogitā.

In fact, the marriage of Rāma and Sitā or Arjuna (Pāndavas) and Draupadi is famous as *Swayamvar* but these are the examples of *Pana Vivāh* in which a contest is arranged and the winner gets the right to marry the girl.

Sambandham: This is another type of marriage. It is prevalent in a particular community in South India. It is a sort of matriarchal family pattern that is still being followed.

Prem Vivāh: The culmination of *Prem* (love) of a girl and boy into marriage is called *Prem Vivāh* (love-marriage). Because of anarchy, lack of discipline and waywardness, love marriages are gaining popularity but as love is the only criterion for this type of marriage so these marriages fail easily only after a few years. The reason of failure is love, which is in reality only physical attraction.

Sevā Vivāh: Till a few decades back, another type of marriage was prevalent in tribal areas when the groom was asked to serve the family of the bride, as he was unable to pay the demand of the parents. When that demand is deemed to be fulfilled the girl is married to that boy. It is known as *Sevā Vivāh.*

Vinimaya Vivāh: It is still performed in different areas and different communities. Due to various reasons when the marriage of a boy is not on its way he gives his sister to another person and in return marries the sister of that person. It is known as *Vinimaya Vivāh.*

Brāhmādishu vivāheshu chaturshwe wānupurvashah.
Brahma varchashwinah putrā jāyante shishta sanmatā.
Rupa satwa guno petā dhanawanto yashashwinah.
Paryāpta bhogo dharmishthā jivanti cha shatam samāh.

ब्रह्मा दिशु विवाहेषु चतुर्ष्वेवानुपूर्वशः।
ब्रह्म वर्चस्विनः पुत्रा जायन्ते शिष्ट सम्मता।।
रुप सत्व गुणो पेता धनवन्तो यशस्विनः।
पर्याप्त भोगो धर्मिष्ठा जीवन्ति च शतं समाः।।

(It is the clear diktat of the scriptures that the children of the couples whose marriage has been performed according to the first four i.e. Brāhma; Daiva; Ārsha; and Prājāpatya; get higher education; possess bright character and career and prove their worth. These children are good looking, healthy, skilled and wealthy. They enjoy a complete life, earn fame and live for a hundred years as a religious and spiritual figure. They are the best.)

Acceptable and Non-acceptable Marriages

Marriage in the following families is strictly prohibited:

- The family that has never done anything good.
- The family that had or has no great figure.
- The family that had or has no learned person.
- There are long hairs on the body of the persons.
- The family that suffers from piles and such diseases.
- The family that suffers from TB.
- The family that has diseases of stomach.
- The family that suffers from epilepsy.
- The family that suffers from white leprosy.
- The family that suffers from rotten leprosy.

Heena kriyam nishpurusham nishchhando romasha ārshasam.

Kshayyā mayā vyapasmāriswitri kushti kulāni cha.

One should not marry the girl who has any one of the following features:

- Yellow colour or has eyes of yellow colour
- Extra part of body
- Taller than the groom
- Very fat

- Suffering from some diseases
- Without a hair on the body
- Full of hair on the body
- Extra talkative
- Has a fearful name

One should always prefer a bride with balanced and shapely body; pleasant name; royal gait like that of a swan; almost invisible hair on body; subtle and long hair; white and small teeth; smooth skin; sweet voice; pleasant personality and appearance.

Time

Early marriage is disastrous and late marriage is unfruitful. The best time is the time of maturity. Scriptures say that a girl should be married three years after the first menstrual cycle. Late marriage destroys the youthful pleasure. The skin grows harder and fails to get the subtle and lasting sensations. The passion and satisfaction is also affected. Then, the best time for the marriage of a girl is between 18 to 22 years and the best time for the marriage of a boy is between 22 to 26 years. That is the age to procreate and the children born during that period are well formed and healthy while the children of early and late marriages are not healthy and usually deformed. They don't get all sorts of nourishment as the secretion of different hormones gets affected due to age. Hence, one must study hard and get needed training so that one can be employed and earn enough to feed a family. One must get prepared for it so that one can get married at the right time.

A comparative study of the physiology and the growth and development of girls and boys must have been taken by the wise men during ancient period and they must have rightly come to the conclusion that the physical and psychological maturity in girls is faster than that of the boys. After deep study they have concluded that the girl should be about four to seven years younger than the boys and their marriage should be performed accordingly. Whenever their marriage is delayed they lose passion, smoothness, vitality, desire; and their satisfaction is reduced to a certain extent. Europe is a cold country. The age of puberty of the girls there is much higher than that of India, so one should not copy the late marriages that are performed there. Naturally, the age of marriage for girls in Western countries will be 24 to 30 and that of the boys 28 to 34. It can't be followed in India. It is up to the parents and guardians to think of it and marry off the girls before the age of 22.

Everyday we see that the persons that marry very late, get retired and their children are still in the teens, studying and yet unmarried. They have many responsibilities left over their head. They can not opt for *Vānprastha*. The answer to all these maladies is the marriage at right time; children at right time; their education at right time and their settlement and marriage also at right time. The society will come to the right track that it has lost after independence because none of us knew the real meaning of independence and our duties and responsibilities as free citizen of a free democracy.

If we marry at right time and have children at right time there will be no need to send them early to school. The government has framed a rule and prescribed minimum age for schools but Prep schools have cropped up. Primary and pre-primary classes have come up to destroy and kill the childhood. We are unable to give love to our own children. Naturally, we won't get the respect. We have paid the money and we may get paid back. We have not shown love and won't get respect. All of us are losers till the time we change our outlook and attitude and become a winner.

Fixing the Marriage

The biggest problem before the marriage is fixing a marriage. It has become a great problem to search out a match. The guardians are getting fewer qualities in girls and boys and numerous shortcomings. They are undecided. The time passes in that state. It is the greatest reason of late marriages.

Lust and dowry also play a great role in fixing the marriage. Most of the people are undecided whether they need a *Kulabadhu* or money. They can't get both the things. Pride will also enter their home with the money and take away peace and happiness in return. All the guardians who have taken a lot of money for the marriages of their sons have lost their sons. They failed to win the respect and loyalty of the bride. Their sons are more loyal, obedient and attached to their in-laws. They feel the loss but it is too late to mend it. The others are unable to feel the pain. They follow suit and lose.

Nowadays, horoscope is playing a dubious role or one can say that the groom's side plays a dubious role in the name of horoscope. If they get the desired amount and articles as dowry, everything is considered all right with the horoscope, but if they have greater demands then the marriage is refused on the false ground of some discrepancy in horoscope. People should either accept the importance of horoscope or deny it. It is degeneration to play tricks with the religious and spiritual faith. They must realise that their great sons and great grandsons will have to pay a heavy price for the misdeeds that they are committing. Though the results have started showing up but it will still take a few decades for us to realise the full impact of the disaster that it is bringing.

It is the age of doubt. Even if there is no doubt, the people remain doubtful till the end. The anxieties grow, as they are not sure of the words of other side. So, even when a marriage is fixed both the sides cannot relax till the ceremony is over.

Var-Rakshā

When the marriage is settled, a formal and short ceremony is arranged and in the presence of some selected persons and relatives. *Var-rakshā* or *Vāgdāna* or *Phaladāna* is performed which is like the engagement ceremony. It varies from place to place and family to family. The *Pandit,* the father, the brother, the uncle or even the grand father can perform it.

At most of the places, fruits, *Janeva* and areca nut or coconut is given; at other places fruits and areca are given but nowadays sweets and fruits are commonly given to the groom along with the clothes, a golden ring or a golden chain.

Usually, as parts of rite, *Shashtopachāra* is performed and then *Var Poojan* is done. After that, taking the articles in the palm, the person performing it takes a vow:

------- *kale agni sānnidhye snātah snāte hya arogini; avyangate apatite aklive* ***pitā*** *tubhyam pradāshayati*

If the father is not performing the rite, the word ***pita*** given in bold letters in the above *Mantra* should be replaced with "***dātā***."

------- *kale agni sānnidhye snātah snāte hya arogini; avyangate apatite aklive* ***dātā*** *tubhyam pradāshyasi*

As marriage ceremony has taken a very large proportion so it has become a very tiresome job for the father of the girl to make arrangements to perfection. He keeps on making arrangements till the end and the family fails to enjoy the function as they hardly get time and opportunity to talk to the *Gharatis* (their own guests) or the *Bārāties* (the family members of the groom). It should not be so. Marriage ceremony should be given its original form of a *Samskār*. On the contrary, due to the shortage of time and often the shortage of *Karmakāndi Pandits,* the *Samskārs* are cut short and it is performed as only formality. It must change and it should be truly performed like a *Samskār*. There is no need to show wealth. One should show character, integrity, wisdom and devotion for greater gain from the Samskār in the form of peace, pleasure and prosperity.

Remember, wealth is only a part of prosperity while prosperity includes all types of growth and development.

Kalash Sthāpana/Haridrā/Matakore

The preparation for the marriage begins one month and a week earlier. Many things are done during that period. Both the bride and groom are physically and mentally prepared for the marriage. Every ritual is meaningful and directly related to physical and mental health of the boy and the girl. Since the girl has to go to some other family, so utmost care is taken.

As the custom prevails in the family, 7, 5, 3 or two days before the marriage, *Ganesh Poojan* is held with *Mandapāchhājana*, a straw canopy with nine bamboo pillars 7 x 9 hands measured by the girl, for performing the marriage rites. A *Kalash* is placed at the central bamboo pillar that has a plough and a yoke. It reminds us that India is basically an agricultural country and only agriculture will save our life. Too many industries will destroy the Earth and the life on Earth. *Ganesha Poojan* and *Satyanārāyan Vrat Kathā* are completed along with different family customs. At many places the bride goes out with other ladies for digging soil ceremoniously. The drum is beaten to mark the occasion. An earthen oven is prepared with that soil and many things of different rituals are prepared on this oven within the next few days for the marriage. This ritual of spading soil is known as *Matakore*. Then, the bride sits in the *mandap* and *haldi-teil*, i.e. turmeric paste mixed with mustard oil is smeared. Nowadays, its form has changed and some selected married men and women touch the paste with mango-leaves and then touch the head, shoulder and knee of the bride at her house and of the groom at his house. Except for the *Mandapāchhājana*, and rites related to it which are for the bride, all the other rites and rituals are performed at both the places.

All the *Samskārs* that have not been performed earlier should be performed at this juncture. *Vedikā* is prepared and *Agni* inflamed to perform the rituals and *Homa*. It is a must at the bride's place and arrangements should be made that the fire is not extinguished for the next few days. *Shānti-pātha; Swasti-vāchan; Punyāhvāchan* are all performed at this time.

When the *Bārāt* starts from the groom's house for the bride's house, the mother and other elder ladies throw money as *Nyochhāwar* (propitiatory offering). The ladies embellish the groom with pestle called *Parchhāwana*. At different places there are different rituals but at every place the *bārāt* is sent ceremoniously and happily.

The groom rides either a palanquin or a mare (nowadays, jeeps or cars are perferred) but in any event the ladies perferm different rites and follow different customs as prevalent in the area or family.

Vivāhsamskār Vidhi

The house of the bride and the place where the guests and the marriage party is to stay must be cleaned and moderately decorated. To spend a lot of money on decoration is wastage. One must avoid it. One must remember that extravaganza destroys a person and misers are not liked.

Pitri-Poojan, Deva Poojan and Matrikā Poojan

These rituals are performed during the day of the marriage under the guidance of a competent *Pandit*.

In *Deva Poojan* Shri Ganesh is worshipped first then other gods and goddesses are worshipped. At least, the following ten *Stuties* must be chanted at the time of the *Poojan* of the respective gods or goddesses:

1. Vināyakam gurum bhānu brahmavishnu maheswarān;
   Saraswati pranamyādau shānti kāryārth siddhaye.
2. Guruh brahmā guruh Vishnu gurudeva maheshwarah;
   Guru sākshāt parbrahma tasmai shri guruwe namah.
3. Shuklāmbaram dharma devam shashi varnam chaturbhujam;
   Prasanna vadanam dhyāyet sarvam vighna upashāntaye.
4. Sarvadā sarvakāryeshu nāsti teshām amangalam;
   Yeshām hridisthau bhagawān mangalāyatano harih.
5. Mangalam bhagwān Vishnu mangalam garuradhwajah;
   Mangalam pundarikāksho mangalāyatano harih.
6. Shāntākāram bhujangshayanam damanābham suresham;
   Vishwādhāram gagan sadrisham megha varnam subhāngam;
   Lakshi kāntam kamalanayanam yogibhih dhyānargamyam;
   Bande Vishnu bhavabhayaharam sarva lokaika nātham.
7. Bande deva umāpatim surgurum bande jagatkāranam;
   Bande pannag bhushanam mrigadharam bande pashunām patim;
   Bande surya shashānka wanhi nayanam bande mukundapriyam;
   Bande bhakt janāshrayam cha varadam bande shankeram.

8. Shuklām brahma vichār sāra parmāmādyām jagad vyāpinim;
Veenā pustak dhārinim bhayadām jādyāndhakārāpahām;
Haste sphatika mālikām vidadhatim padmāsne sansthitām;
Bandetām parameshwarim bhagawatim bhddhi pradām shārdām.
9. Āyātu varde devi akshare brahmavādini;
Gātyatri chhandasām māttāt brahma yonih namostute.
10. Sarva mangal mānglye shive sarvārtha sādhike;
Sharanye trayambake gauri nārāyani namostute.

विनायकं गुरूं भानुं ब्रह्मा विष्णु महेश्वरान्।
सरस्वती प्रणम्यादौ शान्ति कार्यार्थ सिद्धये॥1॥
गुरूः ब्रह्मा गुरूः विष्णुः गुरूः देव महेश्वरः।
गुरू साक्षात् प्रबह्म तस्यै श्री गुरूवे नमः॥2॥
शुक्लाम्बरधरं देवं शशि वर्ण चतुर्भुजम्।
प्रसन्न वदनं ध्यायेत् सर्व विघ्न उपशान्तये॥3॥
सर्वदा सर्वकार्येषु नास्ति तेषां अमंगलम्।
येषां हृदिस्थौ भगवान् मंगलाय तनो हरिः॥4॥
मंगलं भगवान विष्णु मंगलं गरूड़ध्वजः।
मंगलं पुण्डरीकाक्षो मंगलाय तनो हरिः॥5॥
शान्ताकारं भुजंगशयनं पद्मनाभं सुरेशं।
विश्वाधारं गगन सदृशं मेघवर्णं शुभांगम।
लक्ष्मीकान्तं कमलनयनं योगिभिः ध्यानगम्यं।
वन्दे विष्णु भव भयहरं सर्व लोकैकनाथम्॥6॥
वन्दे देवं उमापतिं सुरगुरूं वन्दे जगत्कारणं।
वन्दे पन्नगभूषणं मृगधरं वन्दे पशूनां पतिम्॥
वन्दे सूर्य शशांक वह्नि नयनं वन्दे मुकुन्दप्रियं।
वन्दे भक्त जनाश्रम च वरदं वन्दे शंकरम्॥7॥

शुक्लां ब्रह्मं विचारसार परमामाद्यां जगद् व्यापिनीम्।
वीणा पुस्तक धारिणीं भयदां जाड्यान्धकारापहाम्॥
हस्ते स्फटिक मालिकां विद्धतीं पद्मासने संस्थिताम्।
वन्दे तां परमेश्वरीं भगवतीं बुद्धि प्रदां शारदाम्॥8॥
आयातु वरदे देवि अक्षरे ब्रह्मवादिनी।
गायत्रीच्छन्दसां मात्तात् ब्रह्म योनिः नमो स्तुते॥9॥
सर्व मंगल मांगल्ये शिवे सवार्थसाधिके।
शरण्ये त्र्यम्बके गौरि नारायणि नमोस्तुते॥10॥

Dwār-Poojā

It is an important event. All the *Bārāties* are important persons but the groom is cynosure, the centre of attraction. They should be welcomed and there is a tradition to worship the groom. It is performed by the father or by grandfather or uncle or elder brother in his absence. Customarily, all the *Bārāties* are welcomed with fragrant garlands and served cold drinks and refreshments. At the very entrance, arrangements are made for *Poojā*. The groom is brought there and the *Poojā* is performed. First of all, *Mangal-vāchan* (auspicious words) are chanted:

Aum bhadrah karnabhih shranuyāma devā bhadram pashyem akshabhiryajatrāh.

Sthirai rangai stushtu wānsastanubhih vyashemahi devahitam yadāyuh.

It is important here to note that most of the rites that are given below are performed outside at the time of *Dwār-Poojā* or in the *Mandap* at the time of marriage. It depends on the custom and tradition of the place. Moreover, there are many local variations. At many places, only after a formal *Poojā* the rituals outside are concluded and rest of the rituals are performed in the *Mandap*. At every place, apart from the scriptural instructions, the ladies perform different rituals that are also accepted and encouraged for they help them get acquainted with the groom.

After taking a resolve to worship the groom for the marriage with the daughter, *Pavitrikaran, Āchaman, Shikhābandhan, Prānāyām* and *Nyāsa* etc are performed both by the father of the bride, who sits facing west and the groom who sits facing east. The seat, preferably of deer skin, is offered to him with the *Mantra*:

Aum sādhu bhawānāstārchayi shyāmobhawantam.

He accepts it and sits on it after chanting the following *Mantra*:

Aum vashamaro asmi samānānām udyatāmi wa suryam;
Imam tamabhitishthābhiyomām kachchābhi dāsati.

The feet of the groom are washed. It is called *Pāon Pakhāranā.*

The father says: *Aum pādyam pratigrihyatām*

If any person, other than the father, washes the groom's feet then he chants this *Mantra*:

Aum pādyam pādyam pādyam.

The groom accepts by extending legs and saying: *Aum pādyam pratigrihyāmi.*

The feet are washed amidst the following *Mantra*:

Aum virājo doho asi virājo dohamasheeya;
Mayi pādyai virājo dohah.

The next step is to give the *Arghya* of *Durvā, Akshat, Gandha, Pushpa* and *Phala*:

A third person chants the *Mantra*: *Aum arghyo arghyom arghyah.*

The father chants the *Mantra*: *Aum arghyam pratigrihyatām.*

The groom chants the *Mantra*: *Aum arghyam pratigrihnāmi.*

It is accepted and then the following *Mantra* is chanted:

Aum āpah sthayu mābhih sarvān kāmāna wāpnawāni.

Then the groom's forehead is anointed with *Gandh* and *Akshat* and the following *Mantra* is chanted:

Aum samudram wah prahinaimi swām yonim abhigachchhat marishtā asmākam veerāmāparose chimatpayah.

The groom should pour out the water in the *Ishān Kona*. After that *Āchaman* is given in the following way:

A third person: *Aum āchamaniyam āchamaniyam āchamaniyam.*

The father: *Aum āchamaniyam pratigraytām.*

The groom: *Aum āchamaniyam pratigrahnāmi.*

The groom would take the first *Āchaman* with the following *Mantra* and two *Āchamans* without *Mantra*:

Aum āmāganyashā sa ang srijavarchasā tam mā kuru priyam prajānā adhipatim pashunām arishtam tanunām.

Then curd, honey and refined ghee, called *Madhuparka*, are given in a bronze dish covered by another in the following way:

A third person: *Aum madhuparko madhupakam madhuparkah.*

The father: *Aum madhupakah pratigrihyatām.*

The groom: *Aum madhupakah pratigrahnāmi.*

The groom should look intently at *Madhuparka* and chant:

Aum mitrasya twā chakshushā pratikshe

Then he should take them on his left palm with the following *Mantra*:

Aum devasya twā savituh prasawe ashiwanoh bāhubhyām pushno hastābhyām pratigrahnāmi.

And mix them with the thumb and ring finger while chanting the following *Mantra*:

Aum namah shyāwā syāyānna sheyatt ābiddshamtatte nishkrintāmi.

After mixing it, he should eat it three times and every time he should chant the following *Mantra*:

Aum yanmadhuno madhavyam param ang rupamannādyam tenāham madhuno madhyavyena paramena rupenāntānnadyena paramo madhyavyo annādo asāni.

He should put the remaining *Madhuparka* at such a place where no one could cross over it. After sitting again at his place he should touch the related parts of body with the following *Mantras*:

- *Aum wāngame āsye astu.*
- *Aum nasorme prāno astu.*
- *Aum akshorme chakshuh astu.*
- *Aum karnayorme shrotram astu.*
- *Aum bāhwarme balam astu.*
- *Aum urvarme ojo astu.*
- *Aum arishtāni mey angāni tanuh tanwā mey sah sanru.*

The groom is religiously and formally accepted (*Var-Varana*) that makes him authorised to perform the religious rites. A sacred ring of green grass or the central part of a mango leaf is given to the groom to wear. Only at the end of all the rites that ring is taken out.

The following *Swasti-vāchan*, the auspicious *Mantra*, is chanted:

Aum swasti nah indro briddhashrawāh swasti nah pushā vishwavedā swasti na tākasharyo aeishtanemih swasti no brihaspatih dadhātu.

At this very juncture, clothes and cosmetics are given to the bride also so that she can be ready for the marriage ritual. Although, it should be given in her hand with the *Mantras* but nowadays *Mantras* are chanted and *Akshat* sprinkled on them and sent to the bride, usually with symbolic water for her bath.

The following two *Mantras* are chanted at that time:

1. Aum jarāngachchha paridhatswa wāso bhāva krishti nāma abhishasti pāwā;
   Shatam cha jeevam sharadah suvarchā ravi cha putrān nusanvwayaswa āyushmatidam paridhatswa wāsah.

2. Aum yā ākrinta annyam ya atanwa tayāhshcha devi stantunabhito tantanam;
Tāswā devih arjar sesamvyaya swā yushmamatidam paridhatswa wāsah.

In the same way, the groom is also given new clothes to wear but mostly they take the *dhoti* only and wear it. The meaning is very clear–the bride must wear only the clothes provided by the groom's family and the groom must wear only the clothes provided by the bride's family. The following *Mantra* is chanted when the groom wears the clothes:

Aum paridhāsyaiya yashodhāsyah deerghām āyushtwāya jaradastih smi;

Shatam cha jivāmi sharadah puruchi rāishposhama abhisamvyayishye.

While putting on the *Uttariya* or *Angvastram* (a shawl) the groom should chant the following *Mantra*:

Aum vashasā mā dyāwā prithvi yashashe indrā brihaspati yasho bhagamashchamā vidadya shobhā pratipadyatām.

Then the *Pandits* from both the sides chant the following auspicious *Mantras* (*Mangal Pāth*) in a chorus, both outside at the entrance and inside in the *Mandap*:

1. Aum bhadram karne bhih shranuyāma devā bhadram pashyemākshaabhih yajatrāh. Sthirai rangai stushtu bāsnsatanubhih vyashemahi devahitam dāyuh.
2. Aum swasti nah indro briddhashrawāh swasti nah pushā vishwavedā swasti na tākasharyo aeishtanemih swasti no brihaspatih dadhātu. Aum shāntih! Shāntih! Shāntih!
3. Aum brahmā vedapatih shivah pashupatih suryo grahānām patih shukro devapatih analo narpatih

skandashcha senāpatih; vishnuh yagyapatih yamapitripatih tārāpatimshcha chandramā ityaete patayas suparna sahitāh kurvanto wo mangalam.

4. Shri matpankaja vishtaro hariharo vāyuh mahendro analashcha chandro bhāshkara vittapāla varuna pretādhiya ādi grahāh; pradumano nala kuberau suragajah chintāmani kaustubha swāmi shakti dharashcha lānguladharah kurvantu wo mangalam.
5. Netrānām tritaya mahatpashupateh agneastu pādatrayam tattad Vishnu padatrayam tribhuwane khyātam cha rāmatrayam; gangā bāhu pathatrayam subimalam vedatrayam brāhamanam sandhyā nām tritayam dwijah abhimat kurvantawo mangalam.
6. Laxmih kaushtubh pārijātakāsurā dhanawantari chandramā gāwa kāmadudhā sureshwar gajo rambhā adi devānganāh; aswah saptasukhah sudhā haridhanuh shankham visham cha ambuje ratnāniti chaturdasham pratidina kurvantu wo mangalam.
7. Gauri shrikula devatā cha subhagā kandu suparnām shivāh sāvitri cha saraswati cha surabhih satyavratā arundhati; swāhā jāmbawati cha rukmini bhagini duhswapna vindhashwani belā cha ambunidhe saminamakarā kurvantu wo mangalam.

Every time these *Mantras* are repeated, the sacred rice is first distributed and after the chanting of *Mantras*, returned back. It is redistributed and after chanting the *Mantras* it is sprinkled on the groom or bride or both to mark that the related ritual is over. People have invented different customs for making the ceremony memorable and happy and pleasant ways and moments are created: like lifting up and carrying the groom from one place to another; or asking him to break something or to force him salute some vile animal or statue on the pretext of tradition and custom.

Kanyā Nirikashan

After *Dwār-Poojā,* the groom is given some refreshments; and some people from among the *Bārāties* led by the elder brother of the groom go to the *Mandap;* the bride is brought there and the formality of *Kanyā-Nirikshan* is completed. As *Var-Varana* was performed earlier, in the same manner during *Kanyā Nirikshan* the bride is religiously and formally accepted by the groom's family. It is called *Kanyā Varan.* The same *Swasti-vāchan* is chanted at both the places.

Perhaps it was done at the time when the girl was not seen earlier. Nowadays, photographs are a must for the selection of the bride. A few members of the family, sometimes even the groom, go to see and meet and select the girl but this tradition is continued simply because many others had not seen her and because the girl is seen and accepted here by the elder brother of the groom. It is ritualistic acceptance of the girl. A lot of prominence and many gifts in the form of ornaments and cloths are given to her. She is anointed with a tiara, curd and sacred rice. All the preliminaries of *Poojā* are performed in the *Mandap.* One by one all the gifts are presented to the bride. It is, in a way, asking for the permission of the ladies to allow the groom to come inside for the rituals of marriage. All the ladies wait for this *Kanyā Nirikashan* quite impatiently.

In the Mandap

The rites begin with *Mangal-Vāchana* and after taking a resolve to worship the groom for the marriage, *Pavitrikaran, Āchaman, Shikhābandhan, Prānāyām* and *Nyāsa* etc are performed. The groom also takes a *Samkalp.*

The preliminaries are performed and *Swasti-Vāchan* is completed.

Paraspar Darshana

When the bride has also entered the *Mandap* they are given separate *Āchaman* and then are asked to look at each other when the father of the bride asks both: *Parasparam samanjedhām.*

While looking at each other they chant the following *Mantra*:

Aum samanjantu vishwedevāh samāpo hridya agninau;
Sa mātarishwā sandhātā samudreshtri dadhātu nau.

ॐ समंजन्तु विश्वेदेवाः समापो हृदयाग्निनौ।
स मातारिश्वा सन्धाता समुद्रेष्ट्री दधातु नौ॥

Granthi Vandhana

A knot with *Supari* (areca nut), *Haldi* (dried turmeric), *Akshat* (rice grains), *Pushp* (flower), *Dravya* (coin) is tied at one end of the *Uttariya* (the covering shawl, usually called '*kanyādāna kā chāder*) of the bride and that knot is tied with a corner of the *Uttariya* of the groom. The parents (one or both), elder sister, elder sister-in-law, aunts, *Pandit*, the wife of the barber (as the family tradition may be) can tie the knot.

Tying the knot has various symbolic and psychological significances. This knot is the binding factor that keeps them tied throughout life despite differences, intense pain and great crisis. It is cosmic union – separate yet united through a knot that does not touch either of them but it has its existence somewhere between them. At many places before or after it, both the palms of the bride as well as of the groom are coloured yellow with turmeric paste. With it they are encouraged to keep on performing auspicious rites.

Kanyādāna

Parents usually perform *Kanyādāna* but the scriptures are very liberal about it. Anyone, preferably elder and married, can perform it. *Kanyādāna* is treated as *Mahādāna*. Those who have no daughter happily perform the rituals of *Kanyādāna*. In Indian context, an unmarried girl is not only the problem of the parents but of the whole society. There are numerous examples when the marriages were performed by the society. Even today, community marriages are held in almost every region and all the expenses are borne by the society through donations. India is still full of such charitable persons who spend their own money for performing such *Samskārs* and holding *Yagyas* and other religious and spiritual congregations. It is the main reason of the survival of *Sanātana Dharma*, *Samskārs*, rituals, knowledge, culture, custom and civilisation.

The couple, ready to perform *Kanyādāna* takes the following *Samkalp* (resolve) after the preliminaries:

Aum vishuh vishnuh vishnu shrimad bhagawato mahāpurushasya vishnuh āgyāyā pravarta mānasya shri brahmanoni dwitiye parārdhe shri shweta vāräha kalpe vaivaswatah manwantare ashtāvinshatitame kaliyuge kali pratham charane jambudwipe bhuh loke bhārat varshe bharat khande māsānām māsottame ------- mase ------- pakshe ----- tithau ------- wāsare susnātāyā gandha ādya architāyā vastra yugachchhannāyā yathā shaktya alankritāyāh prajāpati daivatyāyā ------- nāmnyā asyā kanyāyā shatguni krita jyotishto tāti rātra shatphal prāpti kāmah vishnu rupine varāya ------- nāmāya vharana poshana cha chhāwan pālanā deenām swakiyottar dāyitwā bhāram akhilam tawa patnitwena tubhyam aham pradade.

Pānigrahan

Pānigrahan is an emotional union. It is the exchange of warmth and unknown passion. It is unpronounced and solemn promise of cooperation and assistance. Whenever the weakness will try to prevail, two other hands are there to support or push or pull to safety. The parents or the guardians enjoin those hands for protection and fostering, and for remaining united till the end.

The person performing *Panigrahan* takes milk, rice grains, fruits, flowers, sandal, water and puts them in the right palm of the groom and chants the following *Mantra*:

Aum yadaishi manasā duram dishā anupawampno wā;
Hiranya varno vaikarnah sa twā manmanasām karotu asau.

ॐ यदैषि मनसा दूरं दिशाऽनुपवम्नो वा।
हिरण्य वर्णो वैकर्णः स त्वा मनमनसां करोतु असौ॥

Then he gives the palm of the bride in his right hand and chants the following *Mantra*:

Aum dātāham varuno rājā dravyam āditya daivatam;

Varo aso vishnurupena pratigrihanātwyam vidhi.

ॐ दाताहं वरूणो राजा द्रव्यं आदित्य दैवतम्।
वरोऽसो विष्णुरूपेण प्रतिगृहृणात्वयं विधि॥

All the eight palms come one upon the other:

1. The right palm of the father.
2. Right palm of the mother.
3. The right palm of the groom .
4. The right palm of the bride.
5. The left palm of the groom.
6. Left palm of the bride.
7. Left palm of the mother.
8. Left palm of the father.

In this way, it becomes a pyramid. They are blessed by all present there. They need the blessings and they get it.

Var Pratigyā

The parents pray that they have given their tender daughter laden with clothes and ornaments with a wish to perform righteous duties for the fulfilment of the cosmic desires. We pray not to do excesses with her in the pursuit of *Dharma, Artha* and *Kāma*:

Kanyā lakshan sampannām kanakā bharenah yutām;
Tubhyam dadāti hey somya! Brahmaloka jigishayā;
Yastwayā dharmah charitah kartavyāh cha ānayā sah;
Dharmechaarthechakāmechanātícharyātwayākwachid.

कन्या लक्षण सम्पनां कनकाभरणेः युताम्।
तुभ्यं ददामि हे सौम्य ब्रह्मलोक जिगीषया॥
यस्त्या धर्मः चरितः कर्तव्यः च आनया सः।
धर्मे च अर्थे च कामे च नातिचर्यात्वया क्वचिद्।

In return the groom assures them that he will keep her like his shadow in the pursuit of *Dharma, Artha,* and *Kāma* and will do no excesses:

Aham nāti charishyāmi tad ukttam bhawatā mam;
Dharma artha kāma kaih dehachchhāyā wacha sadā.

अहं नाति चरिष्यामि तदुकं भवताममा।
धर्मार्थकामकैः कार्ये देहच्छाया वच्च सदा॥

In order to give confidence to the bride, he takes the following vows known as *Var Pratigyā* (the promises by the groom):

Dharma patnim! Militwaivam dhyekam jivan bhāwayo;
Adyārambha yato mey twam ardhāngini iti ghoshitāh.
Swikaromi sukhena twām grih lakshmi mahantatah;
Mantra yitwā vidhāshyāmi sukāryāni twayā sah.
Devāgni san manushyānām sannidhaye krit nishchaya;
Twām pratyaham bhavishyāmi sahishnu mridulah tathā.
Bhawatyāmasamarthāyāmbimukhāyāyanchamkarmani;
Viswāsam sahayogancha mam prāpsyasi twam sadā.
Madhurām prem sanyuktām vārtā satya vyawahritam;
Dridha patni vrat yekam vattam mey tawa sannidho.
Grihasyārth vyawasthāyām mantrāyitwā twayā sah;
Sanchālanam karishyāmi grihasthochit jivanam.
Yatnashilo bhavishyāmi sanmārga sevitum sadā;
Ādayo matbhedānshcha doshān sanshodhya shāntitah.

धर्मपत्नि! मिलित्वैवं घ्येकं जीवन भावयो।
अद्यारम्भ यतो मे त्वं अर्द्धांगिनी इति घोषिताः॥
स्वीकारोमि सुखेन त्वां गृहलक्ष्मी महन्ततः।
मन्त्रयित्वा विधास्यामि सुकार्याणि त्वया सह॥
देवाऽग्नि सन्मनुष्याणां सन्निधये कृत् निश्चय।
त्वां प्रत्यहं भविष्यामि सहिष्णु मृदुलस्तथा॥
भवत्यां असमर्थायां विमुखायाञ्चं कर्मणि।
विश्वासं सहयोगञ्च मम प्राप्यसि त्वं सदा॥

मधुरां प्रेम संयुक्ता वार्ता सत्यव्यहृतम्।
दृढ़ पत्नीव्रत एकं वतं मे तव सन्निधो॥
गृहस्यार्थ व्यवस्थायां मन्त्रायित्वा त्वया सह।
संचालनं करिष्यामि गृहस्थोचित जीवनम्॥
यत्नशीलो भविष्यामि सन्मार्ग सेवितुं सदा।
आदयो मतभेदांश्च दोषान् संशोध्य शान्तितः॥

(O my rightfully wedded wife! From now on we have become one as you have been declared my better half. I accept you in the most important role of *Grihalakshmi*, the goddess of wealth of the household (the mistress of the house); and declare that I will do everything with your consent. Before the Fire God and all the persons present here I resolve I will remain always soft and flexible, delicate and tolerant. Even when you would be weak or distracted from duties, you would get my faith and cooperation. You will always get my loving words; true behaviour and penance-like sincerity of one devoted to a single wife. I will run the household along righteous path on your advice and with your consent. Even when there is some difference of opinion or something wrong with the deeds, I would peacefully follow the righteous path.)

Kanyā Pratigyā

These are the vows taken by the bride:

1. *Twatto mey akhila saubhāgyam punyai stwam vividhaih kritaih;*

Deva! Sampādito mahyam badhurādye pade abravita.

(O my God! I have had the good fortune of acquiring you with the merits that I accumulated by various deeds in different births.)

2. *Kutumbam pālayishyāmi hyā vriddha bālaka ādikam;*

Yathā labdhena samtushthā vrate kanyā dwitiyake.

(I will look after your entire family from children to the aged and will be happy with whatever is available for sustenance.)

3. *Mishtānna vyanjanādini kāle sampādaye tava*

Āgyā sampādini nityam tritiye sā abravi dwaram.

(I will timely prepare delicious food and follow your orders and directives.)

4. *Shuchih shringāra bhushā aham wāng manah kāyakarmabhih;*

Kridishyāmi twayā svrdham turiye sā vadedwaram.

(I will embellish myself with clean clothes and jewellery and indulge with you in physical pleasure with body, mind and spirit.)

5. *Dukhe dhirāh sukhe hrishtā sukha dukha vibhāgini;*

Nāham partaram yāmi panchame sā abravit dwaram.

(I will face sorrow bravely and bloom during happy days. I will share pleasure and pain with you and never indulge in adultery.)

6. *Sukhena sarvakarmāni karishyāmi grihe tava;*

Sevā swasurayoh cha āmi bandhnām satkritim tathā;

Yatra twam wā aham nāham banche priyam kwachit;

Nāham priyena banchā hi kanyā shashthe pade abravit.

(I will perform all your household chores with pleasure. I will serve the father-in-law and all other relatives. I will be with you wherever you are. I will never deceive you.)

7. *Homa yagyādi kāryeshu bhawāmi cha sahāyyakrit;*
Dharmārth kāma kāryeshu manovrittā anusārini;
Sarve atra sākshinah twam mey pati bhuto asi sāmpratam;
Deho māyā arpitah tubhyam saptame sā abravit.

(I will assist you in all religious rites and rituals, and *Homa*; obey you in righteous deeds, accumulation of wealth and fulfilment of desire. Here in the presence of *Agnideva*, *Brahmins* and relatives you have become my husband and I offer my body to you.)

1. त्वत्तो मेऽखिल सौभाग्यं पुण्यैस्त्वं विविधैः कृतैः।
देव! संपादितो मध्यं वधूराद्ये प्रदेऽब्रवीत्॥

2. कुटुम्बं पालयिष्यामि ह्यवृद्धबालकादिकम्।
यथा लब्धेन संतुष्ठा व्रते कन्या द्वितीय के॥

3. मिष्ठान्न व्यंजनादिनी काले संपादये तव।
आज्ञा संपादिनी नित्यं तृतीये साऽब्रवीद्वरम्॥

4. शुचिः श्रृंगारभूषाऽहं वाङ्मनः कार्यकर्मभिः।
क्रीडिष्यामि त्वया सार्धं तुरीये सा वदेद्वरम्॥

5. दुःखे धीरा सुखे हृष्टा सुखदुःख विभागनी।
नाहं परतरं यामि पंच्रमे साऽब्रवीद्वरम्॥

6. सुखेन सर्वकर्माणि करिष्यामि गृहे तव।
सेवा श्वसुरयोश्चामि बन्धूनां सत्कृतिं तथा॥
यत्र त्वं वा अहं तत्र नाहं वञ्चे प्रियं क्वचित्।
नाहं प्रियेण वञ्चा हि कन्या षष्ठे पदेऽब्रवीत्॥

7. होम यज्ञादि कार्येषु भवामि च सहाय्यकृत्।
धर्मार्थकामकार्येषु मनोवृत्तानुसारिणी॥
सर्वेऽत्र साक्षिणस्त्वं मे पतिर्भूतोऽसि सांप्रतम्।
देहो मयार्पितस्तुभ्यं सप्तये साऽब्रवीद्वरम्॥

Shākhochchāra

The *Pandits* of both the sides chant the *Mantras* for the safety and prosperity of the people. It is called '*Jana Mangal Pātha'*, which is given earlier in this chapter.

Then, the *Pandits* of the groom's side announce the branches of the ancestors of the groom in the following way:

----- *gotrasya* ----- *pravarasya* ----- *vedino* ----- *shākhino* ----- *sutrino* ----- *sharmanah prapotrāya.* ----- *gotrasya* ----- *pravarasya* ----- *vedino* ----- *shākhino* ----- *sutrino* ----- *sharmanah potrāya.* ----- *gotrasya* ----- *pravarasya* ----- *vedino* ----- *shākhino* ----- *sutrino* ----- *sharmanah putrāya Shri* ----- *sharmā.*

Then, the *Pandits* of the bride's side announce the branches of the ancestors of the bride in the same way as given below:

----- *gotrasya* ----- *pravarasya* ----- *vedino* ----- *shākhino* ----- *sutrino* ----- *sharmanah prapotrima.* ----- *gotrasya* ----- *pravarasya* ----- *vedino* ----- *shākhino* ----- *sutrino* ----- *sharmanah potrima.* ----- *gotrasya* ----- *pravarasya* ----- *vedino* ----- *shākhino* ----- *sutrino* ----- *sharmanah putrima Saubhāgyawati* ----- *Devi.*

The groom takes *Samkalp* of acceptance. After the preliminaries of name and place etc as above, the following is added:

----- *gotrotpannām* ----- *nāmni shri rupinim yathāshaktya alankritām upakalpit upaskāra sahitā imām kanyām prajāpati daivatyām savarga kāmah patni twena tubhyam aham sampradade.*

Aum swasti.

Aum dyostwādadātu prithvi twā pratigrahnātu.

It is the time to pay the *Dāna* and *Dakshinā*.

Dāna and Dakshinā

Kanyādāna is not deemed to be complete until *Dāna* and *Dakshinā* are not given. With the *Kanyādāna* there is the provision of ten *Mahādānas* that are the following:

Kanyārthe kanakam dhenuh dāsi rath mahāgrihāh; Mahisha aswashālā gajā shayyā mahānādi wai dash.

कन्यार्थे कनकं धेनुः दासी रथ महागृहाः।
महिष अश्वशाला गजा शय्या महानादि वै दश॥

The *Mahādāna* includes gold; cow; maid; chariot; land; building; buffalo; horse; elephant and bed. It is not necessary to give all of them. It is up to the financial condition of the parents and also as per their wishes. It can't be the demand of the groom's side. The same thing is true of *Dakshinā*. Any amount that he likes and can pay; any amount that he wishes in lieu there of the animals and articles. The binding is *Dāna* but not the quality, quantity or the price.

While offering the *Dāna* and the *Dakshinā*, the father should say the following and include those things only that he is actually giving. Other things should be left out:

Aum adyakritat kanyādāna pratishtārtham idam yathāshakti swarna, ropya, bhumi, bhwanah, gau aswacha ----- gotrāya ----- sharmanah varāya dānam cha dakshinām aham sampradade.

The groom should say: *Aum swasti* in acceptance and chant the following *Mantra*:

Aum kodātkasmā adātkamidātkāmimāyādāt;
Kā modātā kāmah pratigrahitā kāmai tatte.

ॐ कोदात्कस्मा अदात्कमीदात्कामायादात्।
का मोदाता कामः प्रतिग्रहीता कामै तत्ते॥

Māng Bharanā/Sindur Dāna

At many places, *Sindur Dāna* is performed after *Saptapadi* and at other places it is performed before the *Āhuties* because the *Kanyādāna* has already been performed and the *Āhuties* and *Saptapadi* are to be performed together as husband and wife, So, it should be performed here and now. But, like in all other rituals, in this ritual also the local and family tradition will prevail and is accepted.

First the groom performs *Abhisheka* of the bride by sprinkling the water taken from the *Kalash.* Both should sit in the west of the sacred fire facing east and the bride should be seated on his right. The *Kalash* should be placed before him. The groom should take water with the mango leaves and sprinkle over the bride with the following *Mantra*:

Aum āpah shivāh shivatamāh shāntāh shānta tamāh tāste kanvantu bheshajam.

Then the *Dhruva Tārā*, the pole star, is shown to them for the stability in marriage and love. The following *Mantra* is chanted by them:

Aumdhruvamasidhruvatwāmpashyāmi.Aumdhruvaidhi poshyā mayi. Mahyam twādād brihaspath mayāpatyā prajāvati sanjiva sharadah shatam.

The groom places his right hand from over her right shoulder and chants the following *Mantra*:

Aum mam vrate te hridam dadhāmi mam chittam anuchittam te astu. Mam wāchekama manājushaswa prajāpatisht vāni yunukt mahyam.

The groom takes *Roli* (a mixture of Turmeric and lime) on a ring and anoints the forehead of the bride while chanting:

Aum sumangalih yiyavadhuh yiyā ang sameta pashyat. Saubhāgyam asyai datwā thāstam viparetana.

Then the bride comes to sit on the left of the groom who takes *Sindur* (vermilion) with his thumb and fingers (fingers vary from place to place) and puts it in the parting on her head dividing her hair. He chants the following *Mantra*:

Aum vāmamudya savitah vyāmashwo divediveh vāmamasmabhya ang sāvih. Vāmasyahi kshayasya devabhureh yādhiyāvāma bhājah syām.

The married ladies sing songs and bless her (at many places they also put vermilion) with the following *Mantra*:

Aum goryāh sāvitrayāh tawa saubhāgyam bhawatu.

The *Pandits* chant the following *Mantra*:

Aum iha gāvo nishidant vihāshwā iha purushāh iho sahasram dakshina yagya iha pushā nishidatu.

Vivāh Samskārātha Homa

At some places, other relatives lead them to the seat of *Homa* but at other places, the *Var* takes the hand of his wife and escorts her to the place where *Homādi* are to be performed.

As usual *Brahmā* is selected and requested with *Samkalp* to perform the *Homas*. At the close of the *Samkalp* these words are added: *Pratigrihitāyā asyā bhāryāyā patnitwa siddhaye vaivāhika homa karishye.*

He accepts and *Vedi* is prepared. Nowadays, either it is prepared earlier or the *Vedi* prepared at the time of *Matakore* is used.

There are fourteen *Ādhāra Āhuties* which are performed. They include:

- One *Prajāpati*
- One *Indra*
- Two *Ajya*
- Three *Vyāhuties*
- Five *Sarva Prāshchita*
- Two *Swistakrita.*

All these *Āhuties* have been described before. Then twelve *Rashtrabhrit Āhuties* are also performed. The twelve *Rāshtrabhrit Āhuties* are:

1. Aum ritāshāng ritam agni gandharbhah sana idam brahmachhatram pātu tasmai swāhāwāt. Idam amrita āhe ritdhne agne gandharvāya namam.
2. Aum ritāshāng rita dhāma agnih gandharvah stasya aushadhayopsa raso mudonāma tābhyah swāhā. Idam aushadhibhyo apsahomyo mudabhyo namam.
3. Aum sa ang hityau viswa sāmā suryo gandharvah sana idam brahmaksetram pātu tasmai swāhā wāt. Idam sa hitāya viswasāmne suryāya gandhavāya namam.

4. Aum ang sahitau viswa sāmā suryo gandharvah tasya marichayo apsarasà āyuvonāmatābhyah swāhā. Idam marichibhyo apasarobhyo āyubhyo namam.
5. Aum sushumnah surya rashmih chandramā gandarvah sa na idam kshatram pātu tasmai swāhā wāt. Idam sushumnāya suryarashmaye chandramase gandharvāya namam.
6. Aum sushumnah surya rashmih chandramā gandarvah tasya nakshtrānya apsaraso bhekuryo nāmtābhyah swāhā. Idam nakshetrebhyo apsarobhyo bhekuribhyo namam.
7. Aum ishiro viswavya chāwāto gandharvah sana idam brahmakshetram pātu tasamai swāhā wāt. Idam rishirāye viswavya cha sevātāya gandharvāya namam.
8. Aum ishiro viswavyachā wāto gandharvah tasyāpo apsaras urjonāma tābhyah swāhā. Idam adabhyh apsarasobhya ugarbhyah namam.
9. Aum bhujyah suparno yagyo gandharvah sana idam brahma kshetram pātu tasamai swāhā wāt. Idam bhujyawe suparnāya yagyāya gandhavāya namam.
10. Aum bhujyah suparno yagyo gandhavaḥ masya dakshinā apsarasata wānāya tābhyah swāhā. Idam dakshinākshyo apsarobhyah tāwābhyo namam.
11. Aum prajāpati viswakarmā mano gandharvah sana idam brahma kshetram pātu tasmai swāhā wāt. Idam prajāpataye viswakarmane manase gandarvāya namam.
12. Aum prajāpatih viswakarmā mano gandharvah tasya rik sāmāny apsarasa yeshtyo nāmatābhyah swāhā. Idam rik sāmbhyo apsarobhya yeshtibhyo namam.

After this, the following thirteen *Jayā Homa Āhuties* are offered to *Agni*:

1. Aum chittam cha swāhā. Idam chittāya namam.
2. Aum chittishcha swāhā. Idam chittai namam.
3. Aum ākritam cha swāhā. Idam ākritai namam.
4. Aum ākutishcha swāhā. Idam ākutai namam.
5. Aum vigyātam swāhā. Idam vigyātāya namam.
6. Aum vigyātishcha swāhā. Idam vigyātai namam.
7. Aum manashcha swāhā. Idam manase namam.
8. Aum sharkarishcha swāhā. Idam sharkaribhyo namam.
9. Aum darshashcha swāhā. Idam darshāya namam.
10. Aum pornamāsāyacha swāhā. Idam pornamāsāya namam.
11. Aum brihachcha swāhā. Idam brihate namam.
12. Aum rathantam cha swāhā. Idam rathantarāya namam.
13. Aum prajāpatih jayānindrāya brishne prāyachchhadugrah pritnā.
    Tasmai vishah samanamantu sarmāh sa ugrah sa iha vyovabhuva swāhā.
    Idam prajāpataye jayānindrāya namam.

After that, the following eighteen *Āhuties* of *Abhyātāna Homa* are performed:

1. Aum agni bhutānām adhipatih sa mā awatwasmin brahma punyasmi nakshatre ashyāmāshishyashyām purodhāyām asmin karmanasyām devahutyāng swāhā. Idam agnaye bhutānām adhipataye namam.
2. Aum indrayoh jyeshtānām adhipatih sa mā awatwasmin brahma punyasmi nakshatre ashyāmāshishyashyām purodhāyām asmin karmanasyām devahutyāng swāhā. Idam indrāya jyeshthānām adhipataye namam.

3. Aum yamah prithvyā adhipatih sa mā awatwasmin brahma punyasmi nakshatre ashyāmāshishyashyām purodhāyām asmin karmanasyām devahutyāng swāhā. Idam yamāya prithvyā adhipataye namam.
4. Aumvāyuantarikshasyaadhipatihsamāawatwasmin brahma punyasmi nakshatre ashyāmāshishyashyām purodhāyām asmin karmanasyām devahutyāng swāhā. Idam vāyave antarikshasya adhipataye namam.
5. Aum suryo divo adhipatih sa mā awatwasmin brahma punyasmi nakshatre ashyāmāshishyashyām purodhāyām asmin karmanasyām devahutyāng swāhā. Idam suryāya diwo adhipataye namam.
6. Aum chandramā nakshatrānām adhipatih sa mā awatwasmin brahma punyasmi nakshatre ashyāmāshishyashyām purodhāyām asmin karmanasyām devahutyāng swāhā. Idam chandramase nakshatrānām adhipataye namam.
7. Aumbrihaspatibrahmnoadhipatihsamāawatwasmin brahma punyasmi nakshatre ashyāmāshishyashyām purodhāyām asmin karmanasyām devahutyāng swāhā. Idam brihaspataye brhmanā adhipataye namam.
8. Aummitrahsatyānāmahadhipatihsamāawatwasmin brahma punyasmi nakshatre ashyāmāshishyashyām purodhāyām asmin karmanasyām devahutyāng swāhā. Idam mitrāya satyānām adhipataye namam.
9. Aum varuno āpām adhipatih sa mā awatwasmin brahma punyasmi nakshatre ashyāmāshishyashyām purodhāyām asmin karmanasyām devahutyāng swāhā. Idam varunāya āpāyām adhipataye namam.
10. Aum samudrah srotānām adhipatih sa mā awatwasmin brahma punyasmi nakshatre

ashyāmāshishyashyām purodhāyām asmin karmanasyām devahutyāng swāhā. Idam samudrāya srotānām adhipataye namam.

11. Aumannasāmrājyānāmadhipatihsamāawatwasmin brahma punyasmi nakshatre ashyāmāshishyashyām purodhāyām asmin karmanasyām devahutyāng swāhā. Idam annāya sāmrājyānām adhipataye namam.

12. Aumsomaaushadhinām adhipatihsamāawatwasmin brahma punyasmi nakshatre ashyāmāshishyashyām purodhāyām asmin karmanasyām devahutyāng swāhā. Idam somāya aushadhinām adhipataye namam.

13. Aumsavitāprasawānāmadhipatihsamāawatwasmin brahma punyasmi nakshatre ashyāmāshishyashyām purodhāyām asmin karmanasyām devahutyāng swāhā. Idam savitre prasawānām adhipataye namam.

14. Aum rudrah pashunām adhipatih sa mā awatwasmin brahma punyasmi nakshatre ashyāmāshishyashyām purodhāyām asmin karmanasyām devahutyāng swāhā. Idam rudrāya pashunāmā adhipataye namam.

15. Aumtwashātārupānāmadhipatihsamāawatwasmin brahma punyasmi nakshatre ashyāmāshishyashyām purodhāyām asmin karmanasyām devahutyāng swāhā. Idam twashtā rupānām adhipataye namam.

16. Aum maruto ganānām adhipatsya sa mā awatwasmin brahma punyasmi nakshatre ashyāmāshishyashyām purodhāyām asmin karmanasyām devahutyāng swāhā. Idam marudbhyo ganānām adhipatibhyo namam.

17. Aum agni bhutānām adhipatih sa mā awatwasmin brahma punyasmi nakshatre ashyāmāshishyashyām

purodhāyām asmin karmanasyām devahutyāng swāhā. Idam agnaye bhutānām adhipataye namam.

18. Aum agni bhutānām adhipatih sa mā awatwasmin brahma punyasmi nakshatre ashyāmāshishyashyām purodhāyām asmin karmanasyām devahutyāng swāhā. Idam agnaye bhutānām adhipataye namam.

The water called *Pranitodaka* kept in a vessel should be touched after the third, fifteenth and the eighteenth *Āhuti*.

For long life, prosperity and peace in life, the following *Paramamrityuh Āhuties* should be performed:

1. Aum agniraite prathamo devatānām ang sau asyai prajānmunchatu mrityupāshāt. Tadaya ang rājā varuno anumanyatām yatheya ang stri pautrāmagham na rodāt swāhā. Idam agnaye idam namam.
2. Aumimāmagnihatrāyatāmgārhapatyahprajāmasyai nayatu deergham āyuh ashunyopasthā jivatāmastu mātā potram ānandam abhibudhyatāmiva ang swāhā. Idam agnaye idam namam.
3. Aum swastino agne divā prithvyā vishwāni dhehyayathā yajatra. Yadashyām ahidiwi jātam prashastam tad smāsu dravinam dhehi chitra ang swāhā. Idam agnaye idam namam.
4. Aum sugannu panthām pradishanna yehi jyotih madhye hyajaranna āyuh. Apaitu mrituh amritam na āgād vaivaswato no abhayam kanotu swāhā. Idam vaivaswatāya namam. (Touch the water in the pranitodaka.)
5. Aum para mrityo antu parehi pantha anyah itaro devayānāt. Chakshushmate shrinwate te bravimi mā nah prajā ang ririshomota virān swāhā. Idam mritwe namam.

Pradakshinā

In this way sixty-two important Āhuties are given. Then the last *Lāwā Homa Āhuties* are performed. The *Lāwā Homa Āhuties* are actually, taking seven rounds of the fire in the *Vedikā* by the newly wedded couple to mark the journey ahead together, to put the spiritual and divine stamp on the marriage agreement, and to complete the *Vivāh Samskār*. It is performed so that balance and peace can be established.

In *Lāwā Homa,* first three *Āhuties* are given by the bride. The groom and the bride stand up facing east. Her brother fills her cupped hands with *Lāwā* prepared with refined butter and pārched corn. The bride should chant the following three *Mantras*. At some places, the groom chants the *Mantras* after picking her right thumb up. The groom then helps her drop each time one third of the corn:

1. Aum gribhanāmi te sobhagatwāya hasta mayā patyā jaradashtih yathāsah bhago aryam savitā purandhih mahyam twā durgāmah apatyāya devāh.
2. Aum amo ahamasmi sā twā ang sā twamasyamo aham. Sāmaham asmi riktwam dhaurah prithvitwam. Tāwewa vivāhāwahai sahareto dadhāwahai. Prajām pranāyāwahai putrānwi dāwahai bahuna.
3. Tejaridashtayah sampriyo rochishnu sumanasmānau. Pashyewma sharadah shatam jivema sharadah shatam ang shranuyāma sharadah shatāt.

While doing so they should take rounds of the fire. After the first round the bride should offer *Lāwā Homa* and say thrice: *Aum aryamanah*. She should also chant the following *Mantra*:

Aum tubhyam agne paryawahansasuryām wahatu nā sah. Punah patibhyo jāyadāgne prajā sah.

Then the brother should fill her cupped palm again. The entire process would be repeated twice more and every time the bride will be in the lead while taking the round.

A stone is placed in the way in north of the *Vedi*. The bride steps on it. At some places, the groom places her right foot on the stone. The stone symbolises the difficulties in life that have to be crossed over. The groom is always ready to stand by her and help her whenever and wherever needed. The groom chants the following *Mantra* while putting her right foot on the stone:

Aum ārohe mam ashmashānam swayamewa. Twa ang sthirā bhava. Abhitishtha pritayanto awabādhaswa pritanāyatah.

And when she puts her left leg also then he should chant this *Mantra*:

Aum saraswati predamava subhage wājini vratā; Yām twā viswasya bhutasya prajāyām asyāgratah. Yasyām bhuta sama bhava dyasyām viswam idam jagat; Māmadya gāthā gāsyāmiyā strinām uttamam yashah.

ॐ सरस्वति प्रेदमव सुभगे वाजिनीव्रता।
यां त्वा विश्वस्य भूतस्य प्रजायामस्याग्रतः।।
यस्यां भूत समभवद्यस्यां विश्वं इदं जगत्।
मामद्य गाथा गास्यामिया स्त्रीणां उत्तमं यशः।।

In this way, in three rounds *Lāwā Homa* is offered nine times and three times the bride steps on the stone. After that the brother should fill her joined palms with the rest of *Lāwā* and she should put all of it together into the *Vedi* as *Āhuti* with the *Mantra*:

Aum bhagāya swāhā. Idam bhagāya namam.

The bride will lead in the fourth round also but the *Mantras* are not chanted. Then the groom will come into the lead and the bride will follow him.

Saptapadi

At the end the seventh round *Pradakshinā* turns into *Saptapadi.* It is a vow, a promise, a resolve and a declaration that they will move ahead together. The couple, now, takes seven steps together synchronising the timing and steps both. Here too, the bride leads. On each step, they should chant the following *Mantras.* The first one is for grains, the second *Mantra* is for strength, the third is for wealth, the fourth is for happiness, the fifth is for animal wealth, the sixth is for growth according to the seasons and the seventh *Mantra* is for love, compassion and friendship:

1. Aum ishe ekapadi bhava sā mamānuvratā bhava vishnu nayatu putrān vindāwahai vahunste santu jaradastayah.
2. Aum urje dwipadi bhava sā mamānuvratā bhava vishnu ńayatu putrān vindāwahai vahunste santu jaradastayah.
3. Aum rāyasposhāya tripadi bhava sā mamānuvratā bhava vishnu nayatu putrān vindāwahai vahunste santu jaradastayah.
4. Aum mayo bhawāya chatushpadi bhava sā mamānuvratā bhava vishnu nayatu putrān vindāwahai vahunste santu jaradastayah.
5. Aum prajābhyah panchpadi bhava sā mamānuvratā bhava vishnu nayatu putrān vindāwahai vahunste santu jaradastayah.

6. Aum ritubhyah shatpadi bhava sā mamānuvratā bhava vishnu nayatu putrān vindāwahai vahunste santu jaradastayah.
7. Aum shakhe saptpadi bhava sā mamānuvratā bhava vishnu nayatu putrān vindāwahai vahunste santu jaradastayah.

After that the *Brahmā* performs the closing of *Āhuties* and the groom gives the *Purnāhuti* and *Dakshinā*. Then *Bhasma* is anointed to the couple. All these things are performed with the *Mantras* given earlier.

The couple is then led inside. The marriage as *Samskār* is over. The other rituals of *Kohabar* or *Vadhu Vidāi*, *Visarjana* and *Mandap Upavāsana* are performed by ladies and relatives.

When the bride comes to the in-laws' house, the ladies guide the *Vadhu Pravesh*, *Dhruva* and *Saptarishi Darshan* along with *Arundhati*; and *Goda Bharāi* or *Munh Dikhāi* are all performed as a part of the custom that prevails in a particular family. At many places they are blessed and consecrated by sprinkling sacred water.

❋❋❋

Samskār-14

Āwasthyādhāna Samskār (Sacred Fire)

This Samskār is also known as *Vivāhāgniparigrah Samskār*. The sacred fire called *Āwasthya* is related to general activities of the household. Its setting up is called *Awasthyādhāna*. A part of the sacred fire that was started during the marriage is brought and set in the house. All the *Smārta Karmas*, (the rites enjoined by the *Smritis*, the code of Law); like daily *Homa*; *Vaishwadeva Karma* and lighting the hearth are performed with this fire. This fire is known by different names like: *Āwasthya; Grihya; Smārta; Opawasthya; Vaivāhika* and *Aupāsan*. It is initiated by the eldest son. In the case of partition in a family it should be initiated and kept by all the brothers living at different places and houses. Despite partition, if they are living in one house then this fire will not be divided. It should be initiated and set-up on an auspicious day and time.

Once upon a time, the tradition of tending fire started and it was performed patiently and incessantly till or even after the independence. It is very difficult to pinpoint the reasonbutamidsttheinvention,availabilityandpopularity of match boxes and electricity suddenly this tradition vanished. This fire is no longer brought or kept burning. The other fact is that people have become completely materialists and think only of material comforts. Hence, the *Smārta Karmas* are also not performed.

The modern man does not need the fire, nor does he need *Dharma* and *Moksha*. For him money alone will take off all tensions and depression, solve all problems and make each person rule the world. Each one will be the ruler. There will be no one to be ruled. Everyone will have his/her own laws and regulations. In this way, there will be only terror and each one will be thinking to kill others. But a time may come when most of the people will be killed. Then peace and religion will be needed for the survival as *Dharmo rakshati rakshitah* (the religion saves when it is saved). Then the cycle of better, religious, spiritual and *Smārta Karmas* will return.

Agnyādhān Vidhi

On the day fixed for *Agnyādhān* the couple should be ready in every respect and sit on two separate seats facing east and after the *Āchaman*, *Pranāyām* and the preliminaries of *Samkalp* add: *Aum āwasthyāgni aham ādhāsye* to complete it.

Before that, preparation for other rituals must have been completed and all needed articles collected for the rites: pious *Kusha; Ājya Sthāli; Charu Sthāli* of *Udumber*; *Samidās* of *Dhāka*; earthen pots and *Aranies*. The *Vedi* must be the size of 14 fingers measured by the person performing the *Samskār*.

The five *Bhusamskārs* which are performed are:

1. *Parisamuhan*
2. *Upalekhan*
3. *Ullekhan*
4. *Uddharan*
5. *Abhyakshan*

The *Vedi* should be covered by a cloth. In the *Arani* side churning with *Arnies* is completed by the couple with separate *aranies* (wooden drills used for kindling fire by rubbing together). As a deviation from this tradition, at several places the husband holds and presses the mortar (*Okhali*) and the wife performs the act of churning. The fire is produced with the help of firewood and placed in the *Kunda* prepared for it amidst the chanting of different *Mantras* by Pandits and learned men; and amidst the auspicious songs sung by ladies and mild music played by the musicians. At other places, the *Agni* is brought from a wealthy farmer. The songs and music go on when one goes for the *Agni* and when he returns with it.

When the *Agni* is ready then a *Brahmā* is selected and *Samkalp* is given to him for performing the ritual. Everything is done accordingly as done in the *Yagyas* given earlier. He collects all the things needed. *Chāru* is prepared accordingly. When everything is ready he sits with his right knee touching the ground to perform *Āhuties*.

First the fourteen *Ādhāra Āhuties* are given as given in *Vivāh Samskār*. These *Ādhāra Āhuties* include:

- One *Prajāpati*
- One *Indra*
- Two *Ajya*

- Three *Vyāhuties*
- Five *Sarva Prayāshchita*
- Two *Swistakrita*

Then *Ajya Āhuties* should be given with the following eight *Richās*:

1. Aum tawanno agne varunasya vidwān devasya hedo ayavayāsisishthāh. Yajishtho wahni tamah shoshachāno viswādweshā ang si pramu mugdhya sma swāhā. Idam agni varunābhyām namam.
2. Aum sa tawanno agne awamo bhawoti nedishtho asyā usaso vyushtau. Awayakshwa no varunang rarāro wihi mridik ang suhawonayedhi swāhā. Idam agni varunābhyām namam.
3. Aum imam mey varun shruddhi hawamadyā cha mridaya. Twāma vasyurāchake swāhā. Idam varunāya namam.
4. Aum tatwāyāmi brāhmnā vandanmānah tadāshāste yajmāno havirbhih. Ahedamāno varune havidhyurusha ang sa mā na āyuh pramoshi swāhā. Idam varunāya namam.
5. Aum ye te shatatam varun ye sahastramyagiyāh pāshā vitatā mahāntah. Tebhirno adyā savitota vishanuh vishwe munchantu marutah swarkāh swāhā. Idam varunāya savitre vishnave vishwebhyo devebhyo marudbhyah swarkebhyashcha namam.
6. Aum ayāshcha agne asyan na abhishashtipāshcha satyam itwamayā asi. Ayā nā yagyam wahāsyayā no bhehi bheshaja ang swāhā. Idam agnye ayase namam.
7. Aum uduttamam varunam pāshamasmad bādham vimasyam ang shrayāya. Ath āwayam ādityam vrate tawānāgas aditaye swāhā. Idam varunāya namam.
8. Aum bhawatam nah samanasau sacheta

sāvarepasau. Māmagya hi sishtam mā yagyaparim jātavedasau shivau bhawatamadya na swāhā. Idam jāta vedobhyām namam.

After that, *Swistakrita Āhuti* should be given and another Āhuti with the following *Mantra*:

Aum ayāsya agneh vashatkrit yatkarmanātyariricham devāgātuvidahswāhā.Idamdevebhyogātuvidbhyonamam.

Panchāhuti Homa is performed with *Mantras*:

- *Tawanno agne*
- *Satwam no agne*
- *Ayāshch agne*
- *Yate shata and uduttam*

It is repeated again.

Then *Prajāpati Āhuti, Bahirhoma; Sansrava Prāshan* and *Āchaman* are performed.

The ritual comes to an end with the *Dakshinā* to *Brahmā* and feast to a *Brāhmin* and *Prasād.*

❁❁❁

Samskār-15

TRETĀGNISANGRAH SAMSKĀR (CONSERVING FIRE)

Tretāgnisangrah Samskār is the baptism into the conservation of fire, known as *Shrotādhāna*, to start a domestic life. In this Samskār the three types of *Agni*: *Gārhapatya Agni; Āwāhaniya Agni* and *Dakshināpatya Agni* are collected. It is also known as *Agnyādheya*.

It is performed on an auspicious day after marriage and after the Awasthyādhāna Samskār. One should avoid Mala Māsa; Kshaya Māsa; Rikta Tithi; Bhadrā; Mangalvār (Tuesday) and Shanivār (Saturday) along with the months of Āshādh; Bhādo; and Pausha. The best Nakshtras for it are Vishākhā; Kritikā; Mrigshirā; Rewati; Jyeshtā and Uttarā. Shukla Paksha and Pratipada Tithi should be preferred.

In the Morning

The Yagya Mandap should be correctly raised and Vedi for three Agnies should be ready separately. The needed openings should be left in the Mandap. After getting prepared in every way, the man should sit at the right place in the east of the Vedi facing north and his wife should be on his right. He should begin by performing *Āchamana*; *Samkalp*; *Swasti Punyāhwāchan*; *Ganapati Poojan*; *Mātrikā Poojan* and *Nāndi Shrāddha*. He should also accept the *Ritwija* and *Brahmā* along with *Adharvayu* and *Agnidha*. The *Agnies* should be brought and placed in the *Kunds* and kindled.

Then the *Pitars* (ancestors) are called with the following Mantra:

Aum devāh pitara paitaro devā yo aham asmi chja sanyaje. Yasya aham asmina tamantah āmi swambha ishta ang sa ang shrānta swa ang hatam astu.

After calling the Pitars, the husband should enter the Mandap from the east and sit in the west of the Agni facing east; and the wife should enter from the south and sit in the south of the husband. They should take the *Aranies* in their laps and worship them with fragrance etc. The Brahmā and others should bless them. Then after placing the *Aranies* at their right places and saluting the *Brāhmins* they should leave the place as the morning rituals is over. There is no rule for fasting on the day. They can eat or drink anything but vegetarian.

In the Evening

In the evening they should cook *Chātushprāshya* meal on that *Agni* adequate for four *Brāhmins*. After cooking and taking it off, they should mix *Ghee* in it and offer it as *Homa* in the *Gārhapatya Agni* with the following *Mantra*:

Aum samidhā agnim duvyasta ghritaih vodhayatā atithim. Āsmin havyā juhotana swāhā.

Then they should chant the following *Mantra* rhythmically:

Aum sumamiddhāya shochshe ghritam tibram juhotana. Agnaye jātavedase.

After standing up the second *Āhuti* should be given with the following *Mantra:*

Aum tantwā samid ibharangiro ghritena vardhayāmasi. Bahachchho chāya vishthāya swāhā.

And the third *Āhuti* should be given with this *Mantra*:

Aum upatwa agne ahavishmatih tritāchāryantuh aryat. Jushaswa samidho mamam swāhā.

Then with the following *Samkalp* and declaration, wash the feet of the *Ritwija* etc; feed them and give the *Dakshinā* while chanting this *Mantra*:

Asya chātushprāshya pachana karmanah sāngatāsiddhyartham brahmādibhyah ritwigbhyah imam varam dakshinām bhawadbhyo aham sampradade.

During the Night

The couple should remain fully awake during that night and they should be vigilant that the fire should not extinguish any time during the night.

The Next Morning

In the morning they should take bath and change the clothes. They should take out all the fire and the soot, and spread the fire at a wet place so that it gets extinguished by itself. No water should be poured over it.

After taking the fire off from the *Gārhapatya Kunda*; they should perform all the *Homas* up to the *Purnāhuti Homa* under the direction of the *Ritwija* and *Brahmā*. Please note that during this period they should not utter a single other word. The *Adharwayu* should perform *Panchbhu Samskār* of the *Kunda* and paint it thrice. Then he should write inscription known as *Ullekhan*. After that, he should place a piece of gold in the *Kunda* and cover it and make a round at the top with the soil taken from the mice-hole and spread fifty chips with mud over it. The chips are prepared with the soil from mice-hole and water.

Then the *Panchabhu Samskār* of the *Āwahaniya Kunda* is performed and after placing a piece of gold this too is filled up and covered in the same manner but 72 chips are placed at the top with mud.

Then the *Panchabhu Samskār* of the *Dakshināgni Kunda* is completed, water poured, gold piece placed and then this too is filled up and covered. At the top should be the soil from a mice-hole and 22 chips with mud are spread over it.

Agnimanthan

This is the churning of fire. A horse or an ox is brought there and made to stand still, facing west. *Adhar Arani* is placed on the *Kusha* in the south of *Gārhapatya Agni Kunda* and the churning of fire is performed as given earlier. When the *Agni* appears then the *Dakshinā* should be given to *Adhavwaryu*. The person performing this *Samskār* should place dry dung around it and inflame it by blowing air into it with his breath chanting the *Mantra: Aum prānam amrite dadhe*.

When it is inflamed he should try to inhale the heat of the fire with the following *Mantra* at least for five times: *Aum amritam prāna ādadhe.*

Then *Adharwayu* should inflame it with *Dhāka* and set it on *Gārhapatya Kunda* with the following *Mantra*:

Aum bhurbhuwah swah ādityānām twā devānām vratpate vrate na dadhe.

When *Adharwayu* says *Rathantar gāya* then the *Brahmā* should sing the *Rathanatar Sāma.*

Then the *Agni* should be brought to *Awāhaniya Kunda* on a tile. The couple should try to inhale the smoke coming from it. The *Adharwayu* says *Vāmadevyam gāya.*

Then the *Brahmā* sings *Vāmadevya Sāma.* The horse or the ox is brought up and made to touch the *Awāhaniya Kunda* and is taken off; made to take a round and stand still in front of it. The *Adharwayu* says *Brihad gāya* and the *Brahmā* sings the *Brihad Sāma.*

The track made by the horse or ox is touched twice with the fire and the above *Mantra*: *Aum bhurbhuwah swah ādityānām twā devānām vratpate vrate na dadhe*: is repeated.

While touching the top portion of the firewood placed there, the couple should chant the following *Mantras*:

- *Aum dyauriva bhumnā prithvi vyarimnā. Tasya aste prithivi devayajanati prishthe agnim annādm annādye dadhe.*
- *Aum āyangau prishinah krami dasadanmātaram purah. Pitarabhcha prayantswah.*
- *Aum antashchah atirochanā asya pranād pānati. Vyakhyan mahishi diwam.*

- *Aum tri ang shaddhāma virājati vāk patangāya dhiyate prati vastoh hadyubhih.*

After that the inflamed *Agni* from the *Gārhapatya Kunda* is taken on a tile and set in *Dakshinā Kunda* with the given *Mantra*:

Aum bhurbhuwah swah ādityānām twā devānām vratpate vrate na dadhe.

This *Mantra* is also chanted by the couple. Then *Adhavwaryu* says:

Shvaita vāsta anwatiya yagyāyavigyāya gāya

Now the *Brahmā* sings the three *Sāmas* one by one. The *Adharwayu* performs the *Purnāhuti*. The long silence of the couple is broken when they say: *Varam dadāmi.*

Then with the usual *Samkalp* he should give them the *Dakshinā*. The *Prasād* and feast marks the end of this *Samskār*.

❁❁❁

Samskār-16

Antyeshti Samskār (The Funeral)

Life comes to a full circle. It is the working of Nature created by the Almighty that everything that has begun must come to an end and then a new life shall start. The Samskārs which began before the birth with *Punswan* come to an end with *Antyeshti Samskār* that continues till after the death. Every person has to die and there are indications that life continues by taking new births. The end of life on the Earth is a remote possibility as the *Vedas* have said that whenever there will be excess of everything there would be a deluge to delude everything; and a new Manu will appear to restart the process of life. Six Manus have already come and disappeared. We are living in the seventh Manu. The most important part of it is that no one will be there to witness it. That is the immortality of death and the permanence of the system of change and cycle. If death is the truth, it has to come, so we must be prepared to welcome it and must help a dying person to die in peace and with solace that life will continue on Earth and his progeny will multiply happily. All the things that he could not finish in his lifetime would be accomplished; and that the acts of atonement would complete before his death for the mistakes that he committed in his lifetime.

On the Death Bed

When a person is on the deathbed, instead of discussing his illness or other worldly problems, chant the *Mantras* and recite the holy books, particularly the *Shlokas* from the *Gitā* for his peaceful departure. As the scriptures say that in place of weeping one should make provisions for his dependents and the progeny, perform wholesome deeds and complete the works left unfinished by him, for his peace:

Rodanapekshayā kuryāt suvyawasthām mrita ātmnah;
Samāshritā samārthānām putrādinām samācharet;
Kalyānamayā karmābhih mrita ātmnah sushāntaye;
Tachchhesha uttardāyitwam vida chchheda shubhekshāyā.

रोदनपेक्ष्या कुर्यात् सुव्यवस्थां मृतात्मनः।
समाश्रिता समार्थानां पुत्रादीनां समाचरेत्॥
कल्याणमय कर्माभिः मृतात्मनः सुशान्तये।
तच्छेषोतरदायित्वं विदच्छेद शुभेच्छाया॥

For this, when a person is on the deathbed, many rituals are performed mostly for giving his mind relief and rest. They are for psychological benefits. Different types of charities are performed. *Dānas* like *Annadāna*; *Godāna*; *Bhumidāna* and metals like gold etc are also donated. Other worldly materials too are given. Selected things, according to the financial condition and the wish of the dying person, should be donated in charity.

When it is felt that the moribund patient is about to die he should be brought and placed at a clean place on the ground on *Kusha* and *Kambal* with his head in the north and legs in the south or according to family or local tradition. Something fragrant incense must burn incessantly and the *Gāyatri Mantra* or *Mahā Mrityunjaya Mantra* or the *Gitā* or the *Rāmāyana* should be recited, as far as practicable.

After the Death

The moment a person dies, if his body is not on the floor then it should be placed there immediately with the head in the north. Incense sticks must burn there. At certain places, *Mukhāgni* in the form of *Vatti* (wick) is placed in his/her mouth. At some places, drops of *Ghrita* (refined butter oil) are poured into the eyes, ears and nostrils.

Whatever is perfomed immediately after deaths, is performed at the place of death. These rituals are performed for the cleanliness of the atmosphere, to shake off the fear and to slow down the process of deterioration.

Preparations for the final journey should be made quickly. The dead body should not be kept for long on medical grounds. The *Shava Yātrā* (the funeral march) should start as soon as possible. Preferably everything must be performed before the evening.

A temporary structure of freshly-cut bamboo is prepared to carry the dead body to the bank of some lake or river for burning on pyre. Before the journey starts, the dead body is given a bath with the following *Mantras*:

- Aum āpohistā mayo bhuwah.
- Aum tām na urje dadhātana.

- Aum yo wah shiva tamo rasah.
- Aum tasm bhājayatehanah.
- Aum ushatiriva mātarah.
- Aum tasmā arang māmawah.
- Aum asya kshayāya jinwatha.
- Aum āpo janayathā cha nah.

At certain places, 6 or 24 *Pindas* are given which are prepared with stiff dough of flour and refined butter oil. It is given in the *Shamshān Ghat*, the cremation ground. Usually the eldest son performs this ritual with the following *Mantra*:

Adya ----- gotrasya ----- pretasya pretatā nibrityartham uttamlikeprāptyarthamaudharvadaihikakarmakarishye.

While on the way, the dead body is taken off from the shoulders and kept on the ground at five or seven places. At the cremation ground, a wide space is cleaned for constructing a pyre with the following *Mantra*:

Aum shuddha wālah sarva shuddhawālo mani wālasta aswināh shyeta shyetāksho arunaste rudrāya pashupataye karnāyām avaliptā rodrā nabhau rupāh pārjanyāh.

Aum should be written on that piece of land, and four *Samidhā* as pillars should be fixed in all the four directions with the following *Mantras*:

For the East

Aum prāchi digginah adhipatih asito rakshitā aditwā ishawah. Tebhyo nāmo adhipatibhyo namo rakshitribhyo nama ishubhyo nama yebhyo astu. Yo asmāndweshti yam vayam dwishmantam wā jambhe dadhmah.

For the South

Aum dakshinā digindro adhipatih tishchirāji rakshitā pitarah ishawah. Tebhyo nāmo adhipatibhyo namo rakshitribhyo nama ishubhyo nama yebhyo astu. Yo asmāndweshti yam vayam dwishmantam wā jambhe dadhmah.

For the West

Aum pratichi digvaruno adhipatih pridāk rakshitā annam ishawah. Tebhyo nāmo adhipatibhyo namo rakshitribhyo nama ishubhyo nama yebhyo astu. Yo asmāndweshti yam vayam dwishmantam wā jambhe dadhmah.

For the North

Aum udichi dik somo adhipatih swajo rakshitā shani ishawah. Tebhyo nāmo adhipatibhyo namo rakshitribhyo nama ishubhyo nama yebhyo astu. Yo asmāndweshti yam vayam dwishmantam wā jambhe dadhmah.

Drain-like ditches are dug dividing the pillars for passing the air. Then almost half of the firewood and some sandalwood are placed as a pyre. Now the body is placed on the pyre with the following *Mantra*:

Aum agnaye naya supathā rāye asmān vishwāni deva vāyunāni vidwān. Yuyodhyasma ajjurānamejo bhuyishthām te nama ukti vidhem.

The other firewood and the remaining sandalwood are placedonthebody. Towardstheheadofthepyre, *Panchabhu Samskār* is performed and with: *Aum kravyādāya namah*; the fire named *Kravyādāya* (at almost every place this fire is bought from the *Shamshāna* keeper) is kindled and taking round of the pyre, the fire is put into the mouth five or seven times with the following *Mantra*:

Aum bhurbhuwah dyoriva bhumnā prithiviwa tasyāte prithivi devajayani prishthe agnih annādam annādyādyādhe. Agniputam purodadhe havyawāhamuprabruve. Devām yayā sādayādih.

Then with the following *Mantra,* the *Ahuties* are given:

- *Aum prajāpataye swāhah.*
- *Idam prajāpataye namama iti manasā.*
- *Aum indrāya swāhah.*
- *Imam indrāya namam. Ityādhārau.*
- *Aum agnaye swāhah. Idam agnaye namam.*
- *Aum somāya swāhah. Idam somāya namam*
- *Aum bhuh swāhah. Idam agnaye namama.*
- *Aum bhuwah swāhah, Idam wāyawe namam.*
- *Aum swah swāhah. Idam suryāsta namam.*

The following *Ahuties* are performed in order to offer various parts of the body to *Agni*, the God of Fire:

- *Aum lomabhya swāhah. Idam namam.*
- *Aum twache swāhah. Idam twache namam.*
- *Aum lohitāya swāhah. Idam lohitāi namam.*
- *Aum medobhya swāhah. Idam medobhya namam.*
- *Aum mansebhya swāhah. Idam mansebhya namam.*
- *Aum snāyubhyah swāhah. Idam snāyubhyah namam.*
- *Aum asthibhyah swāhah. Idam asthibhyah namam.*
- *Aum majjābhyah swāhah. Idam majjābhyah namam.*
- *Aum retase swāhah. Idam retase namam.*
- *Aum pāyawe swāhah. Idam pāyawe namam.*

Kapāla Kriyā

Kapāla Kriyā is deemed to be the last act in the process of *Shavadāha* (the burning of the dead body). The *Kapāla Kriyā* is also called *Mastakachhedan* as the head is pierced as a part of this rite. When the dead body is almost burnt up, the head is broken and is filled up with *Ghee* and *Til* to enable it to burn completely. The following *Mantra* is chanted at that time: *Asau swargāya lokāya swāhā jwalatu pāwake.*

Stream on the Body

At many places before the final burning of the dead body, *Ghee* is poured as a current with the following *Mantra*:

Aum basoh pavitram asi shatadhāram baso pavitram asi sahasra dhāram. Devah twā savitā punātu baso pavitrena shatdhārena suptwā kāmadhuka swāhv.

After the *Kapāla Kriya*, when the body is completely burned, the place is cleaned. The ashes are immersed in the lake or the river. Some remaining bones and some ashes are kept for immersion into the Ganga or some other holy river.

At many places, the *Kapāla Kriyā* is performed early the next morning.

When the burning is completed then all the persons who had accompanied the dead body take compulsory bath in the river or pond nearby. The following *Mantra* is chanted at that time:

Aum apānah shoshucha daghamanne shushug trayārayim. Apānah shoshuchadagham.

Then they return home but before going inside each of them will have to touch many things according to the local custom that must include an iron object and dried red chilly.

The cycle is completed before the resurgence or rebirth. It is a mystery how the dead persons spend the period of transition before the rebirth or the *Punswan*.

❋❋❋

Vānprastha Samskār

At many places *vānprastha* and *Samyāsa Samskārs* are treated as the 14th and 15th *Samskārs*. But these *Samskārs* are optional and all the persons do not opt for them. Hence, these *Samskārs* are given separately at the end.

Illegibility and Time

Only those people are eligible for the *Vānaprastha Samskār* who are of more than fifty-five years of age; have spent the life of *Brahmacharya* and have finished the responsibilities of the *Grihastya Dharma*; have a son or sons and whose son or sons have at least one son each. According to *Shatpath Brāhman:*

Brahmacharya āshramam samāpya grihi bhaweda grihi bhutwā vani bhaweda vani bhutwā prabrajet.

Vānaprastha Karma

Vānaprastha is a religious consecration. It is baptism into a life away from the house, village and luxury. The investiture into *Vānaprastha* is a penance of a difficult kind. One has to leave the house and the family; one can not take the food of the village; one can leave the wife behind or take her with him but have no physical relations with her:

Santyajya grāmya āhāram sarvanchai parichchhadam;
Putreshu bhāryām nikshipya vanam gachchhet sahai wā.

He should study the scriptures or teach them; have control over sense organs, mind and sex; be friendly with all, be alert, he should give whatever he could and have compassion for all living beings:

Swādhyāye nitya yuktah syādyānto maitrah samāhitah;
Dātā nityamanā dātā sarva bhutā anukampakah.

He should accept alms from only the persons that live in the forests including the students, tapaswis, religious persons and the learned men that are either *Vānprasthi* or *Samyāsi*:

Tāpaseh yeva vipreshuyātrika bhaikshyam āharet;
Grihamedhishu cha anyesu seveta dikshā vipro vane vaset.

In the forest one should remain in the company of great and illuminated souls, with sages and saints and try his level best to get united to the Almighty Brahma.

Vānaprastha Vidhi: The Rite

The *Mandap* should be raised and *Vedikā* constructed for the purpose and the fire should be inflamed and from *Samidhādāna* to *Purnāhuti*, all the *Āhuties* are to be performed. Then *Sāma Gāna* should be sung and *Visarjan* completed. After distributing *Prasād* one should meet the relatives, give the charge and responsibilities to the son and leave the house and village for a life of austerity. ❁❁❁

Samyās Samskār

In *Samyās dridha vairāgya*, asceticism and freedom from worldly desires and *yathārthagyāna*, the knowledge of the reality is essential. These are two great pre-conditions for it. Any one that fulfils these conditions can opt for *Samyās* at any age. It is a declaration of complete detachment and freedom from all lust and all sorts of prejudices. It is a life for others and hence, the greatest life in itself and by itself:

Samyang nyasyantya dharmācharanāni yena wā samyang nityam satkarmasāsta upavishati sthiri bhawati yena sa Samyāsah. Samyāso vidyate yasya sa samnyāsi.

The *Brāhman Grantha* says:

Yadharevavirajettadharevapravrajedvanādwāgrihādwā.

(The day one, whether a *Vānaprasthi* or a *Grihasta*, feels detachment and inner compulsion for serving others, one can opt for *samyās*.

Illegibility and Time

Samyās is recommended to only those that have lived the life of *Brahmacharya* and *Grihasta*; have gone for *Vānaprastha* and have completed it. They can go for *Samyās* at the age of 75 or more: *Manusmriti* says:

Vaneshu cha vihrityaiva tritiyam bhāgam āyushah;

Chaturtham āyusho bhāgam tyaktwā sangān parivrajet.

Samyās Vidhi: The Rite

The person who wishes to take *Samyās* should live only on milk for three days, sleep on bare ground, perform *Dhyāna*, *Prānāyām* and chant *Aum* in solitude.

On the day (the fourth day) of taking *Samyās*, the person should rise at 4 AM and be ready for the Samskārs. He should keep on chanting *Aum*, the *Pranava*. He should get his head shaven and should consecrate it for 108 times with the *Mantras* of *Purusha Sukta*. A *Mandap* should be raised and *Vedikā* constructed for the purpose and the fire should be inflamed. Then from *Samidhādāna* to *Purnāhuti*, all the *Āhuties* are to be performed. He should offer *Purnāhuti* with the following two *Mantras* or *Samkalp*:

Putraishanāyāshcha vitaishanāyāshcha lokaishanāyāshcha utathāyātha bhikshācharayam charanti. 1.

(Only they can make others free from fear by teaching the truth that have freed themselves from the love of the son, the wealth and the fame in the society.)

Putraishanā vitaishanā lokaishanā mayā parityaktā;

Mattah sarva bhutebhyo abhayam astu swāhā. 2.

(I have renounced from today the love for son, lust of wealth and wish of fame. It is my true word that all living beings would live without fear from me.)

He should, then, stand in navel deep water facing east and chant the following *Mantras*.

Aum bhuh sāvitrim pravishāmi tat savitur varinayam.

Aum bhuwah sāvitrim pravishāmi bhargo devasya dhimahi.

Aum swah sāvitrim pravishāmi dhiyo yo nah prachodayāt.

Aum bhurbhuwah swah sāvitrim pravishāmi paro rajase asāwadom.

He should repeat the resolution that he took with the *Purnāhuti* and then chant the following *Mantras* and after every *Mantra* pour water from his joined palms:

Aum bhuh samyastam mayā.

Aum bhuwah samyastam mayā.

Aum swah samyastam mayā.

Aum abhayam sarvabhutebhyo mattah swāhā.

Yenā saharam wahāsi yenāgre sarva vedasam;

Tenemam yagyam no waha swa ardeweshu gantawe.

He should take off the remaining few hair from his head, and the *Upavit* and give it as *Homa* to water with water, hair and *upavit* in the joined palms after reciting the following *Mantras*:

Aum āpo wai sarvā devatāh swāhā.

Aum bhuh swāhā.

After coming out of water he should wear the *Kāshāya vastra* and take the *Danda* with the *Mantra*: *yo mey dandah dhārayāmi.*

Then *Sāma Gāna* should be sung and *Visarjan* completed.

What should a Samyāsi do?

According to *Manusmriti*: A *Samyāsi* should look ahead before stepping on to avoid crushing an innocent insect or other living being; drink water only after filtering it through a cloth; should speak and teach only truth; behave with the greatest purity of heart and mind:

Drishti putam nyaset pādam vastra putam jalam piwet;
Satya putām vaded vācham manah putam samācharet.

A *Samyāsi* should have faith in the self; be free from expectations; a teetotaler; eat only for remaining alive; and teach others the truth:

Adhyātmah atirāsino nirpeksho nirāmishah;
Ātmanaiva sahāyena sukhārthi vichare diha.

He should get shaven from time to time; should wear only *Geruā* vastra coloured in *Geru* or *Kusumbha*, and carry only a stick and a begging pot. He should never inflict injury or cause pain to any living being: human or non-human and truthfully teach all to be true:

Klipta kasha nakha shamashruh pātri dandi kusumbhawān;
Vicharenniyato nityam sarvabhutānya apidayan.

❁❁❁

Samskārs for Prosperity

It is better to start with what should be given at the end: as the beginning is an end (The birth of a child is the end of the pain and torture of the mother.) and the end initiates a fresh beginning. (The end of construction work marks the beginning of occupying and living in the house.) Life is like that wheel whose beginning and end are at the same point and everywhere; it could be at any point on the wheel. The points of beginning and end are important in a limited way; shining (health) and performance (happiness); and continuity and success are more important. The success of life is not in *āhār* (food); *maithun* (sex) and *nidrā* (sleep) it is in incessant growth, continuity and prosperity that is possible with Samskārs. Samskārs make living easier, better and fuller if they are performed as they should with right earnestness.

Shri Krishna declared in the *Gitā*:

"That person easily succeeds in both the physical and spiritual realms (worlds) whose, Samskārs have been duly completed and that has achieved control over senses":

Samskritasya hi dāntasya niyatasya yat ātmanah;
Prāgyasya anantarā siddhih ihloke paratra cha.

संस्कृतस्य हि दान्तस्य नीयतस्य यत् आत्मनः।
प्रज्ञस्य अनन्तरा सिद्धिः इहलोके परत्र च।

With *Punsawan Samskār* we try, expect and get cultured, refined and brilliant children; and are assured of their steady growth, as the act of purification, refinement, growth, progress and prosperity continues through different Samskārs. One may think that it is over after death with *Antyeshthi Samskār*; but no, it continues along with *Shrāddha* and *Tarpans*. The dead are remembered and recalled through many rituals so that they can get peace and either better rebirth or salvation; and so that they can bless the posterity. It is all a continuous process. Growth and refinement should never stop as the universe is growing at its pace and as the soul is immortal.

See and know the **'Chariot of Dharma'** as described by *Tulasidās* in his *Rāma Charit Mānas*, be assured of everything and proceed boldly and confidently on the *'Samskāri Path'* of righteousness and prosperity, and of bliss and salvation:

"**Valour** and **fortitude** are the wheels of the Chariot of Dharma, while **truthfulness** and **good conduct** are its enduring banner and standard. **Strength**, **discretion**, **self-control** and **benevolence** are its four horses that have been joined (yoked) to the chariot of dharma with the cords of **forgiveness**, **compassion** and **evenness of mind**. **Adoration of God** is the expert charioteer (driver); **dispassion** is the shield and **contentment** is the sword; **charity** is the axe; **reason** is the fierce lance; and **wisdom**, the relentless bow. A **pure and steady mind** is like a quiver; while **quietude** and various forms of **abstinence** (*yamas*) and **religious observances** (*niyamas*) are a sheaf of arrows. **Homage** to the *Brāhmins* and to preceptor is an impenetrable coat of mail. There is no other equipment for victory as efficacious as these are. He who owns such a Chariot of Dharma and **piety** shall have no enemy to conquer anywhere."

One person, on his own can't bear the burden of all the responsibilities; can't earn and create all that one needs, and perform all the tasks. One can't be the runner and simultaneously manage and decide the race. As life is all; a lot more than what we can imagine; a strange combination of numerous races; so life is superb and incomprehensible. A person, man, woman or child, needs a lot during the lifetime and can grow to an unknown extent both in height and depth. Samskārs modulate and direct that growth and make the task easier.

Moreover, one person alone can't perform all the experiments and come to a definite conclusion about the quality, quantity and purity of the numerous things needed and used. Samskārs help and give the ability to be better; and lead a happy and prosperous life in different ways, among different people, under different circumstances and at different places. Samskārs stop a person from falling down. They give immense power and ensure success.

A person comes out clean from the grip of lust, desire, jealousy, anger and other mental, physical and moral ailments. He/ she follows a clean path of religiosity and is enriched with moral values and wholesome deeds. Consciousness is strengthened; conscience is empowered; skills improved and life enriched. He does good things and in return gets a better life.

Scriptures have taught us that to keep faith in religion according to the rights and ability is a quality. On the contrary, it is a sin to cross the sanctioned boundary. Vices and virtues are decided according to the rights and deeds. Then it is essential to get rid of lust, anger, jealousy, ego and excessive indulgence in luxury and physical pleasure:

Dharmārtham vyavahārārtham yātrārtham iti cha anagha;

Darshito ayam mayā āchāro dharma mudrahatām dhuram.

Karmanā jātya shuddhā nāmanena niyamah kritah;

Guna dosha vidhānena sangānā tyājane chchhāyā.

धमार्थं व्यवहारार्थं यात्रार्थं इति चानघ।
दर्शितोऽयं मयाऽऽचारो धर्म मुद्रहतां धुरम्।।
कर्मणां जात्य शुद्धा नामनेन नियमः कृतः।
गुण दोष विधानेन संगाना त्याजनेच्छाया।

As with a brush different colours are used to create a beautiful picture; in the same way, if all the Samskārs are performed and the patterns and rules obeyed then life of a person would be worth living, blissful; and pure enough to get bliss and salvation.

Chitrakarma yathānekai rangaih unmilyate shanaih;

Brāhmanyamapi tadwatsyāt samskraih mantrapurvakiah.

चित्रकर्म यथानेकै रंगैः उन्मील्यते शनैः।
ब्राह्मण्यमपि तद्वत्स्यात् संस्कारैः मन्त्रपूर्वकैः।।

A person, with Samskārs and other human attributes, is loving to God. *Shri Krishna* has declared it in the *Gitā*:

Adeshtā sarva bhutānām maitrah karuna yeva cha;

Nirmamo nirahankārah sum dukha sukhah kshami.

Santushthah satatam yogi yat ātmā dridha nishchayah;

Mayā arpita mano buddhih yo mad bhaktah sa mey priyah.

अदेष्टा सर्वभूतानाम मैत्रः करूण एव च ।
निर्ममो निरहंकारः सम दुःख सुखः क्षमी ॥
सन्तुष्टः सततं योगी यत् आत्मा दृढ़ निश्चयः ।
मय्यार्पित मनो बुद्धिः यो मद् भक्तः स मे प्रियः ॥

(The person that loves all the living beings with jealousy to none, has no lust, is kind without expectations, has no longing or affection, no ego and is detached to pain and pleasure; and forgives them that do wrong him, he is a yogi confident and contented; has control over mind, body and senses and is devoted to me; such a person is dear to me.)

In the Convocation Order the Guru, the Preceptor advised his pupil but with a difference. It became the fundamental basis of Samskārs and social life:

संस्कृत	*Roman*	*Meaning*
मातृदेवो भव ।	*Mātridevo bhava.*	*Treat mother as Goddess.*
पितृदेवो भव ।	*Pitridevo bhava.*	*Treat father as God.*
आचार्य देवो भव ।	*Āchārya devo bhava.*	*Treat preceptor as God.*
अतिथि देवो भव ।	*Atithi devo bhava.*	*Treat a guest as God.*
यान्यनवद्यानि कर्माणि। तानि सेवित्यानि । नो इतराणि ।	*Yānyanavadyāni karmāni. tāni sevitāni. No etarāni.*	*Perform only such deeds that are righteous. Do not copy others.*
यान्यस्माकं सुचरितानि। तानि त्वयोपास्यानि। नो इतराणि।	*Yānya asmākang sucharitāni. Tāni tvayopāsyāni. No etarāni.*	*Whatever good is in us, follow them. Do not copy others.*

ये के चास्मच्छ्रेया ॅ सो ब्राह्मणाः।	*Ye ke chāsmachchheyāng so brāhmanāh.*	*The elders are like Brahmins.*
तेशां त्वयाऽऽसनेन प्रष्वसितव्यम्।	*Teshām tvayā āsanena prashvasitavyam.*	*Give them rest, and the best that you can.*
श्रद्धया देयम्।	*Shraddhayā deyam.*	*Give in charity with humility.*
अश्रद्धया अदेयम्।	*Ashraddhayā adeyam.*	*Don't give with ego.*
श्रिया देयम्।	*Shriyā deyam.*	*Give according to financial status.*
ह्रिया देयम्।	*Hriyā deyam.*	*Give with shyness.*
भिया देयम्।	*Bhiyā deyam.*	*Give with fear.*
संविदा देयम्।	*Samvidā deyam.*	*Give with wisdom.*

Don't think of adding years to life; try to add life to your years, Samskārs to the self and righteousness to deeds. Longevity may not be meaningless but pious, cultured and sublime life is more meaningful and thousand times better. A righteous and benevolent person that contributes to the continuity and betterment of life and living conditions lives even after death; death is not his end: *kriti yasya sa jivati:* with deeds and in deeds one lives. So, grow from inside, be human and sublime to ensure life even after certain death. Get Samskārs and live forever. Character and deeds will do the rest. Be a human being and glow with divinity: *manurbhava; janaya vaivyam janam*. Character is ornament for all: *sheelam sarvasya bhusham*. Get and wear the ornaments of Samskārs and thus of character and righteousness. Prosperity, health, happiness, bliss and beatitude will be in your possession.

Hari Aum Tatsat !